What Workers Want

What Workers Want

Updated Edition

Richard B. Freeman

and Joel Rogers

ILR Press *an imprint of*

Cornell University Press *Ithaca and London*

Russell Sage Foundation *New York*

First published 1999 by Cornell University Press
First printing, Cornell Paperbacks, 1999
First printing, updated edition, Cornell Paperbacks, 2006

Printed in the United States of America

Library of Congress Cataloging-in-Publication Data
Freeman, Richard B. (Richard Barry), 1943–
What workers want / Richard B. Freeman & Joel Rogers.
   p.   cm.
Includes index.
ISBN-13: 978-0-8014-7325-8 (pbk : alk. paper)
ISBN-10: 0-8014-7325-x (pbk : alk. paper)
1. Job satisfaction — United States. 2. Employees — United
States — Attitudes. I. Rogers, Joel, 1952–   . II. Title.
HF5549.5.J63F74 1999
331.2'095 — dc21   98-38848

Cornell University Press strives to use environmentally
responsible suppliers and materials to the fullest extent
possible in the publishing of its books. Such materials
include vegetable-based, low-VOC inks and acid-free
papers that are recycled, totally chlorine-free, or partly
composed of nonwood fibers. For further information,
visit our website at www.cornellpress.cornell.edu.

Paperback printing   10 9 8 7 6 5 4 3 2 1

PRINTED IN U.S.A.

To Jennifer Amadeo-Holl

and Alida Castillo-Freeman,

who did the work and kept

at least one of us sane

CONTENTS

LIST OF EXHIBITS

PREFACE TO THE UPDATED EDITION

This updated edition of *What Workers Want* keeps the core text and chapter structure of the first edition (Chapters 1–7 in the current book), while eliminating its appendices. The appendices reported the methodology, telephone questionnaires, and written materials used in the two waves of the Worker Representation and Participation Survey (WRPS), all of which is now available online at www.nber.org/~freeman/wrps.html. That site also offers an integrated dataset of all findings, ready for download by interested researchers, and links to other national surveys, modeled on the WRPS, conducted since.

New to the updated edition are a new introduction and conclusion. The Introduction examines how our original findings stand up in light of survey research that others have done since the WRPS. The Conclusion offers suggestions on how to reform our labor relations system so that it delivers to workers what they want in the form of workplace representation and participation.

Our thanks to Fran Benson of Cornell University Press for suggesting this updated edition and seeing it through production, and to Pablo Mitnik, of the University of Wisconsin graduate program in sociology, for research assistance. We also thank those many colleagues, too numerous to name here, who commented on the earlier work and those who did new surveys on which we draw in this one. Special thanks to Geoff Garin, of Hart Research Associates (HRA), who generously shared some of HRA's proprietary data.

RBF and JR

Cambridge, Mass., and Madison, Wisc.

May 2006

ACKNOWLEDGMENTS

In conducting the Worker Representation and Participation Study (WRPS) and writing this book, we had considerable help.

For the financing that made it possible, we thank the Russell Sage Foundation, the Joyce Foundation, the Alfred P. Sloan Foundation, and the Spencer Foundation.

For their counsel and patience in meeting our many requests or advice or data, we thank Paul Allaire, Marcella Berland, Elaine Bernard, Bruce Carswell, Joshua Cohen, Diane Colasanto, Phil Comstock, Dawn Crossland, John Dunlop, Sam Estreicher, Mike Farren, Larry Gold, Lydia desGroseilliers, Larry Hugick, Susan Jessop, Jack Joyce, Michael Katz, Thomas Kochan, Susan Jessop, Randall MacDonald, Karyn Matchey, Angela McDermott, Nora Cate Schaeffer, Judy Scott, Barney Singer, Ernie Savoie, David Silberman, Elisabeth Smith, Andy Stern, Greg Tarpinian, Paula Voos, Ruy Teixeira, Joe Uehlein, Eric Wanner, Paul Weiler, Erik Olin Wright, and Cliff Zukin.

For extraordinary help throughout, special thanks to Diane Colasanto and the two people to whom we dedicate this book: Jennifer Amadeo-Holl and Alida Castillo-Freeman. Jennifer managed the process of developing the survey and producing the manuscript for the book. Alida did most of the actual data analysis relied on in the study, and is the master of the vagaries of the WRPS data set. They both worked long hours to help us complete this work. We are very grateful.

Introduction to the Updated Edition

The first edition of *What Workers Want* analyzed a large survey of private-sector U.S. workers and managers, the Worker Representation and Participation Survey (WRPS), which we designed to find out how American workers felt about their influence on decisions at the workplace and about possible ways to improve their role in workplace governance. The survey was conducted in the fall and spring of 1994–95. As described in the chapters that follow, finding out what American workers thought about workplace issues was complicated and sometimes vexed by politics; opinion surveys also have their intrinsic limits. But the WRPS was sufficiently successful that scholars in the other major English-speaking countries and in Germany, Japan, and Korea have since completed comparable surveys. These implicitly endorse our general approach and allow analysts to differentiate patterns specific to the United States from those that apply more generally to advanced capitalist economies. The WRPS yielded three main findings for the United States.

First, it uncovered a large gap between the kind and extent of representation and participation workers had and what they desired. This representation/participation gap existed across diverse groups of workers (men and women, different races, skilled and unskilled, etc.) and across many issues (compensation, supervision, training, availability of information on firm plans, use of new technology, etc.). Even workers whose management had instituted employee involvement committees to consult with them on workplace decisions wanted more voice and power in the process. Only a minority of workers — 10 percent to 15 percent, depending on the particular questions — did not want more collective voice at the workplace.

Second, the survey found that workers preferred cooperative relations with management to adversarial ones, where a cooperative relation meant both mutual respect and some degree of power sharing. They believed that greater representation and voice at their workplace would be good for their firm as well as for them. They identified management unwillingness to share power as a major cause for the gap between the representation and voice they wanted and what they had, particularly with respect to efforts to unionize.

Third, workers were open to different paths for increasing their representation and participation at their workplace. Many more wanted unions and collective bargaining than had union representation. The vast majority of union members wanted to keep their unions, though they were cognizant and critical of union weaknesses. Most nonunion employees wanted some kind of elected workplace committee to consult regularly with management, perhaps with third-party arbitration of disputes, and welcomed the idea of workplace committees to aid in workplace regulation in areas like occupational safety and health. In resolving individual disputes, most employees also preferred arbitration to going to court but wanted to make that choice themselves; they were against surrendering their legal rights to a company-based arbitration system. Union members also supported workplace committees, presumably working in conjunction with their union.

The bottom line of the first edition of *What Workers Want* was that the U.S. system of workplace governance had failed the country. It had not delivered to American workers the role in firm decision-making that they wanted and the diverse set of institutions they sought to deal with management at their workplace. Instead, it offered a single choice — collective bargaining, which management often opposed — or no independent representation or participation at their workplace.

With the exception of this Introduction and a new concluding chapter, this updated edition of *What Workers Want* is essentially unchanged from the first. We have made a few very minor corrections to the seven chapters of the first edition, now sandwiched by these additions. That we have limited our revisions to two chapters and not revised the main text may seem odd or reflect indolence on our part. After all, the United States has changed in many ways since the WRPS was completed a decade ago, and it is possible that much of what we found is now outdated.

At the time of the survey, Bill Clinton was in the White House, the Democratic Party controlled Congress, and the AFL-CIO had elected a new leadership to rejuvenate the union movement. In 2005, George Bush is president, the Republicans control Congress, and the labor movement has split into two groups. At the time of the survey, the country was debating

NAFTA and the risk of losing manufacturing jobs due to increased trade with Mexico. In 2005, the country is concerned with the shift of manufacturing jobs to China and the offshoring of service jobs to India, two countries with massively larger workforces and lower wages than Mexico. From 1995 through 2000, the country enjoyed an exceptional period of growth in output and employment and rising wages for all workers, which produced a federal budget surplus that offered opportunities to strengthen the national economy. From 2000 to 2005, average wages stagnated despite continued productivity gains. Following deep tax cuts for the better-off, the federal deficit has returned. New issues figure in our politics. In 2001, terrorists attacked the United States. Shortly afterward, the United States invaded Afghanistan and then, in 2003, Iraq. More recently, Hurricane Katrina devastated the Gulf Coast.

With all the important events and changes since the WRPS, readers of this updated edition of *What Workers Want* might naturally ask: "Isn't this stuff out of date? Shouldn't you guys be conducting a new survey and revising the entire book?"

Our short answer is "no." Of course, if worker attitudes had changed in the period or if the country had reformed the labor relations system, we would have redone the survey, producing WRPS II. But our review of surveys conducted by groups and public opinion polling organizations in this Introduction shows that, perhaps surprisingly, the main findings of the first edition still stand. Much has changed in the economy and politics, but the disconnect between what workers want in the form of influence at their workplaces and what they have remains sizable.

We base this conclusion on a detailed examination of dozens of post-WRPS opinion surveys on the issues that the WRPS survey and Chapters 1–7 of this book cover.[1] The post-WRPS surveys often focus on a particular issue such as job satisfaction, attitudes toward unionization, or attitudes toward employers, rather than on the full spectrum of workplace issues that the WRPS covered. Some surveys adopted our strategy of asking questions in different ways to make sure that the findings did not depend on particular wordings. Some replicated our questions. Others posed the issues in different ways than we did. While the post-WRPS surveys and polls are invariably shorter and less complete than the WRPS, taken together they provide information on almost all the main issues with which the WRPS dealt and give a clear picture of what workers think about workplace governance today.

The new survey results show that workers continue to want to have greater say at the workplace than the U.S. labor relations system offers them. In some cases, the newer studies show that since the WRPS the gap between what workers want and what they have in representation and participation has grown. This is particularly the case for the proportion of workers who say that they want unions to represent them. The post-WRPS surveys also show increased concern about the representation and participation gap and reduced confidence in business leadership. It is because the newer surveys confirm the basic message of the first edition of *What Workers Want* that we have left the core text of the previous edition intact. In addition, we believe that the story it tells — of how we developed the survey and tried to meet the differing concerns and criticisms of unions and management in a highly charged political atmosphere — should still interest students of survey or other applied social science research as they proceed with their own research. The rest of this Introduction reviews the post-WRPS survey findings, organized around our three broad earlier conclusions.

Broad Conclusion I: Attitudes Toward Work and Representation/Participation Gaps

Many opinion surveys ask about job satisfaction with questions like: "how satisfied are you with your job?" and variants thereof. Concerned with worker attitudes toward improving workplace decisions, we focused on more specific issues, such as the state of labor-management relations and worker desires to influence decisions in particular areas, such as provision of benefits, use of new machinery, training, and the like. A worker who was satisfied with his or her job but who wanted greater influence on decisions about training at the workplace was, from our perspective, more interesting or important than a worker who was dissatisfied with his or her job but did not have any thoughts about making the workplace better. However, we did ask respondents one broad satisfaction style question: if, on the average day, they usually looked forward to going to work (66 percent did); wished they didn't have to go (25 percent), or didn't care one way or the other (9 percent). Responses to this question, as well as to diverse others summarized in Chapter 2, lead us to conclude that about two-thirds of workers were contented at their job while about a third were discontented.

The pattern of responses to generic job satisfaction questions in post-

WRPS surveys shows that our decision to avoid the job satisfaction terrain was a good one. The surveys that ask broad satisfaction questions yield considerable variation in reported levels and trends.

Two major surveys show low and virtually constant levels of job dissatisfaction. From 1972 to the present, the General Social Survey (GSS) has asked workers, "On the whole, how satisfied are you with the work you do — would you say you are very satisfied, moderately satisfied, a little dissatisfied, or very dissatisfied?" The results show 14 percent of workers reporting that they were a little or very dissatisfied and 86 percent reporting moderate to high satisfaction, with no trend over time and almost no year-to-year variation.[2] The Gallup Poll also routinely asks a job satisfaction question: "How satisfied or dissatisfied are you with your job?" For the period 1997–2005, 86 percent of workers report being satisfied and 14 percent dissatisfied, again with little yearly variation.

At first blush, you might think that the General Social Survey and Gallup had uncovered what social science rarely finds, a scientific law with a universal constant in the form of the 86/14 division of answers to the job satisfaction question. But polls conducted over the same period that probed about workplace specifics find much higher and in some cases increasing levels of job dissatisfaction.

The most widely publicized job satisfaction surveys subsequent to the WRPS were the 1995 and 2004 surveys conducted by the business research group the Conference Board. The 1995 Conference Board survey found that about 60 percent of workers were broadly satisfied with their jobs, similar to the figure reported in the WRPS. The 2004 Conference Board reported a 10 percentage point drop in worker satisfaction. Just 50 percent of workers were satisfied with their job in that survey, the lowest we have ever seen in a job satisfaction analysis. The decline in satisfaction occurred among all age groups and household income levels and was largest among workers near the center of the age and income distribution.[3] Over the same period neither the GSS nor Gallup showed any trend in job satisfaction.

In 2005, the Harris polling firm found levels of dissatisfaction comparable to those in the Conference Board study and larger than those found in the WRPS. In the Harris Poll, 59 percent of workers were extremely/somewhat/slightly satisfied with their jobs, while 41 percent were not. In addition, Harris found considerable discontent in responses to an innovative set of questions that went beyond the generic "are you satisfied?" design. It found that only 44 percent of workers were glad they had chosen to work for their current employer over others, that one-third felt they were at a dead end in their job, and that 42 percent were trying to cope with feelings of burnout.[4]

The surveys that come closest in spirit to the WRPS focus on particular aspects of the workplace and compensation package as opposed to job satisfaction broadly defined. A particularly valuable set of surveys are the Health Pulse of America surveys conducted by Stony Brook University in New York. While, per their name, the health pulse surveys are focused largely on health issues, they ask about satisfaction with diverse aspects of a person's job. Exhibit I.1 shows that nearly one-fourth (23 percent) of workers were dissatisfied with their salary, while much larger proportions were dissatisfied with or had no health-care benefits (40 percent) nor retirement benefits (46 percent). Despite all the media attention to job insecurity, that issue drew the least amount of dissatisfaction.[5]

We examined other surveys of job satisfaction, whose estimated levels of discontent ranged widely from levels comparable to the GSS and Gallup toward the 1/3rd dissatisfied portion in the WRPS. The variation in results with the standard satisfaction question suggests that responses to this question are less reliable than at first appears to be the case from the near-constant division between the satisfied and dissatisfied found in the GSS and Gallup polls. The analysis in Chapter 3, where we show that the response to questions about wanting influence at workplaces varies considerably depending on whether or not respondents have been previously asked about specific issues and thus have them in the forefront of their consciousness, may apply here as well. In any case, the fact that the surveys that come closest in design or spirit to the WRPS gave results comparable to ours or found higher and rising levels of job dissatisfaction confirms our decision to focus on attitudes toward specific features of the work relationship rather than on satisfaction broadly conceived.

Loyalty and Attitudes toward Management

A key result from the WRPS was that workers had greater loyalty to their firm than they felt the firm had to them. Specifically, while 56 percent of workers reported that they felt a lot of "loyalty" to their employer only 38 percent trusted management "a lot" to keep its promises to them — a gap of 18 percentage points between workers' sense of loyalty and their trust in management.

Post WRPS surveys have found either larger or similar gaps. A 2005 on-

EXHIBIT I.1. Percentage of workers satisfied or dissatisfied with particular aspects of current job.

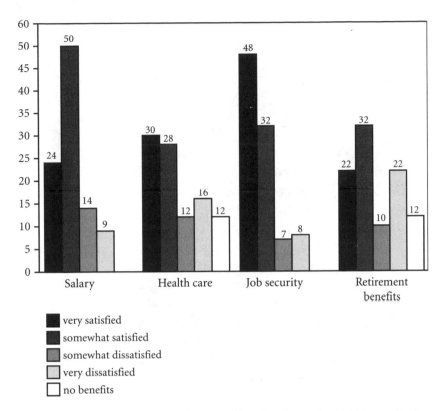

- ■ very satisfied
- ■ somewhat satisfied
- ■ somewhat dissatisfied
- ▫ very dissatisfied
- ▫ no benefits

Source: Stony Brook University, Health Pulse of America, Survey June 2004, reported in ws.cc.stonybrook.edu/surveys/HPAJuly04.htm.

line poll commissioned by Randstad North America reported that 59 percent of workers were loyal to their firm but that only 26 percent thought that management was loyal to them — a 33 percentage point gap.[6] A 2002 *Christian Science Monitor* poll reported that 63 percent were very loyal to their firm, whereas 40 percent believed the firm was loyal to them — a 23 point gap.[7] A 2004 Gallup poll showed a divergence similar to that found in the WRPS: 85 percent of workers professed strong loyalty to their firm, whereas just 67 percent thought the company they worked for had a strong sense of loyalty to them — an 18 percentage point gap.[8] Finally, the 2005 Harris Poll shows a similar pattern of worker distrust toward management. Sixty-three percent of workers reported that they disagreed with the statement that "top management displays integrity and morality." Seventy-one percent did not think that management "is committed to advancing the skills of employees" — a particularly important concern of all but the oldest workers — and an important factor in gaining employee trust and loyalty.

Another way to examine how workers view their relationship with management is to ask whether labor-management relations at the workplace are good, bad, or in-between. The WRPS found that 18 percent viewed relations as excellent, 49 percent saw them as good, 29 percent viewed them as only fair (22 percent) or poor (7 percent). From 1996 to 2005, the survey research firm Peter D. Hart Research Associates asked a more nuanced set of questions about the relationship between management and workers.[9] It asked the public whether management had too much power compared to workers, or workers had too much power compared to management, or if there was a pretty fair balance of power between management and workers. The percentage that said management had too much power increased from 47 percent in 1996 to 53 percent in 2005, while those judging the relationship to be a "pretty fair" balance declined from 41 percent to 36 percent. Just 7 percent thought workers had too much power in both periods. In its 2005 poll, Hart used a split sample design, substituting the word "corporations" for "management" for half the sample. For this half, 63 percent of respondents said corporations had too much power, 28 percent found that the balance with workers was "pretty fair," while just 4 percent thought workers had too much power. The more negative response to use of the term "corporations" probably reflects people's warmer feelings toward management, which consists of real people, than toward the artificial "person" of the corporation, which is just a legal structure. In any case, and consistent with the rising belief that corporations have too much power, in 2002, 58 percent of Americans thought that big business had too much influence on the Bush administration, compared to 22 percent who thought they had the right amount and 8 percent who thought that big business had too little influence.[10]

In the wake of the scandals at Enron, WorldCom, and other major companies, moreover, confidence in business leadership broadly fell. A 2002 CBS news poll reported that only 27 percent of the public believed that most corporate executives were honest, compared to 32 percent who thought that in 1985. Gallup's Social Series 2005 polls show that less than 7 percent of the public reported that they were "very satisfied" with the size and influence of major corporations and that 60 percent wanted the influence of corporations reduced in that year.[11] While the public has never had great confidence in union leadership, in May 2005, a larger proportion of the public said they had a great deal of confidence in organized labor (12 percent) than in big business (8 percent), and a smaller proportion said they had very little or no confidence in labor (25 percent) than in business (31 percent). In short, presumably as a result of the economic and business developments in the 2000s, public support for business has fallen, which has the potential to create greater worker desire for representation and participation to protect employees' interests.

What Matters to Workers

The WRPS found substantial gaps between workers' desire for influence on decisions and their actual influence in several important features of workplaces (Chapter 3). The greatest gap was associated with "bread and butter" issues relating to benefits and pay, followed by training issues, while the smallest gap was between what workers wanted and had in deciding how to organize their work, because in that area most had substantial independence.

In succeeding years, the polls have asked workers how they view employer performance on these and related workplace issues. A 2001 Hart poll asked respondents how important different workplace "rights" were to them and then used the WRPS design of asking them to assign a school letter grade from A to F on how employers were doing in providing that right. In many cases, what the survey called "rights" do not exist in law and are more accurately described as employer fair treatment of workers. Terminology aside, Exhibit I.2 shows substantial gaps between the importance of rights to workers and employer performance, with wide variation among the categories covered in the survey. Differences in questions make it hard to assess whether the Hart results show larger or smaller gaps than those in the WRPS. What is clear is the Hart survey finds large gaps, as did the WRPS.

To see if workers' views changed over time, we rely on a different Hart question, which the survey asked in 1999 and 2005:

Thinking generally about companies and other employers and the way they treat employees, let me mention some different aspects of work, and please tell me how well employers are doing on each item. Are employers doing very well, doing fairly well, falling somewhat short, or falling very short when it comes to . . . [different issues]

Exhibit I.2. Employer performance on the provision of workplace "rights."

	Share of workers thinking the right "essential" or "very important" (A)	Doing well (B)	Gap ratio (A)-(B)
A living wage that provides an income above the poverty line for a full-time worker	87	47	40
Training and assistance if a job moves to another country	81	55	26
Job security unless good cause for termination	85	58	27
Opportunities for education and training	82	59	23
Overtime pay over 40 hrs/week	87	72	15
Personal privacy on the job	82	59	23
Respect from one's employer	94	63	31
Sick leave without losing one's job	90	65	25
Time off to care for a new baby or sick family member without losing one's job	90	66	24
A safe and healthy workplace	98	70	28
Equal treatment, regardless of age	92	55	37
Equal pay for women	95	57	38
Reasonable accommodations for disabled	88	61	27
Equal racial and ethnic treatment	97	63	24
Freedom from sexual harassment	96	73	23

Source: Peter D. Hart Research Associates, Study no. 7704 (August 2005).

Exhibit I.3 summarizes the responses in terms of the proportion of workers who said employers were doing well or falling short and indicates the difference between these responses. To facilitate analysis, we also give the average response for the items in each category. In 1999, there are moderate differences between the proportions who report employers doing well and the proportion who report them falling short on most issues: an average of 5 points for bread-and-butter issues, and 2 points for issues relating to work conditions and future opportunities. The biggest gap is 17 points on workplace relations due to the huge number of workers who felt that companies were not sharing profits with them. The 2005 statistics show an increase in the gap in all categories. The difference between the proportion reporting that employers did well and poorly on the bread-and-butter

Exhibit I.3. Workers' assessment of employer performance on workplace issues.

	Year	Doing well (A)	Falling short (B)	Gap (A-B)
Bread-and-butter issues				
Providing regular cost-of-living raises to employees	1999	43	52	-9
	2005	27	70	-43
Providing adequate and secure retirement benefits	1999	44	52	-8
	2005	31	65	-34
Providing permanent jobs that offer good benefits and job security	1999	50	46	4
	2005	35	62	-27
Paying a fair share of employees' health care costs*	2002	44	50	-6
	2005	38	57	-19
Average of four items	1999*	45	50	**-5**
	2005	33	64	**-31**
Future opportunities/Work conditions				
Providing opportunities for advancement	1999	54	41	13
	2005	44	52	-8
Adopting policies that help working parents	1999	39	56	-17
	2005	35	55	-20
Investing in their employees by giving them the training and education that they need	1999	51	47	4
	2005	50	45	5
Providing women with equal pay	1999	48	54	-6
	2005	42	48	-6
Average of four items	1999	48	50	**-2**
	2005	43	50	**-7**
Workplace relations				
Being loyal to long-term employees	1999	44	53	-9
	2005	32	64	-32
Showing concern for employees, not just for the financial bottom line	1999	39	58	-19
	2005	31	65	-34
Listening to employees' ideas and concerns	1999	46	51	-5
	2005	45	50	-5
Sharing profits with average employees when the company does well	1999	29	66	-37
	2005	24	67	-33
Average of four items	1999	40	57	**-17**
	2005	33	62	**-29**

Source: Peter D. Hart Research Associates, Study no. 7704 (August 2005).
* 2002 data used for the share of health costs.

issues rose on all four items, producing an average gap of -31 points. The differences between employers doing well and poorly in the future opportunities/work conditions domain rose more modestly, by an average of -7. The difference between doing well and falling short in workplace relations, which was already large, rose to reach an average of -29 points. Since 1999 was a booming year in the job market, while 2005 was a weaker year, the changes between the years presumably reflect the impact of the weak recovery from the 2001 recession, as well as structural or secular change in attitudes.

Other Hart surveys that ask somewhat different questions tell a similar story. A February 2005 survey asked workers to name one or two aspects of their job on which they would most like to see improvement and compared the results to those in 1990s Hart surveys. In both the 2005 and 1990s surveys, 18 percent of workers cited job security as one of the two areas they wanted to see improve. Over the same period, the proportion that cited health-care benefits rose from 25 to 39 percent of workers, while the proportion looking for improved wages and salaries increased from 42 to 45 percent and the proportion looking for improved retirement benefits rose from 25 to 29 percent.[12] With a slightly changed question, offering options in response — "which one or two . . . do you feel are the biggest problems facing workplace people today?" — an August 2005 Hart survey gave the following list of top issues: health-care costs (35 percent), jobs going overseas (31 percent), rising gas prices (29 percent), raises that don't keep up with the cost of living (23 percent), lack of retirement security (14 percent), and work schedules interfering with family responsibilities (10 percent).[13] Again, material issues dominate.

In sum, while worker opinions vary across issues, the general pattern is for rising gaps between what firms deliver at workplaces and what workers want. Worker views on specific issues are not constant, as in some of the satisfaction surveys, but change over time as labor market conditions and firm behavior changes.

Broad Conclusion II: Collective Action for Cooperative Workplace Relations

On the WRPS, 63 percent of employees said that they wanted *more* influence than they had over decisions at their workplace compared to 35 percent who preferred to keep things the way they are now. As detailed in Chapters 3 and 5, the survey probed the areas in which workers sought influence and the extent to which workers felt that they needed collective voice to gain influence and resolve workplace problems.

The evidence from ensuing surveys supports the finding that workers want more say in decisions and suggests that the desire for *more* influence has, if anything, increased since we did our survey. The most cogent evidence comes from the California Workforce Survey conducted by the University of California at Berkeley in 2001–2. This asked workers how important it was to them personally to have *more* respect and fair treatment on the job and how important it was for them to have *more* say in workplace decisions. While asking the question about influence differently from us, by using the word "more" in its questions this survey directed attention to the desire for change, rather than satisfaction with the status quo. Answers to the California survey reflect a gap between what people want and what they have, even though the survey did not ask them, as we did, to independently lay out both sides of the gap. In any case, Exhibit I.4 shows that 75 percent of workers on the California survey said that it was very important to have *more* respect and fair treatment on the job. It also shows that 51 percent said it was very important and 38 percent said it was somewhat important to have *more* say in workplace decisions. The sum of these last numbers, 89 percent, exceeds the 63 percent who wanted more influence on the WRPS, though whether this reflects differences in questionnaire design or a trend is unclear.

Turning to the value of collective action, the WRPS found that 43 percent to 56 percent of workers favored collective activity over individual efforts to deal with workplace problems, depending on how we worded the question. Employees differentiated sharply between areas where they sought group support and areas in which they preferred to deal with problems as individuals. The Hart organization asked workers in 1996, 1997, 1999, and 2001 whether group organization or individual action "comes closer to your view about what it takes to improve their situation at work?" As the upper panel of Exhibit I.5 shows, on average 47 percent of persons favored group activity compared to 39 percent who favored relying on themselves, with little variation across years. In 1985, 1993, 2001, and 2003, Hart posed a different question about the efficacy of collective versus individual voice: "Do you think that employees are more successful in getting problems resolved at work when they bring these problems up as a group or when they bring them up as individuals?" The lower panel of Exhibit I.5 gives the responses for 1993, 2001, and 2003. It shows

EXHIBIT I.4. The importance of fair treatment and workplace influence.

How important to you personally is
more respect and fair treatment on the job?

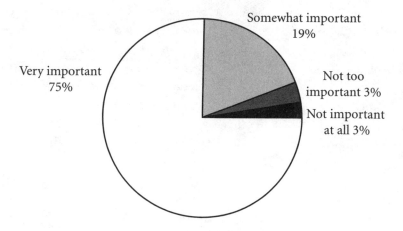

How important to you personally is
having more say in workplace decisions?

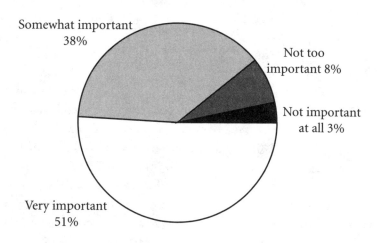

Source: California Workplace Survey was in the field July 2001–January 2002. Data are available at sda.berkeley.edu:7502/archive.htm.

Exhibit I.5. Assessments of the value of collective versus individual efforts to deal with workplace problems.

Panel A: Which comes closer to your view about what it takes to improve the situation at work?

	1/01	3/99	2/97	4/96	**Average**
People need to join together in groups to get what they want	45	48	46	47	**47**
People need to rely on themselves to get what they want.................	40	36	40	41	**39**
Mixed/both (VOL)...............	13	13	13	8	**11**
Not sure.......................	2	3	1	4	**3**

Panel B: Do you think that employees are more successful in getting problems resolved at work when they bring these problems up as a group or when they bring them up as individuals?

	2/03	1/01	2/93	**Average**
More successful as group	70	59	73	**67**
More successful as individuals	18	28	20	**22**
Makes no difference (VOL)	6	7	3	**5**
Not sure.......................	6	6	4	**5**

Note: Before February 2003, the question was phrased, "Do you think that employees are more successful in getting problems resolved with their employer when they bring these problems up as a group or when they bring them up as individuals?" This question was also asked in 1985, with just 54 percent saying they would be more successful as a group; 37 percent said they would be more successful as individuals, 4 percent said no difference, and 5 percent were unsure.
Sources: Panel A, Peter D. Hart Associates, Study no. 6221 (January 2001); Panel B, Peter D. Hart Research Associates, Study no. 6924 (February 2003).

that larger percentages chose the group activity in each year, but by substantially different amounts. Averaging the responses shows that 67 percent chose group activity as more efficacious versus 22 percent who chose individual activity. The 1985 results, summarized in the note to the table, show a smaller advantage for group activity, which suggests that there may be an increase in the perceived advantage of group activity, though again the variability in responses to this question makes us leery of any generalization.

Employer Opposition versus Worker Desire for Cooperation

As detailed in ensuing chapters, the WRPS found that workers viewed cooperation with management as critical to good workplace relations but rated management low in willingness to share power or take account of worker concerns. Most workers were aware that management opposed efforts to unionize. Some said that management's attitude would alter their votes in a secret ballot election.

The post-WRPS surveys confirm that workers are cognizant of management hostility to collective action through unions, and that this weighs heavily in their consideration of unionizing. A 2005 Hart survey found that 53 percent of workers believe that "employers generally oppose the union and try to convince employees to vote no" in National Labor Relations Board (NLRB) elections while less than half as many (26 percent) think that "employers generally take no position and let the employees decide on their own."[14] Another Hart survey found that approximately one in five (22 percent) thought that employers used specific anti-union tactics (ranging from requiring employees to attend anti-union presentations on company time to firing union supporters) "all the time or fairly often," that 25 percent thought employers used the tactics just sometimes, that 23 percent thought employers used the tactics not very often, while 10 percent thought the employers never used the tactics and 18 percent were unsure.[15] Although it is difficult to compare the qualitative survey responses to quantitative estimates of the extent to which firms use the tactics in organizing campaigns, actual use appears to exceed public perceptions.[16]

The public opposes many of these management practices, the legal tactics as well as the illegal violations of the labor laws.[17] At various times, unions have tried to harness this opposition to create the kind of public furor that would lead Congress to increase the penalties on employers for committing unfair labor practices during organizing drives. But the union campaigns have not been successful. In the abstract, a large proportion of the public believes that it is important to have strong laws that give workers the right to form and join unions. In a 2005 Hart survey, 50 percent of the general public said it was very important and 23 percent said it was fairly important to have such laws.[18] But when it comes to placing greater penalties on employers, the proportion of the public who favored adding tough penalties to the law just marginally exceeds the proportion opposed to adding tough penalties. Forty-seven percent of the public said that they approved of changes in the law that would involve tough penalties for violations by employers, 43 percent disapproved, and 10 percent had no opinion. Even among union members, the proportion favoring tough penalties on employers was just 59 percent.[19] In another survey, Hart reports that approximately one-third of respondents approve of anti-union campaigns compared to a bit over a half who disapprove, and that this division varies by party identification, with Republicans evenly split between approval and disapproval, while Democrats are disproportionately disapproving.[20]

In 2003, the Hart survey asked a question that illuminates in one swoop worker concern about employer opposition to unions and the desire of workers for cooperative relations. Hart asked respondents which of three factors was the "biggest disadvantage to having a union": having worse relations between employers and management, being forced to go on strike, and paying more in dues than the union delivers. The biggest factor for the general public, with 38 percent of responses, was having worse relations between employees and management, followed by being forced to go on strike (29 percent) and paying more in dues (20 percent). Among union members 32 percent cited worse relations between employees and management as the biggest disadvantage, while 29 percent cited paying more in dues than the union delivers, and only 18 percent cited being forced to go on strike.[21]

Broad Conclusion III: Workers Want Unions and Nonunion Forms of Representation

As noted, the U.S. labor system effectively offers only one form of collective voice to workers, trade unions that win secret ballot elections. Either a workplace has an exclusive representative collective bargaining contract or workers have no independent collective voice with which to communicate with management. Given this, most labor relations analyses of collective voice have focused on worker desire for unions. To assess whether nonunion workers did/did not want unions, the WRPS asked, "If an election were held today to decide whether employees like you should be represented by a union, would you vote for the union or against the union?" Thirty-two percent of nonunion/nonmanagerial workers said that they would vote for a union — a proportion roughly similar to the proportions found in surveys of the intention to vote in surveys in the 1970s and 1980s. Ninety percent of union workers said they would vote to keep the union. These two statistics implied a desired rate of private sector unionization of 44 percent, which was about four times the actual rate of unionization in 1995.

Exhibit I.6 records the proportion of nonunion workers who say they would vote for/against a union in polls conducted by Hart Research Associates from 1993 through 2005, supplemented with data from a 1984 Harris poll, which asked the same question. The Harris poll shows that in the mid-1980s, 30 percent of nonunion workers would vote union in a secret ballot election — a comparable figure to the WRPS estimate. The Hart estimate for 1993 is higher than the WRPS estimate — 37 percent. What is most striking in Exhibit I.6, however, is the upward trend in the likelihood of voting for a union since then. By 2002 and 2005, the proportion of workers who said they would vote for a union rose above the proportion that said they would vote against a union for the first time in any survey with which we are familiar. If the Hart results are correct, the United States is experiencing a rising tide in the desire for union representation.

Not all recent surveys, however, show such high proportions wanting to unionize as does the Hart survey. A 2005 Zogby[22] poll reports that 36 percent of nonunion workers were likely to vote union, which is 4 points (13 percent) above the 32 percent WRPS estimate for 1994–95 but far below the 53 percent Hart estimate for that year.[23]

From one perspective, the variation in these proportions is irrelevant to understanding the U.S. labor system. After all, they all show that a large proportion of U.S. workers — 32 percent, or 36 percent, or 53 percent — want union representation but are unable to gain it under the existing labor system. The demand for unionism by from one-third to one-half of the U.S. workforce is unfilled.

At the same time, it is important to assess whether the upward trend in the desire for unions is as large as in Exhibit I.6. Are we looking at different measures of what is essentially the same thing, or has that thing — worker desire for more collective voice through unionization — itself changed?

To gauge the extent to which workers have really become more prounion since the WRPS, we examined polls from Gallup and Hart that ask the public about their attitudes toward unions more generally. Our hypothesis is that if there is truly a rising desire for unions, it should show up in diverse questions about attitudes toward unionism, not simply in the voting in a union representation election question. The longest-standing question about unions is "do you approve or disapprove of labor unions" from Gallup. Exhibit I.7 gives the results from this question from 1947 to 2005. The proportion of Americans that approves of unions always exceeds the proportion that disapproves. From 1947 through 1981, however, the difference between the proportion approving and disapproving declined from about 40 percentage points to about 20 percentage points. Since then, the trend decline has reversed, with the proportion of the public disapproving of unions dropping sharply from 1995 through 2005. In 2005, the

If an election were held tomorrow to decide whether your workplace would have a union or not, do you think you would definitely vote for forming a union, probably vote for forming a union, probably vote against forming a union, or definitely vote against forming a union?

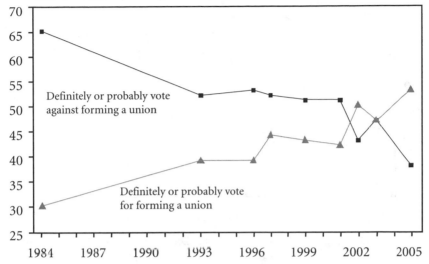

Source: Peter D. Hart Research Associates, various polls, except 1984. Those year's data are from Harris polls, on a slightly differently worded question: "If an election were held tomorrow to decide whether your workplace would be unionized or not, do you think you would definitely vote for a union, probably vote for a union, probably vote against a union, or definitely vote against a union?"

difference between the proportion approving and disapproving reached 43 points, a bit larger than it was in 1947. This is consistent with a large increase in workers wanting to unionize.

Gallup polls have also asked whether people want unions to have more or less influence on social outcomes. The responses here also show that a rising proportion want unions to have more influence. In 2005, 38 percent of persons wanted unions to have more influence, 30 percent wanted unions to have less influence and 29 percent wanted their influence to stay about the same. By contrast, in 1999, 30 percent wanted unions to have more influence — 8 points less than in 2005; 32 percent wanted unions to have less influence, and 36 percent wanted their influence to stay about the same. But, indicative of the problem of the U.S. labor system, in 2005, 53

EXHIBIT I.7. Approval and disapproval of unions, Gallup and Hart polls, 1947–2005.

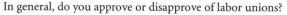

In general, do you approve or disapprove of labor unions?

Source: 1947 through 2000, Gallup. 2001-2005 Peter D. Hart Research Associates, Study no. 7518 (February 2005).

percent of adults said that they expected unions to become weaker over time — a higher percentage than in the 1999 poll, where 44 percent said they believed unions would be weaker.[24]

Judging What Unions Do

Chapter 4 of this book reports how workers viewed unions according to the WRPS. There are two key findings. The first was that an overwhelming 90 percent of union members reported that they would vote to support their union if they were asked to vote to keep it or get rid of it in an NLRB election. One post-WRPS survey replicated the WRPS design of asking union members how they would vote in an election for union representation. The 2002 California survey found, as we did, that union members would overwhelmingly choose their union again: 86 percent said that they would vote to keep the union, whereas 13 percent were for getting rid of it.

The second finding was that, this support notwithstanding, union members viewed unions critically. They were generally satisfied with how their local union performed but were critical of the union movement broadly and of their own union's ability to improve their working lives. As we put it in Chapter 3, union workers love their union, but not blindly. Exhibit I.8 summarizes the results to questions about how workers assess their unions in various areas. It is drawn from post-WRPS Hart surveys and the California Workforce Survey cited earlier. Consistent with the WRPS results, the largest proportion of union members give middling grades to their union in improving wages, benefits, and working conditions (item 1) and in getting members more say in workplace (item 2). A substantial number rated the union as just somewhat effective or not too effective in both these areas. Similarly, asked about the overall performance or experience with the union, the Hart 2003 survey reports that 20 percent viewed it as excellent, 52 percent as good, 20 percent as not so good, and 7 percent as poor (item 3). Despite the different question and sampling frame, the California survey shows a similar pattern (item 4) — a middling assessment of union performance. The 2005 Harris Poll (item 5) finds that while 61 percent of union members say that the union gives them their money's worth for the dues they pay, 39 percent disagree, with 19 percent disagreeing strongly.

The remaining items in Exhibit I.8 consider how the general public views the ability of unions to deliver for their members. The public has a mixed view of the efficacy of unions. Their view is less positive than that of members. In a 2003 Hart survey, the public split nearly evenly around whether unions deliver good representation for the dues they charge (36 percent) or charge too much in dues for what they deliver (39 percent) (item 6). In a 2005 Harris Poll, 7 percent of the public said the unions were doing an excellent job, and 25 percent said they were doing a good job, compared to 48 percent who gave them a fair rating and 17 percent who gave them a poor rating. Union households (not reported in the table) gave only a modestly higher assessment of unions overall.

The WRPS found that workers were least satisfied with union involvement in political activity. The 2005 Harris Poll shows that union politicking remains a sore point for much of the public and for union members. Sixty-seven percent of the public complained that unions were too involved in politics. Sixty percent said that unions are more concerned with fighting change than trying to bring about change, and 55 percent said that unions stifled individual initiative. At the same time, half of the pub-

Exhibit I.8. How workers see union efficacy in post-WRPS surveys.

Panel A: Union members

1. (Hart, 2003) Overall, how effective do you think labor unions are these days in improving wages, benefits, and working conditions for their members?

Very effective	24 %
Fairly effective	36 %
Somewhat effective	32 %
Not effective	8 %

2. (California, 2002) Effectiveness of unions in getting their members more say in workplace decisions

Very effective	22 %
Somewhat effective	48 %
Not too effective	22 %
Not effective at all	9 %

3. (Hart, 2003) Thinking now about the union you belong to, how would you rate the overall performance of your union in representing members like you?

Excellent	20 %
Good	52 %
Not so good	20 %
Poor	7 %
Don't know	1 %

4. (California, 2002) Your personal experience with the union in your company or organization

Highly satisfactory	23 %
Satisfactory	54 %
Not so satisfactory	17 %
Very unsatisfactory	6 %

5. (Harris, 2005) Unions give their members their money's worth for the dues they pay

Agree strongly	26 %
Agree somewhat	35 %
Disagree strongly	20 %
Disagree somewhat	19 %

Panel B: General Public

6. (Hart, 2003)　　Unions . . .

Deliver good representation for the dues they charge	36 %
Charge too much in dues for what they deliver	39 %
Mixed/Both	5 %
Unsure	20 %

Exhibit I.8. (continued)

Panel B: General Public (continued)

7. (Harris, 2005) How would you rate the job being done by unions?

Excellent	7 %
Good	25 %
Fair	48 %
Poor	17 %
Not sure	3 %

Sources: The Harris Poll no. 68 (August 31, 2005), "Negative Attitudes to Labor Unions Show Little Change in Past Decade"; Peter D. Hart Associates, Study no. 6924 (February 2003); 2001–2002 *California Workforce Survey*, sda.berkeley.edu:7502/archive.htm

lic believes that unions get legislation that helps all working people, whether they are union members or not.

Given these nuanced critical views of unions, in what domains do the public and union members have confidence in unions and in what domains do they lack confidence? In 2001, the Hart organization posed this issue by asking workers how much confidence they had that unions "would make a positive contribution to the debate" on a variety of public policy issues. The results in Exhibit I.9 show that the general public and union members discriminate greatly among issues. Both have great confidence in unions when unions speak out on workplace concerns, where presumably they have expertise, have some confidence in unions on issues relating to protecting income standards or helping the poor, but have little confidence in what unions say on broader policy issues, even in areas of obvious importance to average workers, such as taxes, trade agreements, and immigration. Union members have greater confidence than the general public in unions on virtually all issues, but their confidence also drops off sharply beyond workplace issues.

This evidence indicates that the public and union members see unions as their institution of voice on issues pertaining to work but do not regard their views as compelling in other domains where unions have no special expertise. This in turn suggests that to carry weight in public policy, unions have to build on their authority in workplace issues.

Exhibit I.9. Confidence in union contribution to public policy debate.

Percent with confidence unions would make a positive contribution to debates over national issues	"A lot"	Sum of "not much" and "none"	Difference of "a lot" and "not much/none"
Public			
Workplace health and safety	41	10	31
Laws dealing with overtime pay and length of workweek	32	9	23
Work and family issues, such as FMLA	29	13	16
Health care	26	18	8
Policies to help working poor	21	24	-3
Medicare	20	27	-7
Social Security	17	29	-12
Economic policy	12	22	-10
Trade agreements	13	32	-19
Environmental policy	10	35	-25
Taxes	7	31	-24
Immigration policy	10	34	-24
Union members			
Workplace health and safety	60	0	60
Laws dealing with overtime pay and length of workweek	57	0	57
Work and family issues, such as FMLA	48	8	40
Health care	36	16	20
Policies that help the working poor	36	22	14
Medicare	19	16	3
Social Security	28	17	11
Economic policy	24	11	13
Trade agreements	19	26	-7
Environmental policy	17	38	-21
Taxes	12	30	-18
Immigration policy	17	34	-17

Source: Peter D. Hart Research Associates, Study no. 6221 (January 2001).

The Missing Institutions: Nonunion Channels of Collective Voice

Perhaps the greatest innovation of the WRPS was to give workers a wider choice of institutions for representing their interests to management than the union yes-or-no option that the U.S. labor system offers them and on which all other surveys had focused. The striking finding from the survey was that the proportion of workers who wanted workplace committees that could meet with management to discuss problems without the collective bargaining powers that belong uniquely to unions exceeded the proportion who wanted trade unions to represent them (Chapter 7). Given a choice among unions, legal enactment, and workplace committees to increase employees' say in workplace matters and to make sure workers are treated fairly, 52 percent of employees chose workplace committees. Given a choice among "employee organizations that negotiate" (a union in all but name), legal enactment, workplace committees, and nothing, 46 percent of employees chose workplace committees. Union members were generally very receptive to consultative committees as well, while wanting to keep their union.

Subsequent polls have not probed the attributes of workplace committees that workers want in the depth that we do in Chapter 7. But they confirm that workers see these institutions as attractive. Exhibit I.10 shows that in each year in which the Hart survey asked workers whether they supported an association of workers *that was not a union* to represent the interests of the employees and meet regularly with management, nearly 40 percent said they would definitely vote for the association and approximately another 40 percent said they would probably vote for it, compared to just 18 percent who were either definitely or probably against it. In the 1997 survey, Hart asked the workers who said they wanted an employee association but not a union in what ways workers wanted this employee association to be different from a labor union. Ten percent said they did not want to pay union dues, and 7 percent said because the group would not be as powerful or have as much control as a union. But the majority of reasons given reflected the desire to have a voice with management that avoided confrontation: 19 percent favored an association to work as a group with one voice with less antagonism (than a union); 16 percent said they wanted the group to stand by employees: and 14 percent referred to better communication. Thus, about half of those who favored an association over a union wanted an independent voice at the workplace without collective bargaining, irrespective of dues and concern over union failings.

Using the Hart 2001 survey, we have examined the association between supporting a union and supporting an employee association. Among workers who said that they would vote for a union in the survey, 92 percent favored an association, presumably in addition to their union. Among workers who said that they would vote against a union, 68 percent favored the employee association. Along a variety of dimensions, the workers who oppose unions but would vote for an association look very different than traditional union supporters. They are more likely to be Republican, to be

EXHIBIT I.10. Percentage of employed respondents who would vote for or against forming an employee association that was not a union to represent employee interests with management.

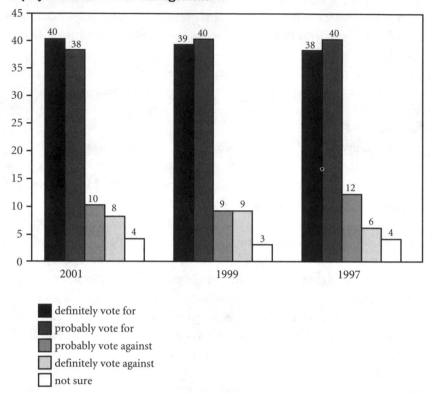

definitely vote for
probably vote for
probably vote against
definitely vote against
not sure

Source: Peter D. Hart Research Associates, study no. 6221 (January 2001). Based on the question: "And suppose there were a proposal to form an employees association in your workplace that was not a union, but that would represent the interests of employees and meet regularly with management to discuss important workplace issues. Would you definitely vote for, probably vote for, probably vote against, or definitely vote against forming an employees association?"

white-collar workers, to have higher incomes, and to be white than persons who say they would vote union.[25] Taking these responses, we have decomposed workers into the four categories shown in Exhibit I.11, depending on whether they favor unions and associations, just one or the other institution, or neither. The largest group consists of the 39 percent of workers who favor unions and an employee association, which makes them the strongest supporters of collective voice. Given the way the current U.S.

Exhibit I.11. Proportion of workers who would vote for the formation of an employee association and who would vote in favor of a union, 2001.

Proportion who would vote for association and union	39
Proportion who would vote for association but against a union	35
Proportion who would vote for union but against association	2
Proportion who would vote against both	14
Remainder, not sure on one or both votes	10

Source: Tabulated from Peter D. Hart Research Associates, Study no. 6221, January 2001

labor system works, unions will never represent most of these workers. The second largest group consists of the 35 percent of workers who want an employee association but not a union. Given the way the current U.S. labor system works, none of these workers will get the form of representation and participation that they want. The only workers who will achieve what they want are the 14 percent opposed to either form of collective voice.

All told, workers seem more supportive of unions in the 2000s than we found in the mid-1990s in the WRPS. But the institution that appeals to most workers, whether they want a union or not, is an independent workplace committee to represent them in workplace decisions.

Conclusion

In sum, the post-WRPS polls support the conclusions in ensuing chapters of this book. In the mid-2000s, as in the mid-1990s, workers see a major gap between the representation and participation they want at the workplace and what they have. In the mid-2000s, as in the mid-1990s, they are open to different options on increasing their say at the workplace, from unionization to nonunion joint committees that meet and discuss issues with management. However, while workers want a cooperative relation with management, they have grown more distrustful that management will take their interests into account. The surveys in the 2000s also suggest that their desire for representation and participation is greater than when we did the WRPS.

That workers want greater say at their workplace as much or more than they did when we conducted the WRPS seems sensible given what has happened in the job market since we conducted our survey. The late 1990s economic boom notwithstanding, the U.S. economy has not delivered rising wages to most American workers despite rising productivity. Employers provide fewer workers with health insurance and pensions than they did in the mid-1990s. Major firms have gone belly-up due to malfeasance of management. Globalization has seemingly reduced job security and the chances for improved wages and benefits. The proportion of workers represented by unions has continued to slide. On the labor front, the labor law that the country enacted in the Depression and amended modestly since then has not changed. In face of all this, our new concluding chapter examines ways the country might improve this situation. But first, knowing that the results are as valid as they were a decade ago, let's look at the detailed WRPS evidence on *What Workers Want*.

CHAPTER 1

Ask the People Who Live There

Do you like going to work? Do your firm's managers treat you and your coworkers fairly? Do you want to have a greater influence on the decisions that affect your job and workplace? If so, how do you think this would be best accomplished: By having more individual discussion with management? By electing a union to represent you? By being part of a worker committee that talks with management? By having more legal protection?

In the United States, more than in any other industrial democracy, how well you do in life depends on how you do in the job market and how your employer treats you and other workers. Americans spend more time at their workplaces than do the citizens of virtually any other developed country. The incomes and benefits from work determine living standards more than in other countries. Many benefits that governments universally guarantee citizens elsewhere — paid vacation, job training, and health insurance — are in the United States decided on at the workplace by employers. And the pay and conditions of work vary more across jobs in the United States than in other countries. Unions and collective bargaining, which require employers in particular fields of manufacture and service to comply with national standards, are relatively weak and limited. Only 10 percent of private-sector workers in the United States belong to unions, and collective-bargaining agreements are generally limited to unionized firms.[1] As a result, the difference between a "good" and a "bad" job in our labor system is greater than is the case for other countries. Our private employers have more authority in deciding how to treat their workers than do private employers in other advanced countries.

Despite the importance of jobs to American living standards and employer influence on the quality of jobs, however, the United States has not seriously examined the basic framework governing employee-employer relations in more than half a century. That framework was established in the 1930s and 1940s, when industrial factories with largely male workforces dominated the economy. The choice then was to encourage unionization and collective bargaining with management as the best way to deal with workplace governance. Today, the structure and demands of the economy are very different, unions are shadows of their former selves, and the law de facto reduces the chances of successful worker organization. Despite an outmoded labor system, however, America has not had a serious national discussion of how the workplace might be governed in the modern economy.[2]

Every few years or so, unions or management groups propose changes in our labor law, but usually these suggestions are limited to tinkering with the existing framework rather than fundamentally reforming it. In their weakened state, unions are suspicious of where an open-ended reform discussion might lead. Because business holds the upper hand over unions, it naturally prefers the present system, despite its inefficiencies. The reform discussions that typically result are classic inside-the-Beltway fights — deadly contested by the parties but generally ignored by the broader public. What is most striking about discussions of American labor policy is that those most affected by it—the workers themselves — are not even part of the discussion. This is indeed a strange situation — rather like having an election without bothering to count votes.

This book's goal is to move the discussion of the laws and rules that govern workplaces and the national debate on ways to improve that governance, so that it addresses what workers want, not what insiders want. The book arose from the fact that one of us (Richard Freeman) served on the Commission on the Future of Worker-Management Relations, a national body that the first Clinton administration appointed to consider some changes in labor law. Early on, the commission's hearings and discussion focused largely on what the insiders thought should be done in the area and seemed oblivious to what American workers might want. To bring the voice of the worker into the debate, we decided to undertake as objective and scientific a survey as we could of worker views toward how workplaces operated and how their workplaces might be improved. This book reports the findings of the Worker Representation and Participation Survey (WRPS).

We hope that the voice of American workers that emerges in *What Workers Want* will someday spur, and guide, a serious effort at reforming our national labor policy and developing the labor institutions and policies that fit modern workers and firms.

Some Background on the WRPS

The WRPS was an ambitious, sprawling project. We view it as the most extensive analysis of American worker attitudes toward workplace relationships and power in more than twenty years.[3] The study sought to determine the levels and kinds of representation and participation workers wanted within their firms; how workers rated existing institutions of workplace governance (for example, unions, management-led personnel policies, and government regulation) as satisfying their desires for representation and participation; and the types of reforms workers desired. It included managers but not top executives and many employees who did some supervision as part of their job.

The WRPS began with a set of focus groups with workers in similar occupations, followed by a half-hour national telephone survey of more than 2,400 workers. It concluded with a mail/telephone follow-up survey of some 800 of the original respondents. This follow-up survey probed earlier responses and gathered reactions to written information on potential labor-law reforms that had been provided in advance. Along the way, it entailed or spawned a number of related surveys, many national in their own right, that were undertaken to check or reproduce our results.[4] We have amassed a huge amount of data that should occupy researchers for some time to come.[5]

The WRPS was also a contentious project — contentious because labor relations are contentious and because, at least briefly, it appeared that our results might influence policy. The ways in which workers participate in a firm's decision-making — be it as individuals, through union representatives, or through other channels — are controversial because they involve the division of power at the workplace. Management and labor regularly argue over this division before Congress and administrative agencies. Certain phrases, code words, and jargon — right-to-work laws, company unions, striker replacement, teamwork, and even labor-law reform — evoke strong emotional reactions on both sides. Such reactions reflect dispute and tension at the ground floor, in the workplaces from which we drew our respondents to the survey. In such an atmosphere, finding out what American workers truly want by way of participation and representation on their job is difficult. Even assuming that we could get workers to talk to us about their jobs, we needed to be especially careful in phrasing our questions. All the usual issues that public-opinion researchers worry about — for instance, the wording of questions, the order in which they are asked, and the scaling of attitudes — could be critical in getting accurate answers.

The survey's potential influence on policy was through the Commission on the Future of Worker-Management Relations.[6] The commission was chaired by John Dunlop (the dean of American labor relations and, among many other things, a former secretary of labor) and was widely known as the "Dunlop Commission." He and other members of the commission welcomed our effort to bring workers' voices into the policy discussion. But both management and labor groups worried that the WRPS might yield findings inimical to their positions.

To navigate these tensions, we tried to ensure that the WRPS was not only fair and accurate but also perceived as such. We enlisted academic survey experts to serve as our informal advisors, and probably more important, we asked for the guidance of management and union representatives. Our operating premise was that only if both groups accepted the WRPS survey design as valid would it have much chance of accomplishing what we wanted: a respectful hearing of the views of American workers. How we worked with management and labor on the survey, and the lessons we learned from that experience, is a story in its own right. We hope to describe not just our findings but also the difficulty of bringing social science to bear in contested issues of public policy.

Basic Findings

So what did we learn? Here's the kind of say workers want in workplace decisions and the barriers they see to attaining it:

- American workers want more of a say/influence/representation/ participation/voice (call it what you will) at the workplace than they now have. We call the difference between the say that workers want and what they currently have the *representation/participation gap*. The gap varies among groups and across workplace issues, but it is ubiquitous.
- Employees want greater say both because they think it will directly improve the quality of their working lives and because they think it will make their firm more productive and successful (which also enhances their work lives over the long run).
- Employees want greater workplace participation as individuals and as part of a group as well. Generally, workers like the open-door policies, suggestion boxes, and other employer-based mechanisms that give them individual access to management. Indeed, on many issues they

prefer to deal with management individually. But on other issues, for example, workplace health and safety, pay and benefit plans — where problems affect workers as a group — , workers want to speak as a group. And here, as in general, workers believe that such collective voices will benefit the firm as well as them.

- Workers want *cooperative relations* with management. Approximately one-third of employees are displeased with how management treats workers, and many give management low scores in concern for employees, trustworthiness, and willingness to share power. But few workers believe that the long-run solution to these problems is institutionalized labor-management conflict. Rather, the vast majority think that a workplace organization can only be effective if it enjoys management participation and support. Employees want a positive relation with management, not a war.

- Workers want some measure of *independence and protection of that independence* in their dealings with management. Having cooperative relations with management does not mean saying "Yes, boss" to any employer wish; it entails some measure of joint decision-making. The ideal organizational form for this cooperation varies across different groups of workers. Union members want to maintain union representation, and many nonunion workers also favor a union. An even larger share of workers want some form of a labor-management committee that stops short of collective bargaining but in which they have some significant independence in selecting representatives and resolving disputes. Whereas most workers favor more government protection of employees, only a handful think it preferable to a workplace-based organization — an organization of the kind very few now have.

- Workers believe that *management resistance* is the primary reason they do not have their desired level of influence at the workplace. They give managers high marks for business competence but believe that most managements are unwilling to share power or permit much independence in worker decision-making. They know that management would fight them if they tried to form a union, and many believe that management opposes independent worker representatives even in advisory workplace committees.

Here's what workers think about the way current institutions of workplace governance and worker protection (unions, personnel policies, and government regulation) operate:

- Unionized workers strongly support their unions, and the vast majority would vote to retain them in an election for union representation. Members believe that local unions represent their interests well but are more skeptical of their national union, particularly when it comes to representing them in politics. Nonunion workers have a less positive view of unions, but about one-third would vote for a union if given the opportunity. Taking union and nonunion workers together, that translates to a private-sector unionization rate of 44 percent, or better than three times the rate of representation among those surveyed and almost five times the national private-sector unionization rate.[7]
- Workers generally welcome management-initiated employee involvement (EI) programs and other advanced human-resource policies, but most think that these programs do not go far enough in devolving authority to employees. Workers in companies with EI programs are more satisfied with their working lives and are less likely to want unions than other workers. But most participants in such programs believe that the programs would work better if management gave greater decision-making power to workers.
- Workers exaggerate their statutory rights at workplaces. They believe that almost anything that seems blatantly unfair is also illegal, when in fact national labor law allows many acts — for example, firing someone without any reason — that most would consider "unfair." Still, most workers seek greater government protection on the job, even while recognizing the burden this might place on the firm. More than one in twenty workers reported that they had brought complaints about their workplace to courts or regulatory agencies, and nearly one in ten said they had seriously thought of doing so. But workers are not particularly pleased with the legal system being the major forum for dealing with workplace problems: Most would prefer to resolve problems through workplace-based organizations or institutions and to have the option of using those organizations for more informal resolution of disputes.

Finally, workers are clear and consistent about the institutions or organizations they would like to see at their workplace:

- Most workers want an organization that is run jointly by employees and management, to which workers elect their own representatives and in which disputes between management and labor are resolved through independent arbitration rather than management discretion.

- The vast majority of workers want the option of resolving problems concerning legal rights at their workplace through arbitration, and most said that they would use such an alternative dispute-resolution system rather than going to court or an administrative agency. But workers do not want firms to be allowed to require that workers forgo their rights to legal redress in favor of company-instituted arbitration systems as a condition for employment. Most workers also favor supplementing current enforcement of labor laws and standards through workforce-based regulatory committees, which would have some power to enforce labor laws and standards.

- Given a choice between improving their position at the workplace through labor-management committees, unions, or other employee organizations that collectively bargained with management or increased government regulation, about 25 percent of workers would choose union or unionlike organizations, and about 15 percent would opt for more regulation. Some 60 percent would prefer labor-management committees, where workers would have varying degrees of independence from management, often including electing representatives and carrying disagreements with management to an outside arbitrator. Overall, 45 percent of employees want a strongly independent workplace organization (which only unions provide in the current system), 43 percent want an organization with more limited independence from management, and the remaining workers want a workplace in which management alone rules.

And here's what the managers had to say:

- Managers broadly confirm worker assessment of their unwillingness to share power. Many are anti-union. Many oppose programs that would keep them from making the final decisions about workplace governance.

- At the same time, much of management favors a more substantial employee voice in joint committees. Perhaps most striking, nearly one-half of managers said that they favored employees electing their own representatives to such committees.

That workers (and managers) have these views may be surprising to some and annoying to many. Managers might be irritated that workers give them such poor marks for sharing power, that the vast majority of workers want some independence from them, and that unions are so popular with their members. Or maybe they'd be angry that half of their colleagues seem to think a bit of democracy through employees electing people to advisory committees is a good thing. Unions, or those believing in old-fashioned class struggle, might be annoyed to learn that workers just don't think workplace organization is achievable without management acceptance, that they seek a cooperative relation with managers, and that they are vitally concerned about the health of their firms.

However you respond to the preceding findings, we hope that this book will convince you that workers have consistent views on, and strong desires for, a workplace-relations system quite different from what now exists. They want a more varied system of participation and representation with a more cooperative and equal relationship to management.

We believe that a system of labor relations consistent with these views is both desirable and feasible for America. We think it would certainly make workers happier, and would probably make firms more productive. But *What Workers Want* is not about arguing for that system; it is not about limning its institutional features or strategizing about how workers, unions, and firms might achieve it. Rather, and more simply, this book seeks to open the discussion by being as clear and accurate as possible on the worker aspirations that would provide its motivation and support.

Why Care about What Workers Want?

Why do we think that finding out what workers want is worth an entire research project and ultimately a book?

We did not ask this question when we began our research. It seemed obvious that in a capitalist democracy in which nearly everyone earns his or her living as a worker, finding out what workers wanted on the job was the sine qua non of developing good labor policies at the company or national level. But in the course of our work, critics and skeptics sometimes put "Why care?" questions to us.

Why care what employees want at the workplace when long-term jobs are a thing of the past? We'll call this the "death of the job" objection, in reference to a *Fortune* magazine story on the topic.[8]

Why care when employees who are dissatisfied with their workplace can always switch to another one? We'll call this the "take this job and shove it" objection, after the country and western song.

Why care about workplace governance at all when overall employment and income are booming in the United States as they were when we wrote this book? We'll call this the "it's the economy, stupid" objection, after the Clinton campaign theme.

And why care what ordinary workers want, when management and labor experts know better about how to design systems of workplace governance and labor laws? We'll call this the "father knows best" objection.

Implicit in these questions are strong views or beliefs about how American labor markets function, and the way in which public policy is and perhaps should be determined. Some of these views are simply wrong; others are inconsistent or, more kindly, not readily commensurate with our country's democratic ideals. But such views are definitely out there. So before presenting our findings about what workers want, we will now take a moment to respond to these objections to the very task we have set for ourselves.

Death of the Job?

Consider first the belief that workers now change jobs so frequently and are so minimally involved in firms that it is silly to look to them for concern or knowledge about ways to improve labor-management relations. This view imagines the firm as a nexus of short-term contracts between capital and skills, suppliers and purchasers. The firm is virtual, hiring contingent workers or consultants for specific projects for most activities. In such a world, workers flit like mayflies from one employer to another, and people lack the information, interest, or standing to provide instruction on workplace governance.

This story has both a critical version and a celebratory one. The critical version stresses the rise in contingent work and subcontractor relations, in which workers lose fringe benefits and protection of some labor laws. The celebratory one exalts independent professionals working at home on short-term contracts — the epitome of the medieval artisan. Common to both versions is the conviction that managers and workers simply do not spend enough time together to develop valid expectations of one another. The romantic equivalent would be leading a life of bar-hopping, one-night stands, and short-term dating rather than entering a permanent relationship.

Despite the popularity of this spot-market view of the U.S. job market, it is wrong. Contingent work and subcontracting have certainly become more important. Temporary help agencies are among the fastest-growing firms. Management consultants, who often hire young professionals for short-term intensive work, are another growth area. Some especially prominent and talented workers — professional athletes under free agency, for example, or recording stars shopping for new labels, or CEO turnaround artists — make bundles under short-term contracts in which their unique skills command unique compensation. Today a Red Sox, tomorrow a Brewer, and next week a Yankee.

These situations are not the norm in the United States, however, nor are they likely to become so in the foreseeable future. Contrary to the claim that the job is dead, the typical American employee still works for the same company for many years (as the staff at *Fortune* themselves undoubtedly do) and thus has good reason to care about how his or her firm performs and how it handles its workplace relations.[9] Respondents to the WPRS reported, on average, that they had been with their current employer for 7.6 years. On standard statistical assumptions, their job tenure — the time they stay with one employer — will average twice as long, or about fifteen years.[10]

Also, the link between an employee and a firm, moreover, is not just a function of time but of the position that the worker holds in the firm and the firm's reliance on that individual. Take the case of supervision, certainly an important firm function. To a striking degree, American firms spread supervisory tasks widely in the workforce. Some 15 percent of WRPS respondents identified themselves as managers, engaged in supervision more or less full time; 31 percent of nonmanagerial employees reported that they supervised other workers as part of their job. Weighting these as shares of our respondent groups, 41 percent of American workers engage in some supervisory activity. At the very least, these are not casual or contingent workers but a critical part of the firm's stock of human capital.

Consistent with these facts, better than 60 percent of WRPS respondents describe their current job as long term or as an opportunity for advancement in the same company. Only 15 percent view their job as part of a career or profession that will probably take them to different companies. But even these workers, who might best fit the spot-market view of virtual corporations, are concerned about how their workplace functions. They might be with the firm only a few years, but those years can be critical in their acquiring the skills needed to advance in their career. And how the firm treats them even during limited periods can still make their lives enjoyable or miserable.

The remaining quarter or so of employees describe their job as something that they will probably leave — a short-term or noncareer position. Nearly one-half of these workers were eighteen to twenty-four years of age;

most were in wholesale/retail trade; most made $200 or less a week. They are in the early search phase of their work lives, or are part of the low-skilled group who have, in recent years, suffered the worst wage losses in the U.S. job market.

Still, it is possible that while the spot-market description of firm relations is wrong, the lack of attachment to firms that it predicts might be right. Perhaps even workers who are with a firm for many years don't give a damn about how it's doing. But this is not so. More than one-half of non-managerial employees describe themselves as having a lot of loyalty to their company, compared with 15 percent who say they have only a little loyalty or no loyalty at all.[11] An even larger portion of managerial employees have a lot of loyalty to the firm, as do employees with greater tenure. To be sure, employees report greater loyalty to their immediate supervisors and to fellow employees than to the firm itself; managers also report greater loyalty to their supervisors and to the people who work for them than to the firm. But overall, the majority of workers report that they have a lot of loyalty to the firm itself.

In short, employees have good reasons to be concerned about workplace governance, and top management has good reason to know those concerns. The two groups are going to be living together, and depending on each other, for quite a while.

Take This Job and Shove It

If the spot-market view of American labor is fundamentally misleading, so, too, is the easy-exit view. This view contends that the labor market is like a consumption market: an environment in which employees can switch companies as costlessly as consumers switch the supermarket where they buy groceries. If the job market were like a supermarket, a worker unhappy at a given workplace could readily move on to the next employer. If his or her current employer was able to determine what it was doing wrong — a big "if" when workers leave[12] — the firm would presumably change, or face the consequences of a shortfall of workers and lost productivity, market share, profitability, and so on.

For most workers, however, telling the employer to "take this job and shove it" is easier said than done. While the United States has one of the most mobile workforces in the world, most workers, as we've just seen, stay with the same employer for a long time. Most workers have invested a lot in their job. It's easy to quit if you are in a low-paying job; you probably won't lose much, and you might end up in a better job. It's easy to quit if you are an unattached young professional or craftsperson whose skills are salable and who has no family concerns in changing location. But it's not so easy when your career is tied to a particular firm and you have bills to pay, kids to raise, or a spouse or partner working in the same locale. Given the relatively low social safety net and employer provision of many benefits at work, workers cannot afford to leave jobs lightly. Leave your job and you lose your health insurance and, if you are not vested, your pension rights. Voluntary quitters are not eligible for unemployment benefits. In the United States, more so than in other advanced capitalist nations, income depends on the particular job one has: Easy exit is not an option for most workers.

For most American employees, then, the opportunity for improving their position is not exit but voice — staying in the employment relationship and communicating or bargaining individually or collectively for desired changes.[13] The analogy with a personal relationship is clear. When you have a problem with your spouse or partner, you can take the easy-exit option and split, or you can stay and talk about the problem and bargain over a solution. Whenever the benefits of a mutual relationship exceed the uncertain benefits of breaking that relationship, it is better to talk and improve the relationship than to break up and start anew.[14] The same holds true for employee-firm relations at the workplace, where the possibility for discussion and change depend critically on worker voice and bargaining power. When both workers and management have some say in decision-making, each group has an incentive to be forthcoming about their problems and preferences, rendering discussion valuable. By contrast, when all the power at a workplace resides with one side, it is often better to keep information to oneself: Why give management facts that it might use for its benefit but not for yours?[15]

It's the Economy, Stupid

The "Why care?" question we have heard most frequently concerns the overall performance of the U.S. economy. Why worry about employee concerns about workplace relations when the national income and employment aggregates look so favorable? (At this writing, low unemployment, rapid employment growth, and low inflation has created the best aggregate economy in fifty years, according to the chairman of the Federal Reserve.) Isn't the economy's overall performance more important in how the average American will fare than what goes on at a particular workplace? Won't any change in U.S. labor relations risk upsetting the economy that is doing well for everyone?

If the economy were doing well for everyone, we might agree with this objection. As important as the quality of work and workplace relations are to employee self-esteem and well-being, full employment and rising incomes are arguably the more important guarantor of living standards. So if the benefits of American economic growth went more or less equitably to all employees, or if changing workplace relations in the ways workers want would upend the economy, perhaps we should not care what workers want in the form of representation and participation at their place of employment.

But the fact is that American workers are not getting their fair share of our economy's benefits. For most American workers, real hourly pay has stagnated or declined for more than a generation, whereas in other advanced countries workers' earnings have risen during that same period.[16] The level of income inequality in the United States has skyrocketed, making the country's economy the most unequal in the developed world. For example, data from the Organization for Economic Cooperation and Development (OECD) show that the top 10 percent of U.S. workers earn 5.6 times as much as the bottom 10 percent. By contrast, the top 10 percent of workers in the European Union or Japan earn, respectively, 2.1 and 2.4 times as much.[17] The United States is, by this simple measure, almost three time more unequal than the world's other great centers of capitalism.

Full-time workers near the bottom of the American wage structure are particularly badly off compared with their peers in the European Union or Japan. American poverty rates are the highest in the developed world, and while the number of professional, managerial, and technical jobs has increased greatly, so, too, has the number of low-paying jobs with no benefits. It is shameful that "prisoner" is just about the fastest-growing "occupation" in the United States, the "trade" of more than 2 percent of American men.

Consider that from 1979 to 1996, peak to peak in the business cycle, U.S. gross domestic product (GDP) increased some $2.5 trillion in real (1996) terms — a gain in average family income of $6,360. But almost two-thirds of that gain went to the top 5 percent of families, whose income rose more than $72,000 on average, and virtually all the rest of the gain went to other families in the top two-fifths of the distribution. As a result, average income of families in the bottom 60 percent of the income distribution was actually lower in 1996 than in 1979. Rather than falling with economic growth, poverty actually increased. The "rising tide lifts all boats" effect of economic growth — the belief that growth benefits all and reduces poverty — ceased to work in the past two decades.[18] It lifted the yachts but sank the dinghies.

No one knows precisely why this happened. Some people blame increased trade with Third World countries. Some people blame technological change. Some blame immigration. But surely workplace relations and the ability of workers to influence decisions at their firm are a major part of the story. Far from being a reason not to worry about workplace relations, recent U.S. economic performance gives every reason to look at those relations closely, in the hope that they might help us to alleviate the one big flaw in our economic performance: the concentration of the gains of growth among the very few.

Father Knows Best

Finally, we come to the "father knows best" view, the idea that matters of workplace governance are best left to the "experts" — be they of the management, union, government, or academic variety — and that there is little to be learned from nonexpert workers. You mean you don't know what a Section 8(a)(3) violation is? Don't tell me how you want your workplace changed! You say you don't know what the Seventh Circuit said about sexual harassment claims last week? How dare you think you've got something to say about the dilemmas faced by working women! Leave it to the experts; they're the ones who know what they're talking about.

We respect expertise. Indeed, we count ourselves among the experts. Which leads us to reject the "father knows best" view more or less completely. As researchers in labor relations, we know that the expert does not in fact know best. The employment relation is dense, rich, and particular. It involves human beings, not arcane law arguments or abstract economic models. Experts can usefully remind everyone that we're operating under a different economy from the one we had in the 1930s — a different economy with different people in it. But even the greatest expert in the world cannot say what that implies for Harry or Juan or Mary's workplace without listening pretty closely to those workers themselves. Experts on workers should heed the wisdom Dr. Spock, the baby specialist, who told worried young mothers: "I don't know your baby nearly as well as you do." Workers know their workplace a lot better than any expert does.

So for those who'd really like to know how to improve the American workplace, we can confidently recommend this: Ask the people who live there! This is what we did in the WRPS. *What Workers Want* tells you what we found.

CHAPTER 2

Finding Out What Workers Want

So, how do researchers determine the kinds of changes a hundred million American workers would like to see in hundreds of thousands of workplaces?

One way, attractive to certain academics, is to sit in an office and ponder what some theory of capitalism tells us workers want. Marxists thought they knew what workers wanted: the destruction of capitalism and the creation of socialist heaven. Some competitive-market theorists think they know what workers want: what they now have, for otherwise the workers would switch jobs until they found the employer that provided the desired workplace arrangements.

Another way, attractive to journalists, is to interview a few selected people. Lunch-pail Lou. Manager Mary. Programmer Pete. With more time, one can mimic Studs Terkel, author of the best-selling oral history *Working*, and interview in depth a few dozen employees around the country.[1] Or one can do what former university president John Coleman did in the 1970s: leave your normal profession and try different jobs in which you interact with coworkers.

A third way, attractive to politicians, is to hire a polling firm to add a one-line question or two to their standard battery: "Are you satisfied with your job?" or "Who do you think can better deal with labor issues, the president or Congress?" Hire a consultant to interpret the results: "And so, boss, what you should be saying on TV tonight is A, because the opposition's vulnerability is B. Here's the wedge issue for our side, and the best sound bite to raise it."

All of these approaches have some value, but had we followed any of them we trust that you would not have accepted our results as anything approaching a systematic and objective representation of the views of American workers. And for our part, we wouldn't have had the chutzpah to ask you to. General theories of labor markets or class struggle can be elegant and exciting, but they often prove vacuous or misleading when it comes to understanding actual workplace practice (again, "father" does not know best, in part because he just doesn't have the details). Intense discussions with small groups of workers can be instructive as to how people are thinking, but such anecdotal evidence is unlikely to represent the views of the broader population of workers. And standard opinion polls, while useful for lobbying, in attack ads, and for gaining some sense of people's everyday anxieties, usually call for snap reactions more than considered judgments. Answers may be sensitive to question wording and sequence and might change when people have more information or time to think about the issues.

Our goal for the Worker Representation and Participation Survey (WRPS) was more ambitious. We wanted it to represent, accurately, the views of the whole of the workforce. We wanted it to capture attitudes on a wide range of workplace issues: human-resource and personnel practices, different modes of representation and participation, legal regulation and alternative means of enforcing the law. And we wanted to allow respondents to reflect on their answers and digest and respond to new information. To bring the American worker's voice into the nation's labor-policy debate, the WRPS, we knew, would require scientific validity beyond your run-of-the-mill opinion poll. On the dynamics of workplace power, it had to be the "mother of all workplace surveys."

As already noted, however, we had to be especially careful because labor policy is an area of such bitter dispute and because our survey threatened to have consequence. In addition to being squeaky clean academically, we needed to involve the protagonists of labor policy in the survey design. In standard academic studies, one worries about scientific critiques. Professor X might question sample design; Professor Y might worry about the sequencing of questions; Professor X^2 might wonder why we did not ask about her pet problem; and Professor Y^2 might criticize us for not using his favorite high-powered statistical technique to analyze the data. Criticism is the name of the game in seminars and classrooms throughout the country, and well it should be. Knowing that other researchers will look for flaws in your work pushes every researcher toward greater rigor and care. But the WRPS risked criticism of a different kind as well: politically motivated attacks where unions or management disagreed with the findings. Their concerns rest mainly with whether the views presented go against those of the AFL-CIO Executive Council, the Business Roundtable, the National Association of Manufacturers, the National Federation of Independent

Business, the Chamber of Commerce, or a host of other groups. If they do, the findings have to be wrong — or at least attacked as if they were wrong.

What to do?

We proceeded with care. Our initial scheme was simple. We would convene focus groups around the country to discuss workplace issues. Based on what we learned from these groups, we would develop a questionnaire and survey a representative sample of employees. To find out how these workers viewed proposed policy reforms, we thought we might produce a short instructional video (one of us wanted to be a Hollywood producer, if only for a day) that would explain these reforms and give examples of how they might work. We'd distribute the video to our sample, employees would watch it on their home VCRs, and then we'd ask them what they thought. Finally, to make sure we interpreted responses properly, we planned to hold focus-group meetings after the survey to discuss our conclusions.

We asked a number of experts in survey research to help us plan the survey, and we interviewed several survey research firms that would administer the project. Some were allied with Democrats and labor, others with Republicans and business. Some were less attentive than we wanted to the difficulties of getting at the data we sought. After a number of these meetings, we finally settled on Diane Colasanto and Princeton Survey Research Associates. In addition to being tireless, and smart, Diane and PSRA were politically neutral in a way many polling firms are not. She also seemed genuinely interested in the project's objective, not just in the fee our foundation supporters could provide. And, as if to clinch the deal, she was a former academic who had researched and taught survey design, and was thus fully current on the sometimes arcane methodological concerns that troubled us. Unlike many pollsters, she actually knew Professors X and X^2 — even the supercritical Professor Y^2.

Focus Groups

Setting up focus groups sounds simple. You invite some people to meet somewhere to talk about something you want to learn about. You give them coffee or soda and sandwiches and cookies, and you listen to what they have to say. Afterward you review a tape or transcript of the session, and *presto!* you now know what America thinks about a particular issue. If you are a politician of a certain type, you get an extra dividend: After deep deliberation, you finally know what you yourself think about that issue!

But it's not quite that easy. Many decisions in organizing a focus group can affect what people say and what you learn from them. The first decision is to determine the composition of the group itself. Should it include a heterogeneous collection of workers, whose variety reflects the working population as a whole? Or should it consist of a more homogeneous collection defined along the lines of common race, sex, occupation, age, or whatever? This decision is important not only because variation in the group can affect the questions that the researcher can pursue in depth but also because the group's composition can affect what participants had to say. Women and minorities often speak less in a group that mixes sexes or races than in one that does not. Blue-collar workers might talk differently in the presence of professionals or managers than in their absence. Young workers might feel uneasy criticizing seniority rules in the presence of older workers. And so on.

In addition to deciding who's in the group, issues about how to guide the discussion in useful ways also need to be resolved. It's important that everyone in a focus group gets a chance to talk, but some people are more comfortable speaking, and they often speak much more than others. Unless the group discussion is sufficiently focused, and the group facilitator sufficiently disciplined and forceful, the meeting can degenerate into the dictatorship of the blabbermouth. But there is also a danger that the group facilitator might exert too much influence on how discussion proceeds, inducing responses rather than letting them arise naturally. For instance, if we thought that workers were particularly upset about how firms regard issues of workplace safety, we could instruct the focus-group leader to ask bluntly, "Who's upset about safety?" Or we could allow the focus-group leader to talk generally about issues that make people happy and unhappy at workplaces and hope the safety issue arises by itself.

Yet another issue is how to deal with situations when the group is confused about the facts. Ought the facilitator to introduce expert knowledge about the information in question, or should he or she let the workers' confusion run its course? In the case of workplace safety, what should one do if everyone in the group agrees that the United States has the best workplace safety record in the world, when in fact its record ranks poorly among those of advanced countries? Or what if everyone in the group thinks that half of the U.S. workforce is unionized, or that American labor laws provide certain protections when in fact they do not? If you do not intervene, the discussion may give an accurate picture of how people view matters at a particular moment but not what they would think if provided the evidence necessary to make an informed decision. If you intervene by correcting misconceptions, you risk putting one or two facts before the group, but not the full spectrum of evidence on an issue.

To prepare for our focus groups, one of us attended a meeting of employees organized by a pro-union research group in New York City. These employees were divided by gender: Women met separately from men. Listening to the discussion behind a one-way mirror (standard practice in focus-group research) taught us two things in developing the WRPS focus groups.

The first lesson was that sex and race are less important in talking about one's job than is occupation. Gender might matter in many areas of discourse, but when it came to workplace issues, the major variation in attitudes among these people was by occupation rather than by demographic characteristic. Female blue-collar workers had similar concerns to male blue-collar workers. Female professionals and managers had similar concerns to male professionals and managers. Blue-collar workers were interested in unions; white-collar workers were not. The only demographic factor that mattered considerably was that blacks in all fields of work favored unions more than whites.

The second lesson was that whereas employees know a lot about their workplace, their knowledge tails off quickly on issues and people related to the Washington labor scene. Consider the following exchange at a session with women workers in New York City:

Focus-Group Leader: "Can anyone here name a living American union leader?

Dead silence.

Women Worker 1: "There's that Puerto Rican man who leads the hospital workers, but I don't know his name."[2]

Focus group leader: "Anyone else?"

Dead silence.

Focus Group Leader: "Well, has anyone heard of Lane Kirkland?" (the then-head of the AFL-CIO, nominally the nation's most prominent trade union leader).

Woman Worker 2: E-laine Kirkland? I know her. That's the fat lady who did the grapefruit diet on Oprah Winfrey last week."

Unbelievable?

Believe it. In highly unionized New York City, workers, including union members, hadn't a clue about the man who was the longest-presiding leader of the AFL-CIO since Samuel Gompers spoke oodles about the presence of American labor leadership in the public. It told us to direct the WRPS at the issues employees faced at their workplace, about which they had direct knowledge, and to stay away from references to Washington policy debates. If we were to find out how workers felt about potential alternative dispute-resolution systems or possible changes in the National Labor Relations Act (the Wagner Act of 1935), we would have to provide information about how those specifics would affect their working lives. Reflecting this, the WRPS contains a lot of "How are you/your employer doing at your workplace?" questions and very few "How are employers or employees in America doing?" questions.

For our focus groups, we assembled workers by occupation and varied the regions of the country from which they were drawn. The occupations covered were (1) less skilled workers in small firms (participants included a cashier, a cook, a waiter, a porter, a roofer, and an automotive service worker), (2) less skilled service workers in large firms (a cable technician, a janitor, a deli clerk, a cocktail waitress, and a truck driver), (3) manufacturing workers (a machinist, a tool designer, a pipe fitter, a metal polisher, a warehouse worker, and a forklift operator), (4) low- to mid-level office workers (a financial database analyst, a customer sales representative, a bookkeeper, and an insurance underwriter), (5) knowledge workers (a defense analyst, a computer software engineer, a medical technologist, and a computer programmer and technical writer), and (6) middle managers (from firms ranging from steel manufacturers to health-care providers to retail and computer support services). We held two groups in each of the following locations: Charlotte, North Carolina (Groups 2 and 4); Pittsburgh (Groups 3 and 6); and San Diego (Groups 1 and 5). These groups discussed workplace issues in February of 1994, while we watched from behind the one-way mirrors.

What the Focus Groups Said

It is standard practice in focus-group analysis for the professional firm that conducts the meetings to review the outcomes and offer a summary interpretation of what the people said. This qualitative assessment is based both on particularly memorable or insightful comments and on a general sense of how the meetings went. Princeton Survey Research Associates summarized the comments and meetings as follows:

- Focus-group participants were eager to talk about conditions in the workplace and their relationship with management. (This was good news for us, as interest in talking about these issues was critical to doing a lengthy telephone survey on them.)
- Workers pleased with their employer cited a responsive boss and policies and practices that eased communication with management and gave workers some say in the firm's decisions. (This began to tell us what workers were looking for.)
- Most participants believed that companies undervalued worker input and effort and expressed some distrust of management, and many complained that management was not communicating well with them about what was happening at the workplace. (This told us that issues of voice and representation, on which the WRPS was to probe, were indeed important to workers.)
- Many workers viewed new forms of worker representation or participation suspiciously. (This alerted us to the problem of getting workers to assess alternative institutions — a point that labor and management representatives reinforced strongly.)
- Workers recognized and accepted that the reason companies exist is to make a profit, and that bottom-line considerations must dominate management decisions. (This told us that regardless of the changes workers wanted in their participation in the firm's decision-making, they understood that these changes needed to fit into competitive business operations.)

Beyond the points highlighted by PSRA, however, what most impressed us was the wide variation in each group in the quality of labor-management relations that employees experienced. In nearly every group, one or two workers would tell a glowing story about good relations between workers and management at their workplace. Maybe there was an employee-involvement (EI) program that was working well or a management that empowered workers to make important decisions, or that did something else that showed that managers viewed workers as a company asset. Other employees would look at them and sigh: "You're really lucky. I've got nothing like that where I am." At which point someone would invariably say, "Why is that? Why such a difference?" To which nobody had an answer, except "That's just the way it is."

From these discussions, we drew three conclusions that played a major role in developing our national survey.

The first conclusion was that any labor policy or practice must allow for the substantial diversity in the American workforce and in the concerns workers had about their jobs.

Blue-collar workers had different specific worries from those of white-collar workers. Factory workers were troubled about safety conditions and job security, and recognized that the market dictated some trade-offs between them. "We know there are violations of OSHA [Occupational Safety and Health Administration] regulations, but if the union demanded change, it might just put the company out of business," said one factory worker in our Pittsburgh meeting. White-collar employees worried more about job security and opportunities for advancement. "The new CEO says he's more geared toward employees," commented one, "but in this last lay-off he was looking for people over fifty. Those were the people he wanted to get rid of. So everybody over fifty basically was gone, which makes you think about what will happen after you put in the time." Knowledge employees generally had a sense that their skills gave them some employment security, although not security at a particular job. A defense analyst in San Diego ruefully reported his previous boss once making this credible threat: "Do any of you want to leave? Go ahead, we can replace you in five minutes." But many of these workers could get a job fairly quickly.

The least-skilled, though, were something else entirely. Here job insecurity, and consciousness of being expendable, combined to produce a sort of despairing anger. In focus groups that we found difficult to observe, these employees felt lucky to have a job; they seemed afraid to think about it much and beaten down by the job market. A food service worker in Charlotte complained of feeling "walked on":

I'm the welcome mat. I must have welcome printed on my forehead or something, because I get the crap jobs to do, and I'm the one that gets — I mean, I've been through three stores in the past year, and they just all treat me bad. [My present employer] thinks their employees are expendable. . . . And I'm the type of person, I've taken too much crap for too long, and I ain't gonna shut up no more; I'm gonna stand up exactly for what I believe in, and on that day he told me that . . . I said, "I don't agree with you," and I said, "If that's the way you think, you can kiss my butt, and I'll leave." But I'm still there.

A custodial worker commented, "[In] every job, mostly every job I've had, management always felt like there's too many people out there that need jobs for us to have to put with you, you know, put up with you. Well, you either do what we say, or we'll let you go and it wouldn't be hard to fill it in, you know."

In short, the focus groups gave real faces and voices to the inequality of the U.S. earnings distribution that we described in Chapter 1 — the division of our society into the "haves" and the "have-nots." Inequality shows up not simply in earnings but also in the way people look at their jobs, their employers, and the way they interact with their employers.

Second, although most employees are committed to their firm and want to contribute more to their workplace than they are doing, there is discontent about how firms run workplaces that surfaces when employees start talking about specific issues and problems. In the first few minutes of general discussion, most people said that their workplace was OK: "I have no real complaints. I'm pretty satisfied." But when the discussion moved to specific issues — for instance, independence on the job, communication with management, and safety — people began raising problems. Employees have a clear notion of what constitutes a good employer, and many found their firm falling short of this notion. Many workers said their firm had an EI program, total quality management, teams or quality circles, or whatever label management had chosen, and they welcomed these initiatives. But a few thought the programs a complete hoax, and most felt the programs failed to live up to their promise. As participants got more comfortable with the discussion, they volunteered all sorts of problems. This is how our Charlotte focus group ended:

Moderator: "I'm done. I've covered everything I need to cover. . . . Is there anything else you want to tell me?"
Participant 1: "Oh, yeah, a couple little stories in . . . " *(laughter)*
Participant 2: "I've realized how much I mistrust my employer, and I don't think about that on a regular basis."
Participant 3: "That's true."
Participant 4: "And that's depressing."
Participant 1: "It's like wearing blinders."
Participant 3: "Yeah."
Participant 5: "Because in the beginning I was like 'my company's perfect.'"
Moderator: "Well, you did say that in the beginning."

Participant 1: "But I think you now realize there's some things that . . . "
Participant 5: (interrupting) "Yeah"
Participant 4: "It's not our life."
Participant 1: "But you can't have a life . . . "
Participant 4: (interrupting) "Without it."

That people changed their tone in talking about workplace problems as the focus groups proceeded confirmed our unease with standard job satisfaction questions that fail to probe attitudes about workplace specifics. For our survey to work, we would require much more time and attention from respondents than the standard opinion poll.

Third, after reflection or discussion, we found that employees can specify the type of representation or participation they want at the workplace. The focus group of white-collar employees in Charlotte was again the most striking. The discussion started with several employees making a clear statement about workplace representation, along the following lines: "We're southerners. We don't like unions [the image of a fat balding union leader with a mustache seemed to float in the air, not Norma Rae], so let's not talk about them." "Fine, let's not talk about unions," said the focus-group leader. "Is everything fine at your workplace, or do you have problems you wish you could address with management?"

These employees went on to raise a host of problems regarding their say in their job and how their firm was run. "We wouldn't dare go to management on these issues by ourselves." "Why not?" "They'd label us trouble-makers." "So, what should you do?" "Elect someone to take our concerns to management. But the spokesperson would have to say he had no problems and was just telling management what others thought, or else his career would be endangered . . . on second thought, maybe it would be safer and less disruptive to hire an outsider, though there might be other problems with that."

Shades of a trade union!

Other focus-group discussions, however, went in different directions. The knowledge workers in San Diego did not want any collective solution to their problems. And the least skilled seemed to be too beaten down to imagine that they could improve their lot. If we hadn't fully appreciated it before, this brought home to us the fact that for a country and workforce as heterogeneous as ours, no single design for workplace representation or participation was likely to be effective nationwide. One shoe of a single style and size would never fit the diverse feet of the American workforce.

Double-Checking, Moving On

Some weeks later, we wondered whether we and PSRA had drawn the right broad conclusions from the discussions. Could it be that we heard what we expected or wanted to hear or paid too much attention to the most articulate at the exclusion of the soft-spoken? To check our conclusions, we hired two students to watch videotapes of the focus groups and to code the responses of employees along various dimensions. This gave us a quantitative measure of what people said to complement PSRA and our qualitative reading of the results. The student coding told us that the professional focus-group report and our impressions were on target. People had areas of discontent. They wanted more say at their workplace. They differed, along occupational and educational lines, on the issues that concerned them most. And they had some ideas, albeit vague ones, about the changes that might resolve their job problems and improve their working lives.

Of course, the comments of sixty-odd employees in six focus groups is scarcely representative of the American workforce. But the point of holding focus-group meetings was not to reach any general conclusions but to shape our inquiry. The groups gave us a better sense of (1) the sorts of issues that seemed to concern a large number of employees and (2) the ways that people talked about those issues. They also gave us a sense of the difficulties of getting answers to problems at the workplace right away, and thus the need for conducting fairly lengthy interviews with workers and for posing probing questions on specific issues. And the focus groups told us which issues were more or less susceptible to easy answers, and thus which questions should be asked as close-ended (whereby the interviewer asks the respondent to give one of a specified set of alternatives) or open-ended (whereby respondents answer in their own way, and the interviewer transcribes what they say and codes it later).

So, equipped with what we had learned, we proceeded to draft our national telephone survey. This included numerous questions on current workplace practices and numerous questions on possible reforms.

Hold It!

Our next step was to ask the business and labor advisors we had recruited but hadn't yet met with as a group to review our survey and general project design. Again, we wished to include them early on so as to get the benefit of their wisdom and to minimize possible future objections. At this early point in the process, we thought we had matters pretty well in hand. The focus-group results were instructive and verified. We had an excellent pollster working with us. The kinds of questions we needed to ask were pretty clear, and we were confident that we knew how to ask them.

At a meeting in Washington, D.C., we presented our plan of action. In the room were people on opposing sides of what some might call "the great class war" — employers and business lobbyists, trade union presidents and staff. Many of those on one side knew those on the other; they'd been fighting on Capitol Hill for years. Going into the meeting, our principal concern was that it would descend to aimless wrangling. How could we keep the two sides focused on improving the survey rather than arguing with each other?

The meeting went in an utterly different direction. It wasn't business and labor arguing against each other; it was business and labor united against the way we planned to find out what changes workers might want:

Business Lobbyist: "That will never work. There are so many problems with what you want to do that I don't know where to begin. For starters, you can't show a video of how laws or rules will work at the workplace and ask people to judge them, and get anything I'd believe. Who's going to play the manager — a fat balding guy with a mustache?"

Union President: "I agree. You can't do that. Who's going to play the union organizer — a fat balding guy with a mustache? You'll never get people's real views. They'll go for whoever looks like Robert Redford."

Employer: "You've got to be careful about how you give information to people. It's easy to get the answers you want. . . . I know." (ha, ha)

Union Lobbyist: "Lots of workers will be scared to answer your survey. How do they know this isn't a company scheme to find out who might favor a union?"

Business and Labor in Unison: "It's OK to ask people about their workplace and relations with management, but you cannot ask them to think about policy reforms. You can't ask hypotheticals about what to do. Leave changes in labor law to us."

It was ugly. Instead of gaining the backing for the WRPS we expected from the meeting, it looked as if we'd become pin cushions for labor and management representatives. Business and labor lobbyists, divided on almost everything, agreed that we shouldn't be doing what we were. What did a couple of pointy-headed academics know about workplaces or labor problems anyhow? Leave it to the Beltway crowd.

Time to regroup.

Redesigning the WRPS

People calmed down after the meeting, and when it became clear that we were determined to proceed and would respond to their criticisms, they helped — at first a little, and then a lot. Over the next few months, we had innumerable conversations with business and union representatives, and with their own survey experts. "Don't just criticize us," we kept saying. "Help us make this work! Show us the surveys you've done, and tell us what questions you found worked and what questions didn't give useful information."

Many did, revealing confidential internal surveys they had conducted of employees or union members. Some of the surveys conducted by firms were revealing. One showed that many middle managers and professionals at a major company utterly distrusted the top management, leading us to wonder if the CEO had a bodyguard, or had read the survey himself before handing it over to us. A leading manufacturing firm directed the consultant who designed their internal surveys to review every one of our questions — again and again it seemed (but with definite improvements in question wording through the process). A top-level staffmember at the AFL-CIO helped to coordinate the union oversight of what we did. He also reviewed every draft of the survey (we eventually got to seventeen different complete drafts) and called us regularly with comments.

In short, business and labor got into the spirit of the enterprise. Business pollsters warned us against wordings of questions sure to evoke exaggerated pro-business responses. The AFL-CIO staffer and union pollsters corrected question wording likely to exaggerate pro-union response. And throughout, we checked in with our outside academic experts, who warned us about many other problems.

The improvements made in the WRPS were substantial. Originally, we had designed the survey to deal almost exclusively with workplace representation without thinking much about how management viewed their own participatory human-resource practices. The "P" in the WRPS, and the module of questions focused on EI programs, reflect the suggestions of management representatives. One question, suggested to us by a union-organizing director, came to play a major role in our analysis:

You know what I would really like you to show? Show that when workers think about organization, what they most worry about is how business will react. We hear all the time that workers don't want unions because unions aren't offering them what they want, or aren't offering enough variety, or whatever. That's BS. It's what management does, and their power to act, and workers sensitivity to that, that really determines worker choice. What else explains the difference between public-sector and private-sector organization? The workers aren't that different. The only thing that's different is management and how it acts.

Good point. So we devised a question to probe whether in their desire for representation or participation workers were more sensitive to management behavior than to the characteristics of a worker organization. Specifically, we asked if workers would rather have a weak employee organization with which management cooperated at their workplace, or a stronger organization with which management did not cooperate. As we shall see, the answers to this question made some union activists livid.

But it was not only on broad issues that management and labor representatives helped form the survey. Virtually every WRPS question benefited, in one way or another, from somebody's criticism. Meanwhile, Diane Colasanto brought us up to speed on modern survey technique. To deal with the possibility that question wording or placement might bias responses, we became enthusiastic practitioners of "split questions" and "alternative sequencing." With split questions the researcher asks different parts of the sample the same basic thing, but in different ways. With alternative sequencing, the researcher puts questions in a different order to different respondents; this allows you to track the effect of the survey itself on respondents. To make the most efficient use of our time with respondents, we also posed numerous "skip questions"; these enabled us to pursue issues that were a particular concern to some members of the sample without boring those for whom the issues had no concern. If someone said they were in a union or an active participant in EI programs, we'd ask a series of additional questions; if they said they weren't, we'd skip down to the next appropriate question. Computer-assisted telephone interviewing, which we used, makes it easy to do this, as the ordering of questions is programmed on a computer and appears on the screen as the interview is conducted. This permits interviewers to take a single general survey instrument and tailor its questions to particular respondents: Different questions can be asked in different ways, or different people can be asked different questions.

By summer's end we had something that everyone thought was scientifically defensible, good, and possibly dangerous — just what we wanted! We pretested the redesigned survey among a large group of respondents to learn (1) how long it took people to answer the questions and (2) which questions people found troubling, boring, or tending to lead them toward certain conclusions. The most important thing we learned from the pretest was that respondents seemed interested. If asked, people like to talk about their work: perhaps not as much as they like to talk about their kids, or the latest scandal in Washington, or the hottest television show or sports event, but enough to stay on a telephone for nearly half an hour answering serious questions.

Oh, and we also chucked the video idea — to the disappointment of one fat balding actor with a mustache. So now we were just about ready to go into the field — that is, to get on the phones and ask folks about their workplace.

What to Do about Managers?

One in every ten or eleven American employees works as a manager, and many more employees are supervisors of some form or other. Because managers are workers, it is reasonable to ask them many of the questions that one asks other workers. But some questions that apply to nonmanagerial workers are irrelevant or peculiar to managers. The problem that management faces when employees seek to form a union, for example, is not whether to join the union but whether to try to convince employees not to join, and how hard to try. In nonunion firms, management decides, more or less unilaterally, how much authority to give to EI committees, how to discipline workers who are not living up to expectation, how to treat grievances, and other vital labor-relations matters. It made little sense to ask management to judge management activity in these and other areas.

Given this situation, we decided to exclude managers from some questions, just as we excluded nonunion employees from questions about how their union functioned or excluded employees who said their firm did not have an EI program from questions about how that program operated. But Erik Wright, an academic colleague of a leftist bent (some might call him the last living American Marxist), reviewed our survey design and came up with a better idea. Why not rephrase the questions to get management's perspective? Ask them if they would oppose an employee effort to unionize and why, how they feel about dealing with workers individually as opposed to in a group, and so on.

This would let us compare management and employee views of the same issue as seen from their differing positions within the firm. A capital notion! We would be able to report on how managers felt about issues as employees and also as managers. Ensuing chapters exploit this feature of the WRPS.

If You Could Choose . . .

Our meetings with business and labor representatives led us to develop a new strategy for trying to determine the workplace reforms employees wanted. But we still felt employees were capable of assessing how alternative reforms would function at their workplace and that their views had as much or more validity as those of Washington power groups. But how could we discover what reforms employees might want when they had no experience with those reforms?

The problem of getting people to express their true views to a hypothetical situation is a classic one in survey research. Everything depends, of course, on how the situation is described. Consider, for example, whether people think it is fair or unfair for a landlord to raise the rent on a long-standing, elderly widowed tenants in a rent-stabilized apartment. If the background is described as "City taxes and maintenance costs have risen, so the landlord raised the rent," a large share of people will judge the rent hike to be fair. But if it's described as "The real estate market tightened, the neighborhood was gentrifying, and the landlord saw an opportunity to squeeze old tenants out," then obviously that share will decline. If it's described as "Some drug dealers said they wanted the apartment to conduct business and offered to double the rent" it would drop to close to zero.

To avoid having the context determine answers, one needs either questions that give as neutral a context as possible or split questions to reflect different contexts. Because the disagreement about workplace issues is considerable, even the most careful survey design risks inadvertently leading the respondent in one or another direction on hypothetical questions. Moreover, there is the danger that this bias could color answers to succeeding questions.

Our solution was threefold.

First, we asked how respondents viewed particular reforms or institutional choices at the end, not the beginning, of questioning. In this way, even if we inadvertently phrased these questions in leading ways, we ensured that these questions would not bias responses to other questions in the same area.

Second, when we tried to infer worker preferences about possible new labor institutions or reforms, we usually asked the respondents to choose among narrowly focused attributes of those institutions, rather than inviting respondents to choose between comprehensive institutional schemes. So, for example, in asking about a hypothetical "workplace organization," we separately asked about how employee participants in the organization might be chosen, what the powers of the organization would be, how disputes within it would be settled, and so on. The typical form of these questions was "If it was your decision alone and everyone went along with it, would you prefer Attribute A or Attribute B (for example, "an organization with access to confidential company information or one without that access," "an organization of just similar employees or everyone in your plant," "an organization funded by workers alone or one jointly funded by management")?" By focusing on attributes and dealing with them precisely — and always referencing the respondents own workplace, not Capitol Hill — we could tease out preferences for new institutional forms without the fear of straying too far into never-never land, even if we couldn't specify those forms themselves.

Third, as we shall detail momentarily, when we did ask participants to consider specific reforms, we gave them a short write-up on them. These descriptions made arguments for and against the reform, as blandly and symmetrically as we could. We then asked respondents how, on reflection, they thought that reform would or would not work — again and always, at *their* workplace.

Wave 1 of the WRPS: The Big National Survey

Wave 1 of the WRPS was a national telephone survey of about 2,400 employees in private-sector establishments of twenty-five or more employees. Excluded from the survey were top managers, the self-employed, owners or relatives of owners of firms, public-sector workers, and employees in small firms. We excluded these various groups because we believed that they would have different problems and might prefer different institutional solutions from those of employees in larger, private-sector firms. You can't really ask the self-employed about relations with their employer, nor can you sensibly ask employees in a firm with three to four workers about EI committees. Although we thus cannot report on the attitudes of some workers, we covered the vast majority of the U.S. workforce. The population from which our sample draws covered approximately 75 percent of all private-sector workers — some 70 million workers at the time of the survey.

The sample size of 2,400 was also roughly double the standard national opinion survey. We chose this size because we wanted to test different wording or sequencing of questions (which we would ask of only part of the sample) and to assure ourselves of a substantial number of employees in select groups, such as unions or EI committees. The survey averaged twenty-six minutes, which pressed the outer bounds of conventional telephone surveys.

The survey was conducted in mid-September to mid-October of 1994. We had a high response rate[3] and a lower-than-feared cut-off rate from people terminating the interview part-way through. We evaluated only completed questionnaires. The demographics — age, race, sex, education, location, and so on — were nationally representative for the target population. The estimated sampling error on the responses of the entire group was very low — plus or minus 2 percent.

Verifying the Scaling

We did have one last scare, however. Shortly after we went into the field with our main design, our principal advisor from the AFL-CIO called up, very upset. He had made many suggestions. We had followed some of them but had also rejected some, and one of the ones we had rejected he thought was crucial to getting an accurate result. It involved a technical issue on which he (and, we presumed, AFL-CIO survey experts) disagreed with the decision of our survey firm, PSRA: the scaling of certain variables. The convention used through most of the WRPS was to scale responses using a four-point scale: (4) very, (3) somewhat, (2) not too, and (1) not at all. For example, we ask, "Would you say you are very satisfied, somewhat satisfied, not too satisfied, or not at all satisfied with your say in training?"

Our friend at the AFL-CIO had problems with this. First, if we were to do a four-point scale, he preferred a division that treated satisfaction and dissatisfaction equally. For example, he wanted to ask, "Would you say you are very satisfied, somewhat satisfied, somewhat dissatisfied, or very dissatisfied with . . . ?" Second, he wanted the WRPS to use more five-point scales, with a neutral position marked clearly between satisfaction and dissatisfaction to give respondents the option of saying that they were neither satisfied nor dissatisfied.

The motivation for both criticisms was the fear that our wording and structure biased responses toward reported satisfaction. He argued that the answers "not too satisfied" and "not at all satisfied" are less meaningful than "somewhat dissatisfied" and "very dissatisfied." Fewer people would choose them, and the largely nonunion U.S. workforce would look more satisfied with workplace arrangements than it truly was. Failure to allow respondents to take a neutral position, combined with general reluctance to admit dissatisfaction, would have the same result. "You're setting us up for a survey that will just show happy workers!" he yelled at us on the phone.

We believed that he was wrong. Once they got to talking, employees in our focus group were outspoken in their views. PSRA found four-point scales superior to five-point ones: They take less time and force people to come down on one side or the other of an issue rather than waffling in the middle (say, giving a "3" value to most questions). This is why we had rejected his suggestion of alternatives when he had made it earlier, but less vociferously than he was making it now. But our promise to the business and labor groups was that we would respond to their criticisms. What could we do? Was there a scientific way to determine who was right?

It was too late to alter the WRPS, but we found out that we could add questions to a national weekly "omnibus survey" (so-called because polling companies conduct these surveys weekly with an omnibus of questions, submitted by various clients). We could ask respondents the same questions we had asked on our own survey, but we would scale half the responses our way and half the way our critic at the AFL-CIO wanted. This would be expensive and risky. If he was right, parts of the main survey would be invalid, but we had to respond to any criticism for the results to be beyond reproach.

We dipped into a dwindling budget and bought some questions on a national omnibus to test the alternative wording, and to see what people would do if permitted a neutral response. This omnibus supplement was conducted in two waves in November 1994. It expanded our sample by an additional 1,100 workers. And what a relief! The results from different scaling were not noticeably different. If anything, asking questions the way our critic wanted produced more satisfied responses than our own — the opposite of the effect he had predicted.

Wave 2 of the WRPS: The Follow-Up

Even though our survey was long and detailed, we still wondered whether respondents might have answered some questions differently if they possessed additional information or could reflect longer on a particular issue. And we wanted to do one thing that our business and labor critics had advised us against — ask employees to judge specific feasible policy reforms.

We devised an inexpensive way to accomplish this goal: We conducted a follow-up survey of some of the participants of the national telephone survey. At the end of the Wave 1 questionnaire, we asked survey participants if they would be willing to read written descriptions of possible changes in national labor policies, to think about those proposals, and then to give their opinion of these changes. Although respondents had already talked with us for half an hour, a sizable proportion said they would look at additional materials.

And so, with preliminary results from Wave 1 in hand but not yet announced to the world, we set about Wave 2. In November we mailed written descriptions of three policy proposals to a sample of respondents who said that they would be willing to look at such material and talk to us again. A few weeks later we telephoned these respondents to get their reactions to the policy proposals and to ask a few other questions. We received responses from some 800 persons. The follow-up sample did not differ noticeably in its demographic or economic characteristics from our initial sample and was large enough to qualify as an independent national poll in its own right.

Unique to the U.S. Private Sector or General?

You'd think this would be the end of "the mother of all workplace surveys." But mothers have kids, even mother surveys.

Any survey can speak with confidence only about the population from which the sample was drawn during the period of sampling. We wanted the WRPS to be more than a snapshot. We wanted it to capture the fundamental attitudes of employees in the U.S. private sector as the country approached the twenty-first century — what in grandiose moments we sometimes called "the deep structure" (whatever that means) of employee feelings about their workplace. Had we done that? Or did the responses simply reflect feelings in the particular setting of the U.S. job market in the mid-1990s?

One possibility, in particular, troubled us. One of our major findings was that, in response to the question about worker preferences for a strong labor organization or management cooperation, employees preferred a cooperative management. They were, to put it bluntly, the antithesis of

Karl Marx's vision of a class in conflict with capitalism. We wondered if this reflected labor's weakness in the 1990s rather than deep-seated employee attitudes. If unions were stronger and wages growing for normal workers as well as for CEOs, maybe the desire to cooperate would diminish and workers would be more militant. The standard measure of labor militancy — the incidence of strikes — certainly varies over time and over the business cycle. Maybe our snapshot was limited in time or place. We could see Marx's ghost rising from his grave in London's Highgate Cemetery, denouncing us for mistaking ephemeral attitudes for genuine class unconsciousness.

One way to probe whether our findings represented workers in general, or were unique to American private-sector workers in a particular period, would be to compare the responses of workers in our own survey who faced different job markets. We could ascertain whether union workers had different attitudes from nonunion workers, whether those workers who believed they could easily find a comparable job at similar pay had the same attitudes as those who said they would have trouble if they lost their job, and so forth. The smaller the variation in attitudes among these groups, the more likely it would be that we had identified some universal attitudes rather than time/place contingent attitudes. (We make such comparisons in the ensuing chapters.)

Another way to try to probe would be to compare the responses of U.S. private-sector employees to the responses of private-sector employees in another country with a stronger labor movement. The obvious other country for the United States is Canada. With a labor-relations system that is in many ways very similar to that of the United States, Canada has a private-sector union density that is about twice as high as the United States'; its laws are much more protective of workers, and its business community historically has been less fiercely opposed to unionism than has American business. Why not take our survey (en Français pour les Quebecais) and see how Canadians responded? Because so much of the work had been done, the expenses would be modest, and we would be able to respond to Marx's ghost. In November 1995, we conducted the Canadian WRPS, which covered 1,000 Canadian workers, making it the largest such survey conducted up to that time in Canada.

Yet another way to test whether our results held generally would be to look at public-sector American workers. While unions are weak and declining in the private sector, they have been strong and stable in the public sector. In 1995, about 40 percent of public-sector workers were organized. If we could ask public-sector workers similar questions to those we had asked private-sector workers, we would have a good contrast. The problem was that identifying public-sector employees through a national survey is very expensive. Because about only 10 percent of the workforce is in the public sector, the number of calls necessary to obtain a nationally representative sample is large, and we had very little budget left. But, luckily for us, the Clinton administration had appointed a panel on public-sector labor-management relations with the ungainly name of The Secretary of Labor's Task Force on Excellence in State and Local Government through Labor-Management Cooperation.[4] After listening to our early findings from the WRPS, the task force asked if we could replicate our study with public-sector employees. Yes, we said, but only if they could provide a good sample of employees. The sample they provided was imperfect: membership lists of unionized public-sector workers and a sample of largely nonunion public-sector workers in one southern state. While this was hardly ideal, we decided to proceed: We figured that even an assessment by only some public-sector employees would be useful. If their views agreed with those of the private-sector employees on our main survey, we could tell Karl's ghost to go back to the grave, although maybe not too loudly. In any case, in November 1995 we conducted a survey of the public-sector.

Enough? For us, yes, but a British management group that read our study decided that they wanted to find out how workers in the United Kingdom felt about their jobs. This management group commissioned two Oxford experts to develop a British version, which gave us another country of comparison. At this writing, parts of the WRPS are also being replicated in Japan and Australia (but fortunately not by us).

Here we do not report on the "children" of the basic WRPS. We simply note that Canadian private-sector workers express much the same attitudes as American private-sector workers, that U.S. public-sector workers differ only modestly from private-sector workers,[5] but that British workers seem less cooperative and more aggressive in their attitudes toward management than either Americans or Canadians. Nothing in these follow-up surveys leads us to question our findings about private-sector U.S. workers.

The Final WRPS Design

As you can see, the WRPS on which this book is based consists of much more than a single survey or opinion poll. We ended up with a four-part study, with each part designed either to add additional knowledge or to test

EXHIBIT 2.1. The WRPS and its progeny: more than a survey.

The WRPS

Focus groups
One-and-a-half-hour discussions with 56 workers in six occupational groups; designed to give us a better sense of the general workplace concerns and appropriate language for asking about them.

Wave 1
Twenty-six-minute national survey of 2,308 employees; extensive use of split questions and alternative sequencing to minimize bias.

Wave 2
Fifteen-minute follow-up survey of 801 respondents to Wave 1 questionnaire who had also read mailed fact sheets on workplace alternatives; designed to probe initial responses and to allow respondents to consider alternative policies described by fact sheets.

Omnibus
Ten-minute survey of 1,000 respondents, designed to test the WRPS's four-point scaling questions against five-point alternatives.

The follow-ups

Canadian survey
Twenty-six-minute combination of questions from Waves 1 and 2, administered to 1,100 respondents; designed to see which U.S. employee responses reflect specifics of the U.S. private sector and which generalize to private-sector workers in a closely related economy.

Public-sector survey
Twenty-five-minute survey of 1,002 unionized and nonunionized public-sector employees; designed to see which private-sector U.S. responses reflect specifics of that sector and which generalize to public-sector workers in the same economy.

British survey
Twenty-five-minute survey of 1,000 private-sector employees; designed to illuminate the "new employment contract" between workers and firms, using many questions from Waves 1 and 2 of the WRPS.

the reliability of other parts, and three additional surveys that probe the universality of the results' specificity (see Exhibit 2.1). We took care to establish the study's authority by basing question design on what employees said in focus groups; by using split questions and sequencing questions differently; by taking criticisms seriously; by using a follow-up survey to push the survey instrument to its limit; and by comparing the results with responses abroad, and in the very different climate of public-sector employment.

We have shared some of the nitty-gritty details of our survey design for two reasons. First, we hope to convince you that the findings reported in *What Workers Want* are as valid as we could make them and, more likely than not, correctly capture the attitudes of American workers. We cannot conceive of the nation dealing with its workplace problems without responding to these attitudes. Second, we want to make it clear that social-science surveys do not appear by magic from some survey organization or government agency but in fact are designed as scientific tools by fallible folk who seek answers to important social problems.

Does all of our effort and safeguards mean we got it right? Social science is not laboratory science, a discipline in which you vary the variable or parameter of interest while controlling (mostly) everything else. People are not quarks. They can and do change. Social movements arise suddenly. We think we got it right. We wouldn't have written this book if we didn't think so. It's undoubtedly more "right" for America in a period of high inequality and labor quiescence than for all time, but we would be surprised if most of the attitudes we report will change all that much in the foreseeable future.

CHAPTER 3

What Workers Want and
Why They Don't Have It

Shortly after we completed the Worker Representation and Participation Survey (WRPS), we rushed our top-line findings to business and labor groups and to the Clinton Administration's Commission on the Future of Worker-Management Relations. Some plaudits and some brickbats came back. Union representatives who had hoped our study would support the AFL-CIO line on all issues took offense at the finding that workers wanted cooperation over a strong organization and that most workers wanted joint committees at their workplace. Press reports that played up these results irritated them to no end. The Republican victory in the 1994 congressional elections made business representatives mellow about our finding that workers wanted greater input in workplace decisions and that many nonunion workers wanted unions, for they knew they could prevent any changes in labor legislation inimical to their interests. One lobbyist told us cheerfully that labor policy would be set by his lobbying firm, which represented the bosses of the world, not by any commission or survey, so who cared what we found workers wanted?

In Washington, what matters is the immediate. If something is not on this week's policy talking points or this session's legislative calendar, who cares? From this perspective, the capsule summary in Chapter 1 suffices to tell the story of the WRPS. Our desire to capture the "deep structure" of worker attitudes toward employee relations and to demonstrate that workers could contribute to improving labor relations were looked on as the mad rantings of ivory-tower pinheads.

But a capsule summary of the "mother of all workplace surveys" did not satisfy us, nor, we venture, will it satisfy you. By its nature, a summary can neither give the details that underlie our interpretation of the evidence nor document the variation in attitudes toward the workplace among the diverse American people. Nor can it examine the reasons why some workers are dissatisfied with their influence on workplace decisions and want new arrangements at their workplace while others are happy with their situation.

In this chapter we examine how workers' desire for more say at the workplace depends on the characteristics of workers and their workplaces. We provide a brief narrative to help you put our findings into a broader perspective. We address objections that we imagine the critical reader might have to our interpretation of the survey, much as we would respond to objections in an academic seminar.[1]

Workers Want More Influence

The WRPS shows as conclusively as any survey can that the vast majority of employees want more involvement and greater say in company decisions affecting their workplace. This finding is not grounded in a single question — "Do you want more say or not?" — but in a battery of questions that poke and probe at such desires.[2] We poked and probed at the desire for influence because every other part of our study hinges on this issue.

One way to determine whether workers want more influence on workplace decisions is to ask if they are satisfied with their say on the job. But employees might answer such questions without carefully considering their situation. In our focus-group discussions, people often expressed critical attitudes as they considered their workplace concerns in greater depth than they had at the outset. It is easy to reply, "I'm satisfied, sort of," to a stand-alone question, without giving it much thought. It is harder to give such a cursory response after talking for a while about various aspects of the workplace.

We used a split-sample design to deal with this potential problem. In two spots in the survey, we asked, "Overall, how satisfied are you with the influence you have in company decisions that affect your job or work life?" For half the respondents we asked it *before* we asked workers to discuss particular workplace decisions; for the other half we asked it *after* a battery of questions about particular workplace issues. We hypothesized that the *after* group would be more critical than the *before* group about the amount of influence they had at the workplace.

Exhibit 3.1 shows that this was indeed the case.[3] In the *before* sample, 28 percent of employees reported that they were "very satisfied" with their influence on the job, whereas 19 percent said that they were "not too satis-

EXHIBIT 3.1. Percentage of workers who are satisfied or dissatisfied with their influence on workplace issues.

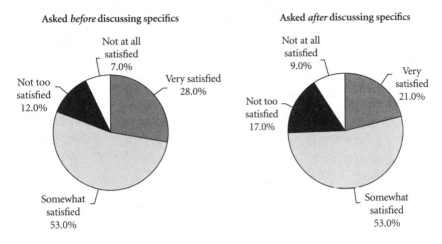

Asked *before* discussing specifics

Not at all satisfied 7.0%
Not too satisfied 12.0%
Very satisfied 28.0%
Somewhat satisfied 53.0%

Asked *after* discussing specifics

Not at all satisfied 9.0%
Not too satisfied 17.0%
Very satisfied 21.0%
Somewhat satisfied 53.0%

Percentage of workers who want more influence at workplaces

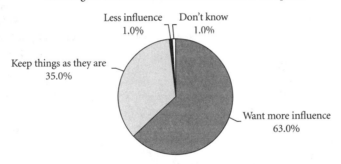

Less influence 1.0%
Don't know 1.0%
Keep things as they are 35.0%
Want more influence 63.0%

Note: Pie-chart portions must add to 100 percent, so some numbers have been rounded up.
Source: Based on these WRPS questions: (Wave 1.14_1,2,3,4) "Overall, how satisfied are you with the influence you have in company decisions that affect your job or work life?" (satisfied, somewhat satisfied, not too satisfied, not satisfied at all); (W1.14b) "If it were your decision alone, and everyone went along with it, would you generally like to have more influence in these areas, less influence, or would you want to keep things the way they are now?"

fied" or "not at all satisfied," a 9-point difference in favor of greater satisfaction. In the *after* sample, 21 percent of employees said that they were "very satisfied" with their influence on the job, whereas 26 percent were "not too satisfied" or "not at all satisfied," a 5-point difference in the opposite direction. The most plausible interpretation of this 14-point swing is that workers gave a more accurate and less perfunctory response after discussing workplace specifics.

Using yet another split design, we asked employees with whom we had discussed particular workplace decisions, "If it were your decision alone, and everyone went along with it, would you generally like to have more influence in these areas, less influence, or would you want to keep things the way they are now?" This puts the "Are you satisfied?" issue into the more dynamic terms of changing workplace conditions. It offers a way to judge whether workers who are "somewhat satisfied" want some change in their situation. Nearly two-thirds of the workers reported that they wanted more influence, compared with 35 percent who were content to keep things as they are and 1 percent who actually desired less influence (see Exhibit 3.1). The workers who wanted more influence were better educated, worked more hours, and had greater tenure than other workers.[4]

Do these results offer any news, or is this just social science reporting the obvious? Surely most people want more influence on decisions affecting their job, as influence is likely to improve their work lives. If we asked people if they want more money, they would all say, "Yes. Big deal."

To address this objection, we asked about the benefits that workers would get from greater influence at the workplace. Eighty-seven percent of workers told us that employees would enjoy their jobs more if more decisions about production and operations were made by employees, instead of by managers. But that was not the only benefit workers saw as flowing from having greater influence on workplace decisions. Three-fourths said that their company would be stronger against its competitors and 79 percent said that the quality of products or services would improve if employees made more decisions about production and operations. In addition, most employees thought that if employees had more say in how workplace problems were addressed at their company, those problems would be solved more effectively.[5]

Still, you might wonder if workers are simply giving self-serving answers. Say your spouse claims that if he or she made more household decisions, everything would run more smoothly, but what might actually happen is you ending up doing more of the dirty work. If this was the case, managers should have told us that giving workers a greater say in decision-making would be harmful to the firm and make problem-solving less rather than more efficient. To the contrary. Fifty-eight percent of managers agreed with workers that workplace problems would be more effectively solved at their company if employees collectively had more say. If the workers and managers are right, the bottom line for companies is better performance.[6]

Many managers have, moreover, acted on their belief that empowering workers can improve the firm's effectiveness. More than half of the workers in the WRPS are employed by firms with some sort of employee-involvement (EI) program, and one-third participated in that program. But, as we shall see in Chapter 5, most EI participants believe that the programs would be more effective if employees collectively had more say in how the programs were run. And most managers of such programs agree that even when firms try hard, they do not give employees enough authority in decision-making.

The Discontented Third

On the average day, what best describes your feelings about going to work? Would you say you usually look forward to it, or wish you didn't have to go, or don't care one way or the other?

Overall, how would you rate relations between employees and management at your company/organization? Would you say they are "excellent," "good," "only fair," or "poor"?

To see whether worker desire for greater say reflects a general malaise with how management treats workers in the United States or is a stand-alone problem, we asked the preceding two questions. We found that, on average, two-thirds of workers were reasonably satisfied with their work lives, but that the other one-third were dissatisfied, and their dissatisfaction was closely linked to their lack of influence on the job.

Exhibit 3.2 shows the responses that constitute the "discontented third." The first pie chart shows that 25 percent of respondents wished that they didn't have to go to work, while 9 percent said they didn't care one way or another. Together these figures imply that about one-third of the workforce are not eager to do their job. The proportion dissatisfied is particularly high among workers in the lower part of the earnings distribution — that is, among the less educated, black workers, and manufacturing workers[7] — as compared with workers in stronger positions in the job market. In this sense, inequality in job satisfaction mirrors the inequality in the earnings distribution. But then 28 percent of college graduates and 39 percent of workers with some college education also wished they didn't have

EXHIBIT 3.2. One-third of workers are dissatisfied.

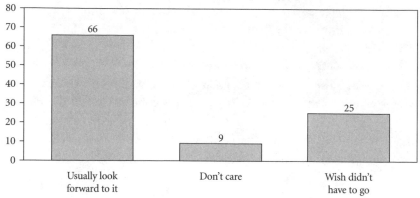

Percentage of workers by attitude toward work

Percentage of workers judging employee–management relations as:

Source: Based on these WRPS questions: (W1.8) "On an average day, what best describes your feelings about going to work? Would you say you usually look forward to it, wish you didn't have to go, don't care one way or the other"; (W1.10b) "Overall, how would you rate relations between employees and management at your company/organization? Would you say they are excellent, good, only fair, or poor?"

to go to work or didn't care one way or the other, and 30 percent of white men also placed themselves in this boat.

A similar pattern is found in employee ratings of employee-management relations. Eighteen percent of workers rate relations between employees and management at their company as being excellent, and nearly one-half label them as good; more than one in five, however, rate labor relations as only fair, and one in fourteen rate them as poor. Cumulating the "fair" and "poor" responses gives us, again, our discontented third. Discontent with labor-management relations is not, moreover, a case of workers thinking "the grass is always greener on the other side." Fifty-one percent of our respondents viewed labor-management relations at their firm as about the same as in other places, and 38 percent thought they were better than average. Only 9 percent thought their company's labor relations were worse than average.

Discontent with labor-management relations shows up in how workers see trust and loyalty at workplaces.

How much loyalty would you say you feel toward the company/organization where you work — "a lot," "some," "only a little," or "no loyalty at all"?

How much do you trust your company/organization to keep its promises to you and other employees — "a lot," "somewhat," "only a little," or "not at all"?

Exhibit 3.3 shows that considerably more workers feel "a lot" of loyalty to their firm than trust their firm "a lot" to carry out its promises to them and to other employees. Approximately two-fifths trust their company somewhat, while one-fifth trust it only a little or not at all. At the individual level, one-third of workers reported a greater amount of loyalty than trust, compared with 10 percent who said they trusted their firm more than they felt loyalty to it.[8] Again the discontented third.

Discontent and Lack of Say

To what extent, if at all, is discontent with jobs and labor-management relations linked to dissatisfaction with influence on workplace decisions?

Extraordinarily so, according to the data summarized in Exhibit 3.4. This exhibit shows how workers with different degrees of satisfaction with their say on decisions responded to other questions about their attitude toward their workplace: whether they look forward to going to work, their rating of employee-management relations, and their trust in their firm. The linkages between satisfaction with influence and these other attitudes is strong. Workers satisfied with their say look forward to going to work, report excellent employee/management relations, and trust their firm. By contrast, workers dissatisfied with their say in workplace decisions disproportionately do not look forward to work; they report fair or poor labor management relations and distrust their employers.

EXHIBIT 3.3. Workers' loyalty and trust of their firm.

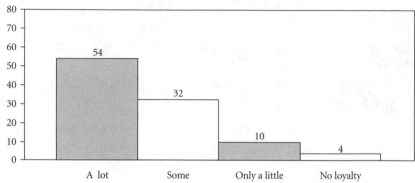

Percentage of workers feeling loyalty to their firm

Percentage of workers who trust their firm to keep its promises

Source: Based on these WRPS questions: (W1.9C) "How much loyalty would you say you feel toward the company/organization you work for as a whole?" (a lot, some, only a little, no loyalty at all); (W1.10a) "In general, how much do you trust your company/organization to keep its promises to you and other employees?" (a lot, somewhat, only a little, not at all).

By organizing the data to show how worker discontent differs by satisfaction or dissatisfaction with say, we do not mean to imply that dissatisfaction with say is the primary cause of discontent. Our data show correlation, not causality. We could just as easily have organized the cross-tabulations the other way around: We could have documented that workers distrustful of their employer, who rate labor relations as poor, who do not enjoy going to work, or who give management a low grade in concern for employees are exceptionally dissatisfied with their say at the work-

EXHIBIT 3.4. Percentage of workers with positive attitudes toward their jobs and firm, by satisfaction with influence on workplace decisions.

	Satisfaction with influence on workplace decisions			
	Very	Somewhat	Not too	Not at all
Looking forward to work				
Usually look forward to work	85	69	46	32
Wish didn't have to go	10	21	43	59
Trusting firm to keep promises				
A lot	65	36	14	8
Little or none	4	16	40	65
Rating employee/management relations				
Excellent	39	15	5	0
Poor/fair	10	27	56	80

Note: We do not adjust for the effect of asking the overall satisfaction question both before and after.
Source: Based on WRPS questions given in Exhibit 3.2 and 3.3 cross-tabulated with (W1.14_1,2,3,4): "Overall, how satisfied are you with the influence you have in company decisions that affect your job or work life?"

place.[9] The key point is that dissatisfaction with say at the workplace is not a trivial issue: It is intrinsically tied to how workers feel about other aspects of their jobs and employers.

The Influence Gap

Very well, you say, a chunk of American workers are unhappy with their influence on workplace decisions and are concomitantly dissatisfied with working life overall. But in your organization, or in any other one for that matter, no one gives people influence in an abstract sense. People have a say in particular decisions by conferring with management in those areas, or by sitting on committees that deal with specific problems, and so on.

Exhibit 3.5 shows worker attitudes toward influence on the job in eight different areas of workplace decision-making. Column 1 records the proportion of workers who said that having influence in a particular area was very important to them. The proportion of workers reporting that it is very important to have influence on decisions varies considerably among items. Over three-quarters of workers (76 percent) said it was very important to have influence on how to do their job and organize their work, while only

EXHIBIT 3.5. A big gap exists between the importance of wanting and having influence on workplace decisions.

	Wanting influence	Having Influence	Average gap	Individual gap
	Percentage of workers for whom it is very important to have a lot of influence	Percentage of workers who said they had a lot of direct influence and involvement	Difference between the columns "wanting influence" and "having influence"	Percentage of workers with less involvement than they want
Deciding what kinds of *benefits* are offered to employees	60	6	54	83
Deciding how much of a *raise* in pay the people in your work group should get	41	6	35	76
Deciding what *training* is needed for people in your work group or department	62	29	33	53
Deciding how to work with new *equipment or software*, if that's ever been needed	52	28	24	46

Setting *goals* for your work group or department	55	32	23	43
Setting *safety* standards and practices	55	35	20	45
Deciding *how* to do your job and organize the work	76	57	19	31
Setting work *schedules*, including breaks, overtime and time off	42	30	12	47
Average	55	28	27	53

Source: Based on these WRPS questions: "How much direct involvement and influence do *you* have in (W1.12aa and 12ba) Deciding *how* to do your job and organize the work? (W1.12ab and 12bb) Deciding what *training* is needed for people in your work group or department? (W1.12ac and 12bc) Setting work *schedules*, including breaks, overtime, and time off? (W1.12ad and 12bd) Deciding how much of a *raise* in pay the people in your work group should get? (W1.12ae and 12be) Setting *goals* for your work group or department? (W1.12af and 12bf) Deciding how to work with new *equipment or software*, if that's ever been needed? (W1.12ag and bg) Setting *safety* standards and practices?" (W1.12ah and 12bh) Deciding what kind of *benefits* are offered to employees? (a lot, some, only a little, no direct involvement at all); (W1.13a) "Suppose you *could* have a *lot* of influence in all these areas at work — regardless of whether you do now or not. As I read each area again, please tell me how important it would be to you to have a *lot* of influence on these decisions. First, how important would it be to you to have influence in (ITEM)?" (very important, somewhat important, not too important, not important at all).

41 percent said it was very important to have influence in deciding general pay raises; this gives a range in the desire for influence of 35 percentage points. Relatively many workers also said that it was very important to have influence in deciding the training workers get and the kind of benefits the firm offers them. Averaging the responses across areas, 55 percent of employees report that it was *very important* to have a lot of influence on these decisions.

Column 2 records the proportion of workers who said they actually had "a lot" of influence in an area. The proportion of workers reporting that they have a lot of influence in an area also varies across items. Just 6 percent of workers said they have a lot of influence setting pay or benefits at their workplace, as compared with 57 percent who said they have a lot of influence deciding how to do their particular job. This gives a 51-percentage-point range across areas, which is larger than the range in the desire for say. The implication is that people are more alike in what they want than are workplaces alike in providing them what they want. Finally, averaging the responses in Column 3 across areas, we see that 27 percent of employees reported that they had a lot of influence on these decisions. That twice as many workers consider it "very important" to have influence in workplace decisions than who say that they have "a lot" of influence in workplace decisions supports the notion that firms are not giving workers their desired say at the workplace.

Column 3 measures the gap between wanting say and having say as the difference between the percentages for whom having influence is very important and the percentages who have a lot of influence. Averaged across items, this influence gap is our bottom-line indicator of how the U.S. job market is falling short of meeting employee desires for say at their workplace. The average gap is a valuable summary statistic, but it is also an imperfect one — imperfect because it collapses four responses to each question (and thus sixteen possible combinations of answers) into a single number based on whether the respondents answered "very" to both items. This lumps together people who, for instance, said influence is "somewhat important" to them with those who said it was "not at all important."[10] The summary statistic is also imperfect because workers who have less influence than they want on items are grouped with workers who have more influence than they want on items.[11] Both of these imperfections imply that the summary gap understates the degree to which workers want more say on the job than they have.

To resolve this problem, we calculate in Column 4 the proportion of workers who want more influence in an area than they report having. Because many workers say it is somewhat important to have an influence on workplace decisions (and thus do not fit into the group in Column 1) but do not have much influence on decisions, this measure shows much greater representation/participation gaps than Column 3 does. Averaging across items, 53 percent of workers have less involvement in a workplace decision than they want — almost twice the difference in the average gap in Column 3.[12]

So, in which specific areas do workers want more say at their workplace? The biggest individual gaps involve deciding on benefits and pay raises for their group. These are issues regarding the division of the pie in the firm, where more influence for workers might benefit them at the expense of management or shareholders. The next largest gap is for something quite different: deciding on the training needed for workers, as the right training can improve productivity, profits, and wages. The gap is large here not because workers have exceptionally little influence on outcomes, as in determining benefits and pay, but because they have an exceptional desire for influencing this outcome. The representation/participation gap is smallest in the area of deciding how to do one's job and in setting work schedules, although for different reasons. Many workers have a great deal of direct influence in deciding how to do their job and organize their work, while relatively few workers regard setting schedules as being very important to them.

Differences in the Influence Gap

Does the gap between wanting and having an influence on workplace decisions vary among workers with different demographic or economic characteristics?

To answer this question, we formed a *summated rating* of the amount of influence each worker wanted and the amount that he or she had across all of the items discussed. A summated rating[13] is a simple scale that scores answers on each item and then sums the scores across items. Because the WRPS used a four-point scale, we accorded a 4 to a respondent's highest influence category and a 1 to his or her lowest influence category. The split design of the WRPS meant that each worker was asked about four items, so the scale takes a value from 4 (when the worker either had or wanted the least influence) to 16 (when the worker either had or wanted the most influence).

Exhibit 3.6 contrasts the value of our summated rating for workers of different types. Column 1 gives our measure of the influence workers want to

EXHIBIT 3.6. Summated rating measures of how much influence workers want and have on workplace decisions (by groups of workers).

	Measure of influence they want	Measure of influence they have	Influence gap
	On a scale from 4 to 16		
Sex			
Men	13.6	10.3	3.2
Women	13.6	9.7	3.9
Race			
White	13.5	10.0	3.5
Black	14.2	9.8	4.4
Education			
College graduate	13.5	10.5	3.0
High school graduate	13.7	9.9	3.8
Occupation			
Professional	13.6	10.8	2.8
Laborer	13.7	9.6	4.1
Union status			
Nonunion	13.6	10.0	3.6
Union	13.6	9.6	4.0
Employee involvement (EI)			
EI participant	13.8	11.2	2.6
Nonparticipant	13.5	9.4	4.1
Weekly earnings			
Upper quartile	13.6	10.8	2.8
Lower quartile	13.5	9.3	4.2

Note: The summated rating scale is based on a coding that gives the highest category a 4, the next highest a 3, the next highest a 2, and the lowest a 1. It simply sums these values for the four items about which we asked each worker. Thus it has a maximum value of 16 and a minimum value of 4. The higher the score in the text, the more a worker said that he or she wanted or had influence in decisions in the areas covered. *Source:* Tabulated from WRPS questions listed in Exhibit 3.5.

have. It shows that diverse groups have similar desires for influence on decisions. Men and women, union and nonunion workers, professionals and laborers all get the same score in terms of the amount of influence they want. Where differences occur, they are relatively modest: high school graduates want a bit more influence than college graduates; blacks want more than whites; participants on EI committees want more than nonparticipants. The overriding impression, however, is that, regardless of how we divide the workforce, employees want comparable amounts of influence on workplace decisions. Column 2 measures the influence that workers say they actually have. Here we find considerable variation. Workers in weaker positions in terms of their education or occupation, earnings, or sex or race have less influence on decisions than workers in stronger positions. Union workers report somewhat less influence than nonunion workers, while participants on EI committees report considerably more influence than do nonparticipants. (We examine these two groups in detail in Chapters 4 and 5.)

Similarity in the amount of influence people want and differences in the amount of influence they have necessarily translates in Column 3 into differences in the magnitude of the influence gap among workers. Most striking here is that influence gaps are large for all groups. To appreciate the magnitude of the summated scale, note that a four-point gap implies that, on average, a worker's influence on the job falls short of that worker's desire for influence by one category — that is, the worker wants a lot of influence and has only some influence, or wants some and has only a little, or wants a little and has none.

However we measure the difference between the say workers want in workplace decisions and the influence they actually have, the gap turns out to be large.

Collective or Individual Voice?

Workers can have a say on workplace decisions as individuals or as part of a group. Individually, employees can exert influence at their workplace by speaking directly with a supervisor. In companies with open-door policies, they can take a problem to higher management. In companies with internal grievance mechanisms, they can use a formal complaint procedure when they have a problem. In many large firms, workers can also voice their concerns through the opinion surveys of workers that these firms regularly conduct. They can also send e-mail or use suggestion boxes.

Collectively, employees can affect decisions by meeting as a group with management or by electing representatives to meet with management. In some companies, management gathers all workers together in "town meetings" to discuss common workplace problems. In other companies, management might set up committees of employees to deal with problems. Independently of management, workers might form unions to represent their collective interests. In most European countries, national law establishes works councils in which all workers — white collar as well as blue collar, nonunion as well as union — elect representatives to meet regularly with management.

When U.S. workers express a desire for more say about their jobs, do they want greater say only as individuals, or as part of a group?

This is a critical question in American labor relations because most employers prefer that employees speak out as individuals and are uneasy dealing with workers as a group. Groups invariably have greater power than the individuals who constitute them, and the strongest worker group in capitalism, the trade union, forces management to negotiate decisions rather than to decide as management feels best.

The WRPS examined the preferences of workers for these forms of exerting influence on workplace decisions in various ways. In one part of the survey, we asked half of the respondents, "Do you agree or disagree with the following statement: 'I'd feel more comfortable raising workplace problems through an employee association, rather than singly.'" We asked the other half: "How would you prefer to solve a workplace problem of your own? Would you feel more comfortable dealing directly with management yourself, or would you feel more comfortable having a group of your coworkers help you deal with management?" We asked the question in two ways to eliminate possible biases owing to differences in wording, context, or sequencing. The first question put the group process first and refers to workplace problems in general. The second question put individual action first and refers to a problem faced by the individual worker.

As Exhibit 3.7 indicates, the sequencing, context, or precise wording of the questions affected the responses. When the first response in the question was *through an employee association*, 56 percent of employees said they preferred to deal with a workplace problem through an association. When the first response was *by self*, 55 percent said they preferred dealing with their problem directly with management, with 43 percent preferring the group approach. The safest conclusion is that workers are evenly divided in their preferences between individual and group ways of dealing with problems.

The preference for a group or an individual solution to problems depends on the particular problem workers face. Most elected to deal with instances of sexual harassment, unfair treatment, and insufficient job training directly with management, whereas for issues involving workplace heath and safety and benefits, they wanted the help of other employees. Many who favored collective voice in general still preferred to deal with harassment/unfair treatment issues individually, while many who said they

EXHIBIT 3.7. Some employees prefer individual voice; others prefer group voice.

Percentage who feel more comfortable raising workplace problems . . .

Through an employee association	56
As an individual	38
Don't know	5

Percentage who prefer to solve a workplace problem of their own . . .

With the help of fellow employees	43
By self	55
Don't know	2

	Depending on the problem				
	Benefits	Health/ safety	Training at job	Unfair treatment	Sexual harrassment
Percentage who prefer to solve workplace problems					
With the help of fellow employees	66	53	44	39	34
By self	33	36	54	59	65
Don't know	1	1	2	3	1

Source: Based on these WRPS questions: (W1.34a) "Do you agree or disagree with the following statement: 'I'd feel more comfortable raising workplace problems through an employee association, rather than as an individual'?"; (W1.34b) "How would *you* prefer to solve a workplace problem of your own? Would you feel more comfortable dealing directly with management *yourself,* or would you feel more comfortable having a *group* of your fellow employees *help* you deal with management?"; (W2.36a–e) "How do you prefer to deal with any complaints you might have about something at work? For each of the following problems, please tell me whether you would prefer to deal directly with management *yourself* or prefer to have a *group* of your fellow employees help you deal with management."

favored individual voice in general preferred to deal with health and safety/benefits collectively.[14]

How much meaning should we attach to workers saying that they want collective input in workplace decisions? After all, it's one thing to say, "Yes, I want to participate in decisions that affect the overall workplace"; it's another matter entirely to put time and effort into such an activity. We asked workers if they would be willing to volunteer two to three hours per month to participate in an employee organization that met with management. One-third of employees said they would definitely be willing to do so; 44 percent said they would probably be willing to meet with management. Because you don't need many folks to represent employees in discussion with management, even if workers vastly exaggerated their willingness to give time to such an activity, there would seem to be an ample supply of employees to serve in any workplace organization.

In sum, employees want greater say at the workplace not simply as individuals but as a group as well. They differentiate between those areas in which they prefer to deal with problems by themselves and those in which the collective or public-goods nature of the decision — health and safety, benefits, a system for resolving problems — would seem to require a group input to be effective.

Cooperation and Independence

In the focus groups, the survey, and the follow-up probes, employees consistently said they wanted a cooperative relationship with management, and that they preferred workplace arrangements that produced such cooperation. The first indication of how sensitive workers were to management's attitude toward an employee organization came in response to a question toward the end of the survey: "Thinking now about any kind of employee organization, not just unions, how would *you* like it to work? If it was your decision alone to make, and everybody went along with it, would you prefer . . . ?" On governance, we offered two choices: one run jointly by employees and management or one run by employees alone. We imagined that most workers would choose "by employees alone," but an overwhelming majority of nonmanagerial employees chose an organization "run jointly" by employees and management (85 percent) to one run "by employees alone" (10 percent). Even union members supported the jointly run organization (82 percent favored this, as compared with 14 percent who favored the employee-run organization). This floored us.

Recognizing that there are two potential determinants to workers' having an influence on workplace decisions — the strength of any employee organization and the attitude of management toward that organization — we asked employees to choose between two hypothetical organizations, "one that management cooperated with in discussing issues, but had no power to make decisions," and "one that had more power, but management opposed." Exhibit 3.8 shows that 63 percent of nonmanagerial employees favored management cooperation and no power, as compared with 22 percent who wanted more power even if management opposed it. Unionized employees, whom we expected to be less concerned about managerial attitudes, gave almost identical responses, preferring the weak organization with cooperation to the stronger organization.

EXHIBIT 3.8. Management cooperation perceived as essential.

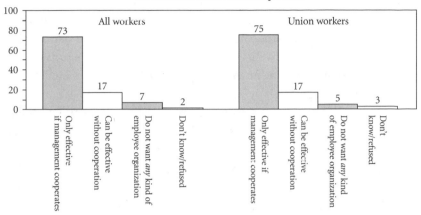

Percentage of workers who think that an employee organization
cannot be effective without cooperation

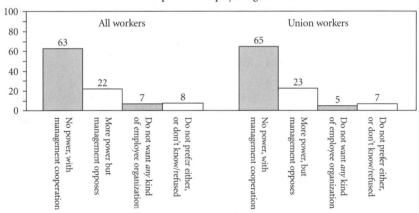

Percentage of workers who prefer management cooperation
to a powerful employee organization

Source: Based on these WRPS questions: (W1.49b) "Do you think employee organizations can be effective *even if* management does not cooperate with them, or do you
think they can *only* be effective if management cooperates?"; (W1.49c) (TO NONMANAGERS)
"Which *one* of these employee organizations would you prefer (ROTATE ORDER): one that
management cooperated with in discussing issues, but had no power to make decisions, or one that had more power, but management opposed?"

Finding that workers prefer a cooperative management to a powerful workplace organization by such an overwhelming number stunned us, as it did the business and labor groups to whom we presented this discovery. The employer representatives were pleased with the result. Union representatives were unhappy. But, as we shall detail, we also found that employees wanted independent authority and standing from management in making workplace decisions along with cooperation. This runs counter to the desire of most management to prevent the formation of independent employee groups, particularly trade unions.

Why were employees so sensitive to management's attitudes about a workplace organization that they preferred a cooperative management to a strong worker organization? The main reason is that most employees believe that management cooperation is essential for any workplace organization to succeed. We asked, "Do you think employee organizations can be effective even if management does not cooperate with them, or do you think they can only be effective if management cooperates?" Three-fourths declared employee organizations could "only be effective with management cooperation" — four times the percentage who thought management cooperation was not required. And once again, union members responded similarly to nonunion members (see Exhibit 3.8).

But what do employees mean by "cooperative management"? A management that smiles and says nice words while it does what it wants? A management that lets workers do what they want? Had the WRPS been a one-shot poll we would have been left wondering or speculating. But we were able to question workers about how they interpreted cooperation on our Wave 2 follow-up. We asked, "what do you think employees get when management is cooperative?" Thirty-one percent said some power to influence company decisions; 66 percent thought employees got a chance to give their opinions and ideas. This pattern of response suggests that most employees expect a cooperative management simply to hear employee views. But we asked further, "If a company always listens to what employees have to say but doesn't follow their advice, is management being cooperative or uncooperative?" Seventy-one percent declared such a management to be uncooperative. Even those who said that the most that employees get from a cooperative management is the chance to give their opinions and ideas thought that a management that listened but never followed employee advice was uncooperative.

We conclude from these responses that employees choose a cooperative management over a strong workplace organization and want workplace organizations to be jointly run by labor and management, because they believe that this gives them a genuine influence on decisions, either through group decision-making or by management's listening to what they have to say and following their advice at least some of the time. Most workers believe that management must be on board for any workplace representation or participation system to work effectively. Management cooperation implies real employee influence.

At the same time, preference for influence through a cooperative management rather than through a strong worker organization does not mean that workers reject an independent organization. In fact, most workers wanted an organization with some independent authority. This opinion came out strongly when we asked employees to specify the characteristics of any workplace organization that dealt with management (see Chapter 7). The majority of workers said that they wanted an organization in which

- either management or employees can raise problems for discussion as opposed to one in which management alone decides the problems that should be discussed.
- employees and management have to agree on decisions as opposed to one in which management makes the final decision about issues.
- conflicts are resolved by an outside arbitrator rather than by management.
- employee representatives are elected or volunteer themselves rather than being chosen by management.

A similar pattern of preferences emerges when we ask employees their views of different existing organizations at the workplace, including unions. Current union members, for example, overwhelmingly prefer a cooperative management to a powerful workplace organization, but they want to keep the organization they have: 90 percent of them would vote to keep their union if a new election were held today. A cooperative management and a union would presumably be their ideal world.

Thirty-two percent of nonunion/nonmanagerial employees would vote for a union "if an election were held today to decide whether employees like [them] should be represented by a union." For these workers, the ideal would also presumably be a union and cooperative management.

Finally, as Chapter 7 shows, many nonunion workers favor a worker organization that is independent of management rather than one that is more compliant to management, while relatively few favor an organization that is management-dominated.

Perhaps we should not have been so surprised at worker sensitivity to management attitudes at the workplace. A workplace has many of the features of a marriage. Cooperation is as essential for a pleasant working environment and high productivity at a workplace as it is for a successful marriage. In most work settings, management has most of the power to effect changes. If you are in a room with a 900-pound gorilla, better that it be good-natured and friendly than hungry and angry. And, to return to the question whose answer first stunned us, workers did not choose an organization run by employees; they chose an organization run *jointly* by management and labor.

One Important Bottleneck: Management Resistance

So why don't workers have the workplace influence they want? We asked employees, "Given the way things are set up now in your company, how likely is it that you could get the influence you want, if you tried to get more influence?" Fifty-six percent of those who wanted more say in workplace decisions indicated that it was "not too likely" or "not likely at all" that they could get the influence they wanted, "even if [they] tried." Only 10 percent thought it "very likely."

Most workers believe that the bottleneck is management. Most believe that management will not voluntarily give them more voice and representation than they currently have. Most believe that management will actively resist employee attempts to establish the one form of independent workplace organization nominally encouraged by U.S. labor law — unions. As with virtually all of the findings in this chapter, this conclusion is based on responses to several questions rather than to a single one.

Consider first how workers grade management's willingness to share power and authority. We asked workers to give a report card to their management in various areas using a five-grade school scale (A, B, C, D, and F). We have all been graded in this manner long enough to have a similar notion of the difference between an A and an F. As Exhibit 3.9 shows, employees gave management high grades in their understanding and knowledge of the business, and reasonably high grades on overall company leadership. If your kids came back with mostly A's and B's, you'd be pleased.

EXHIBIT 3.9. Report card for managers.

Understanding and knowledge of the business

Overall company leadership

Concern for employees

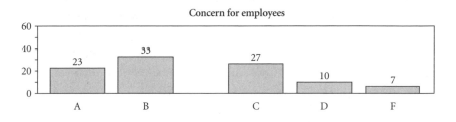

Giving fair pay increases and benefits

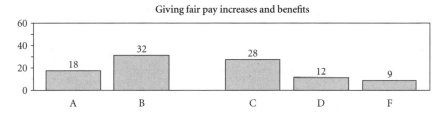

Willingness to share power and authority

Note: Numbers represent percentage of workers who assigned each grade.
Source: Based on this WRPS question: (W2.16aa–ae) "If you were to rate the performance of management on a scale similar to school grades — A for excellent, B for good, C for fair, D for poor, and F for failure — what grades would you give management in the following areas?" (overall company leadership; concern for employees; giving fair pay increases and benefits; understanding and knowledge of the business; willingness to share power and authority).

But the grades drop precipitously when it comes to issues about how management treats workers. Forty-four percent of workers gave a C grade or lower for management's concern for employees. Forty-nine percent gave a C or worse in giving fair pay increases and benefits. But the worst grade of all was for willingness to share power or authority: 55 percent of workers awarded management a C or lower in this area. Workers see management as hogging power in their organization. If your kids came back with mostly C's or lower, you'd probably want to have a serious talk with them about their future.

This is not, moreover, an aberrant finding: It comes up repeatedly throughout the survey. In the part of the WRPS focused on employee involvement, we asked those workers who believed that greater employee participation would be good for their company's performance[15] why they didn't have this participation. Fifty-five percent cited the reason as management's unwillingness to relinquish power. In the part of the WRPS focused on unionization, we asked respondents who had worked at a company or organization at a time when employees were trying to form a union[16] how management had responded. Two-thirds said that management had opposed the organizing campaign in ways that ranged from information campaigns to threats against or harassment of union supporters.[17] Nonunion employees, most of whom had not experienced a union campaign, also expected significant management opposition to any union drive: 55 percent who said they wanted a union gave management opposition as the central reason for not having one.

Managers tell a similar story. The majority in nonunion firms said that they would oppose any unionization effort; one-third said that it would hurt their advancement in the company if the employees they managed formed a union; and most of them said that it would hurt their career a great deal. Under U.S. labor law, a manager who refuses to oppose a union can be summarily dismissed. Three-fourths of managers said that they felt more comfortable dealing with workers on workplace problems individually, as compared with only 14 percent of managers who said that they would prefer dealing with workers in a group. By contrast, about half of workers preferred to deal with management as a group rather than on a one-to-one basis. Most managers reported that they were willing to meet with employee organizations,[18] but 55 percent said that in dealing with any employee group, they wanted to maintain final decision-making powers in cases of dispute. Twenty percent wanted to pick employee representatives for any joint employee/management committee, as compared with 12 percent of employees who wanted management to pick representatives. In fact, in nonunion companies with employee committees, management picks committee members in 27 percent of the cases, fills the committee with volunteers in 43 percent of the cases, and allows employees to elect them in 17 percent of the cases.

In short, the chief reason that workers have less influence at their workplaces than they want is that management is unwilling to cede power or authority to them. Because management has effective hegemony over workplaces, it is easy to understand why workers so highly emphasize managerial cooperation as the key to any successful employee organizational activity.[19]

Conclusion: Employee Voice in a Competitive Market

This chapter shows that workers want more influence or say in workplace decisions than they have, and that this unsatisfied desire for influence pervades U.S. labor-management relations. It also shows that workers want to express this influence through a more cooperative relationship with management, as well as a more equal one. That workers in the most flexible labor market in the advanced world want greater say in workplace decisions will surprise competitive market theorists who believe that market forces solve all problems. That workers in the labor market with the most unequal income distribution in the advanced world want to work cooperatively with their management will distress those who still believe in zero-sum class struggle.

But this chapter's findings fit well with a view of the labor market in which management and employees are intrinsically linked in a relationship that is both cooperative and conflictual — cooperative because both sides are needed to produce output, and conflictual because people invariably disagree about the best way to execute different activities and about the division of the output from those activities.

Considering workplace disagreements, the economists' favorite solution is to increase the possibilities of *exit* — the ability of dissatisfied workers to quit a firm ("take this job and shove it") or of dissatisfied bosses to fire them ("you're toast, buddy"). But exit is an incomplete solution to workplace problems, and it's one that most workers and management reject in favor of some form of dialogue. Exit creates search costs, as workers look for a new job and management looks for new workers; it obviates the firm-specific skills that workers acquire through experience; and it is a poor way to communicate the precise nature of problems, and thus to learn how to correct them. This is as true for disagreements between managers and employees as it is for disagreements between spouses, or children and parents.

As discussed in Chapter 1, the alternative to exit is *voice* — talking about a problem and seeking to resolve it through discussion, argument, and bargaining. Political scientists, sociologists, psychologists — perhaps everyone but economists — like voice.[20] While voice has its own costs (Another committee meeting? Help!), in many circumstances its benefits outweigh its costs. Voice is far more informative than exit, because it permits the exploration of problems. And the process of exploration itself often helps induce the mutual trust needed to act together on new information. Voice is also more democratic, because it requires the cooperation of both sides: It takes one to exit but two to voice. Both sides need to talk, and both sides need to listen.

That most American workers want more individual and collective voice at the workplace, and believe they cannot get it, tells us that most workers feel they do not have enough of that conversation. At least in the view of workers, the current U.S. labor-relations system is generally failing to support this productive way of dealing with workplace problems.

CHAPTER 4

How Workers Judge Unions

Three different institutions govern American workplaces and the relations between labor and management: collective bargaining between unions and management, management-initiated personnel policies, and state and federal government laws and administrative regulations. We asked what workers thought about these different governing institutions, and this and the next two chapters report what workers told us.

Because we found that most workers want more say at their workplaces, and that many are dissatisfied with existing labor-management relations, one critical thing to learn in these chapters is *why these institutions have not met worker desires for greater say*. It could be that existing institutions are inadequate or defective in some way — that unions, firms, and governments are not competent enough to deliver what workers want. It could be that these institutions are simply inadequately supplied — that more unions, more management-led human-resource programs, more laws and government regulators would solve the problem. Or it could be that the mix of these institutions is off-kilter — that strengthening or weakening one might induce the others to provide what workers want.

Another focus of these chapters is how worker attitudes toward these institutions depend on the worker's personal attributes — for instance, age, sex, ethnicity, or income — and on the work conditions he or she experiences. Perhaps different kinds of people want different kinds of voice, for systematically different reasons. Maybe professionals desiring a greater voice want more private dealings with management, whereas office workers seeking greater voice want more regulations and shop-floor workers want unions. Perhaps if you are employed by a good firm that is open to worker input, a consultative committee can give you your desired voice. If your employer is a mean SOB, however, you might want a full-fledged union. What, in short, explains the variation among workers in their attitudes toward current institutions? Is it you or your workplace that makes you favor or oppose unions, employee involvement (EI) committees, or greater governmental regulation of labor market outcomes?

This chapter examines attitudes toward unions and collective bargaining; Chapter 5 turns to attitudes toward management-led policies; Chapter 6 treats attitudes toward legal regulations.

Unionization and Collective Bargaining: Headed for Oblivion?

Remember "big labor" — George Meany with his cigar, Walter Reuther bargaining against General Motors, Jimmy Hoffa with his National Master Freight Agreement? In the 1950s and 1960s, and in some industries through the 1970s, private-sector unions were powerful actors in the U.S. economy. American labor law, grounded in the National Labor Relations Act (NLRA) of 1935, formally encourages collective bargaining as the preferred mode for determining the rules of work and governing labor-management relations. In the aftermath of World War II, collective bargaining arguably influenced the wages job rules for most workers. Some 40 percent of private-sector workers were organized into unions. Nonunion firms widely copied union workplace conditions such as grievance procedures, seniority rules on job bidding, competitive wages and benefits — if only to keep their own workplaces "union free." Although pay and benefits differed markedly between highly organized sectors such as manufacturing and construction and largely nonunion sectors such as services and the retail trade, many experts believed that the broad direction of American labor outcomes was set in those primary sectors in which unions were key actors. If the United Automobile Workers (UAW) set a contract with General Motors, many other unions and firms would follow the UAW-GM pattern, at least in part, and GM would give its nonunion employees wage and benefit increases matching the collective-bargaining agreement. If GM didn't give all workers the union-won increases, the nonunion workers might want to unionize, or they might suffer from morale problems. In Canada, where collective bargaining is more prevalent than in the United States, union wage settlements still greatly affect nonunion wages. In 1997 workers in the only unionized Canadian Starbucks store gained a $0.75 wage increase (roughly 10 percent); Starbucks extended the increase to the chain's 95 nonunion stores, presumably to reduce the incentive for those workers to organize.

But as the United States enters the twenty-first century, collective bargaining outside the public sector is no longer a major force in the economy. Unions represent less than 10 percent of the private-sector workforce and are concentrated in declining industries such as manufacturing and in older firms and plants within those industries. With union density so low, collective bargaining no longer takes wages and benefits out of competition among firms. The greater number of nonunion competitors reduces the spillover of union gains to nonunion workers by increasing nonunion managerial resistance to matching union wages and benefits. If most of your competitors are low-paid nonunion firms, you face market problems if you follow union contracts and pay higher wages and give better benefits. For the same reason, the decline in unionism reduces the ability of unions to win wage and benefit gains for their members. How can you ask for a large wage gain if it is going to put union firms at risk of going out of business or losing market share? And the diminished threat of unionization reduces the pressure on nonunion firms to match union wages or benefits so as to convince workers that they do not need a union to represent their interests.

Despite the great decline in unionism in the private sector, however, the status of unions still lies at the heart of disputes over national labor policy. From one perspective, this is understandable. Unions are the *only* major workplace institution that workers control. To the extent that national labor policy is about guaranteeing workers the right to associate inside the firm (which is the expressed intent of the NLRA), the ability of workers to form and defend unions is the best test of that guarantee. But the current marginality of unions also makes the discussion a little odd. De facto, it excludes labor policy toward 90 percent of private-sector workers even as it does nothing to relieve the intensity of the union-management argument in Washington.

What reconciles these observations is that the diminished position of unions is exactly what makes that discussion so heated. Most firms welcome the steady decline of private-sector unions and oppose any reform that might reverse the decline, however justifiable the reform. Once only Neanderthal ideologues dreamed of a "union-free" economy; now, however, as that reality approaches, many businesses support this goal and are prepared to expend substantial resources to achieve it — lobbying to prevent union-friendly changes in existing law and resisting attempts at new organizing. For unions, reciprocally, the stakes could not be higher. They are in the fight of their lives, and they're losing. They blame current law and policy for providing them little protection against management attack, and they blame management attack for their problem in organizing workers.

This is not an atmosphere conducive to rational debate about what might best serve American workers. It's more a war zone than a policy discussion. Nor does it help that in that zone, the voices of organized interests (labor or management) fully dominate. The views of average American workers are not heard, or are ignored, even though in principle they should be the governing force in national policy.

So how do American workers view unions? What do members like and dislike about them? Given a choice between working union and working nonunion, how many unorganized workers would want unions to represent them? And why don't those workers, however many or few they are, have the union representation they want?

To Know Unions Is . . . to Love Them?

Our entry into the war zone is a simple question that we asked nonunion and union workers alike: Would they vote for or against a union in an National Labor Relations Board (NLRB) election at their workplaces? The question has two virtues. It requires respondents to give a bottom-line assessment. You can recognize the benefits of unions and still decide to vote no, or you can recognize the flaws of unions and still decide to vote yes. And, while it is hypothetical, the question relates to a choice that people have or might readily make at some point in their working lives. The precise question we asked nonmanagerial/nonunion employees was, "If an election were held today to decide whether employees like you should be represented by a union, would you vote for the union or against the union?"

Exhibit 4.1 shows that nearly one-third of respondents said they would vote for the union. Finding that one-third or so of nonunion workers say they want unions in response to questions of this sort is nothing new. Similar figures are reported in many other studies, including those conducted by management groups.[1] We added a twist to the standard question, however, by also asking nonunion workers how they thought their colleagues would vote in such an election. We asked this because if the one-third of the workforce that wanted a union was evenly distributed among workplaces, unions would lose all NLRB elections by a two-to-one majority, whereas if those workers were in workplaces where most workers wanted unions, unions could win elections at those sites. The results show that 82

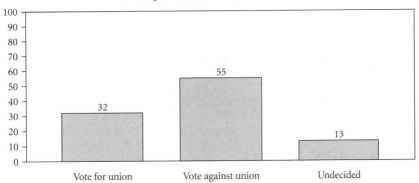

Percentage of nonunion workers who want unions

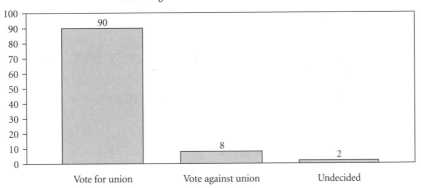

Percentage of union members who want unions

Source: Based on these WRPS questions: (W1.41a) (TO CURRENT UNION MEMBERS) "If a new election were held *today* to decide whether to keep the union at your (company/organiza-tion), would you vote to keep the union or get rid of it?"; (W1.41b) (TO NONMANAGERS WHO ARE NOT CURRENT UNION MEMBERS) "If an election were held *today* to decide whether employees like you should be represented by a union, would you vote for the union or against the union?"

percent of pro-union unorganized workers thought a majority of their colleagues shared their views, while 10 percent of unorganized workers who opposed unions thought themselves in the minority in their workplace in that view. Putting these numbers together, one-third of disorganized workers believe that were an election held tomorrow, workers at their firm would support a union. This is roughly identical to the share of workers who would themselves vote union.

We also asked union members a nearly identical question about their attitude toward their union: "If a new election were held today to decide whether to keep the union at your company, would you vote to keep the union or to get rid of it?" Few surveys ask union members whether they would vote to keep their union or to disestablish it.[2] The reason is that analysts and practitioners generally believe that most members support their union. After all, votes to disestablish unions are rare; workers queue up for union jobs, and those who do not like a union setting can readily move to a nonunion job, as most jobs are nonunion. The figures in Exhibit 4.1 show that this assumption is true: The vast majority of union members support their union.

The surprise in the exhibit is not that union workers support their union but that they support it so much more than nonunion workers. Nearly 90 percent of current union members said they would vote for the union if an election were held tomorrow. Just 8 percent said they would vote against the union. Underlying these voting intentions are the personal experiences of workers with the union at their firm. More than 70 percent of union members described those experiences as positive, 26 percent described them as very good, and 45 percent described them as good. By contrast, just 5 percent of union members described their experiences as bad, and 2 percent described them as very bad. The remaining 22 percent reported mixed ("neither good nor bad") experiences, but a majority also said they would vote to keep the union were a new election held, indicating that the good outweighed the bad in their bottom line.[3]

The 58-percentage-point difference between the 90 percent support for unions from current union members and the 32 percent support from nonmembers contrasts sharply with the broadly similar attitudes of union and nonunion workers on many other Worker Representation and Participation Survey (WRPS) questions. Recall that we found that union members were just as likely to prefer a cooperative management over a powerful employee organization as were nonunion members, and that union members were nearly as likely as nonunion members to want any workplace organization to be jointly run by management and workers rather than to be run solely by workers. The only issue on which union and nonunion workers' views differ by anything approaching 58 percent is in worker desire for a union. What gives? If we are to understand how American workers view unions, it is essential to explain why union workers are so much more supportive of unions at their workplace than are nonunion workers.

The first explanation that comes to the mind of a social scientist is that

EXHIBIT 4.2. Percentage of workers who want unions (by characteristics of workers).

Sex

Men	27
Women	35

Age

18–24	44
25–34	32
35–44	26
45–54	32
55 +	24

Race

Nonblack	28
Black	59

Education

Less than high school	44
High school graduates	34
Some college	32
College graduates	21

Occupation

Professional	25
Laborer	42

Weekly earnings

Upper quartile	22
Lower quartile	45

Source: Tabulated from WRPS for all nonunion/nonmanagerial workers (W1.41b).

union members and nonmembers are different types of people working in different types of jobs. In the private sector, union members substantially differ from nonmembers in several demographic and economic characteristics.[4] They are, for instance, more likely than nonunion workers to be blue-collar and less educated and male. Could it be that workers with these or related characteristics favor unions more than others?

Exhibit 4.2 shows that nonunion member support for unions varies by occupation, education, income, age, and race. The highest level of demand for unionization is by black workers, the majority of whom would vote union today in an NLRB election. Disproportionately large numbers of lower-wage workers, blue-collar workers, and younger workers also support a union. These data indicate that, in general, employees in weak labor market positions tend to favor collective representation. But demographic factors do not explain the huge difference in the desire for unionism between organized and unorganized workers. The reason is simple. Because union members almost unanimously would vote union, there is almost no variation among members for demographic factors to explain.

To document statistically the (in)ability of demographic factors to explain the union/nonunion difference in the desire for a union, we used a linear probability model to relate workers' intention to vote union (1 = vote for the union; 0 = vote against the union) to measures of the individual's demographic characteristics and whether the person was a union member. As Exhibit 4.3 shows, this regression does not reduce the difference between member and nonmember pro-union response at all: The difference actually rises to 60 percentage points.

A second possibility is that an "innate" desire for collective action to obtain a say at their workplace is greater among union members than nonunion workers. Union members might want workplace influence to a greater extent than do observationally equivalent nonunion workers. Or, wanting the same say, union members might prefer solving problems through groups of workers than individually. Perhaps persons with a bent for dealing with problems through collective action are more likely to seek union jobs than are persons who prefer to deal with problems individually. These are variants of the "different types of people" explanation, although in this case the difference between union and nonunion workers is in terms of preferences rather than demographic and economic characteristics.

We examined the extent to which differences in the desire for collective action might explain why union workers are so much more favorable to unions than are nonunion workers by comparing the likelihood that union and nonunion employees would vote for a union contingent on their desire for say and on their preference for group solutions to workplace problems. The results summarized in Exhibit 4.3 fail to explain why union members and nonunion workers view unions so differently. After we take into account the attitudes toward collective action and say, we have a difference between union and nonunion worker opinions that is just 1 percentage point less than it was in the raw data.[5]

A third possible explanation is that workers who are unhappy with unions leave them, so that members consist only of workers who approve of unions. Because about 85 percent of all U.S. jobs are nonunion, workers who don't like unions have a lot of jobs to choose from and can easily vote with their feet. This is a selectivity or sorting argument: People who like unions end up in unions, whereas those who don't like unions work nonunion. But differences in the typical wages and benefits associated with

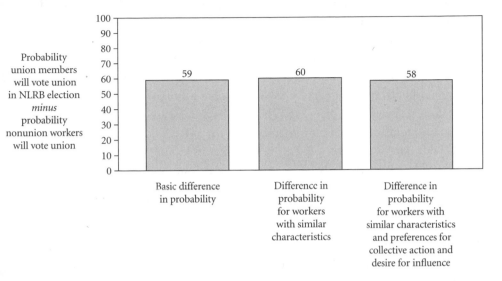

(NLRB = National Labor Relations Board.)

Source: Based on linear probability regression. The "basic difference" is from the regression of the 0/1 dichotomous variable voting for a union on union membership. The "difference in probability for workers with similar characteristics" adds a set of dummy variables for five age groups (18–24, 25–34, 35–44, and 45–54), for two race groups (black and nonblack), for sex, and for five education groups (less than 12 years, high school graduate, technical school post-high school/some college, college graduate, and postcollege graduate). Workplace characteristics were a set of three dummy variables for whether workers were very, somewhat, or not satisfied with their influence on workplace decisions (W1.14_1,2,3,4); two dummy variables for whether they participated in an employee-involvement program (W1.24) or were in a company with a program (W1.23); three dummy variables for the quartile of their weekly earnings in the earnings distribution; one dummy variable for those who did not report earnings; and one dummy variable for worker preferences for preferring to deal with workplace problems with a group of employees rather than as an individual. The latter variable is based on persons who answered that they preferred the help of fellow employees to the WRPS question (W1.34b), "How would *you* prefer to solve a workplace problem of your own? Would you feel more comfortable dealing directly with management *yourself*, or would you feel more comfortable having a *group* of fellow employees *help* you deal with management" (ASKED OF HALF THE SAMPLE), or to the WRPS question (W1.34a), "Do you agree or disagree with the following statement: 'I'd feel more comfortable raising workplace problems through an employee association, rather than as an individual'?" (ASKED OF THE OTHER HALF).

union and nonunion jobs could push the selectivity in the reverse direction. A worker unhappy with a union might stay in that job anyway, as it will generally offer better pay and benefits than a nonunion job would. By contrast, a nonunion worker unhappy with her job might more readily switch employers. The net effect would be more disgruntled workers in the union setting. The democratic nature of unions also argues against explaining the difference in views in terms of sorting. After all, if you don't like how your union works, you can campaign against the leadership and vote for new policies.

One way to assess the selectivity effect is to examine the views of workers who had previously been in a union but were now working nonunion. If people who leave unions do so because they don't like unions, they would be exceptionally likely to vote against a union at their new workplace. Because union density has been falling, there are many more former union members than union members in the WRPS. But former members do not appear to have voted with their feet in leaving unionized settings. Asked how they would vote in an NLRB election, former union members said they would support a union at a moderately *higher* rate than would nonunion workers with no experience of unions: 35 percent of former members said they would vote union, as compared with 30 percent of workers who had never been in a union. Even when we compare workers with the same economic demographic characteristics, we find that former members are slightly more favorably inclined to unions than are persons with no experience with them.[6]

Still, former union members are much closer to other nonunion workers in their intention to vote union than they are to union workers. A 5-percentage-point differences is not a 50-percentage-point one. Why?

One reason is that former members report their union experience less favorably than current members. A smaller share describe their experiences as "very good" (14 percent versus 26 percent) or "good" (24 percent versus 45 percent), and a larger percent describe it as "bad" (13 percent versus 5 percent) or "very bad" (12 percent versus 2 percent). Exhibit 4.4 shows that both current members and former members who say they had good experiences with a union are more likely to vote union than those who say they had a bad experience. These differences in experiences help to explain some of the lower support for unions among ex-members than current members. But ex-union members and current members who had the same experiences with their union differ greatly in their attitudes toward the union. Among workers who report their union experience as "very good," *all* union members would support the union, compared with 74 percent of former members. Among workers who report "bad" or "very bad" union experiences, 44–47 percent of union members would still vote union compared with very small proportions of ex-members.

So the puzzle deepens. Two workers with comparable experiences with

EXHIBIT 4.4. Union members are more likely to vote union than are former members with similar union experiences.

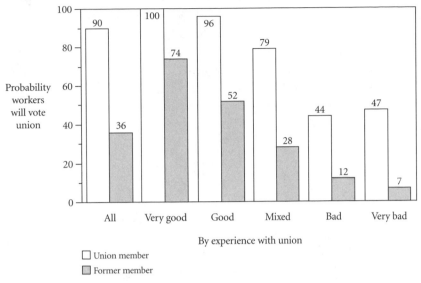

Probability workers will vote union

By experience with union

☐ Union member
▨ Former member

Source: Based on these WRPS questions: (W1.39b) (TO NONMANAGERS) "Have you *ever* been a member of a union?" or (W1.39c) "Before you said there is no union at your (company/organization). Have you *ever* been a member of a union?"; (W1.40a) (TO CURRENT UNION MEMBERS) "How would you describe your personal experience with the union at your (company/organization)?"; (W1.41a) (TO CURRENT UNION MEMBERS) "If a new election were held *today* to decide whether to keep the union at your (company/organization), would you vote to keep the union or get rid of it?"

unions report different intentions to vote depending on their current union status. What is going on?

We think the best explanation for the huge difference in support for unions between members and nonmembers is the "to know them is to love them" hypothesis. This hypothesis is grounded in a well-established psychological phenomenon called the *endowment effect*.[7] Psychologists have found that, in general, people are conservative in their preferences, in the sense that they value what they have more highly than something else of identical value that they don't possess, *simply because they have the former*. Say you are indifferent between two *What Workers Want* coffee mugs: a blue mug and a green mug. You are indifferent between blue and green (it's the gross pink mugs you can't tolerate). You'd just as soon take a blue mug as a green mug. We give you the blue mug, and you use it for a week. We come back and offer to trade you a green mug for your blue one. If you are like most people, you decline the trade. Simply possessing the blue mug raises its value to you. In experiment after experiment, people show that they become attached to what they have or are initially endowed with.

What does the endowment effect imply for our problem?

Assume that workers with neutral feelings about unions are placed into a union setting, and assume that the union is doing a reasonable job at that workplace. Then, by the endowment effect, these workers would end up more favorably inclined to the union than they would otherwise be. They would find that the union does some valuable things for them — for instance, ensuring that the employer treats them fairly in various ways. They might wonder, "How can I be sure the employer will treat me fairly without my union?" In fact, in workplaces where unions win NLRB elections, they usually win by a small majority, but after a short period of time they gain the confidence of the bulk of the workers, with the result that neither management nor workers who opposed the union will seek an election to disestablish the union. This has certainly been the experience at a workplace one of us knows well, Harvard University, where after many years and NLRB votes, clerical and technical workers chose to organize by a slim majority, but where today most workers strongly support the union.

But the same endowment effect should operate on nonunion workers as well. If we put workers with neutral feelings about unions into a nonunion setting, and if the nonunion workplace operates essentially as well as the union workplace, these workers would end up more favorably inclined to the nonunion workplace. They would find that the employer's labor policies did valuable things for them, such as ensuring that supervisors treated them fairly and giving them direct access to management. They might wonder, "How can I be sure things will work well if there is a union intervening between me and the employer?" Maybe the workplace will be rife with conflict.

Assuming that both settings produced the same well-being for workers, and that the endowment effect was working, we would expect that the proportion of workers in the union setting who would vote to keep the workplace union and the proportion of workers in the nonunion setting who would vote to keep the workplace nonunion would be roughly the same. In each case, workers would prefer the mug that they had. It held their coffee without leaking. Who knows if the other mug would do the same?

But the statistics do not show that equal proportions of workers favor the status quo at their workplace. Using the argument that the endowment effect predicts a positive response to the current workplace, we treat workers who are uncertain about how they vote as opposing their current status. Some 55 percent of nonunion workers said they would vote to remain nonunion, as compared with 90 percent of union workers who would vote to remain union. This contrast gives a smaller (35-percentage-point) gap than that in Exhibit 4.1, but it is still huge.

That proportionately more union than nonunion workers want to maintain their current workplace institution suggests that the endowment effect must be working on different outcomes. On average, union workplaces must be fulfilling the desires of their workers better than nonunion workplaces are fulfilling the desires of theirs. Because, contrary to the "let's stay put" endowment effect, 32 percent of nonunion workers want to change the status quo at their workplace as compared with just 8 percent of union workers, unions must be doing something right. That in nonunion settings former union members are more desirous of unions than workers with no experience with unions is consistent with this explanation.

. . . But Not Blindly

When we first conceived the WRPS, we did not intend to ask union members to judge their union. We believed that we had enough on our plate trying to figure out what workers wanted from their workplace than to also try to figure out what they wanted from their union. Our sample of organized workers would necessarily be relatively small — 250 or so union members — which is not enough to permit the type of detailed cross-tabulations and comparisons that we would ideally want to make. And individual unions survey their own members regularly and thus can probe in greater depth the various issues faced by workers in their jurisdiction.

But both the business and labor representatives advising us thought that failing to ask union members about attitudes toward say in their union would be a serious omission. The business representatives said, "It won't look right to the business community if you find that workers are dissatisfied with their say in companies, and you never ask the same things about unions. You're giving workers a chance to gripe about us but not about them." The union representatives said, "It won't look right to unions if you ask union workers a lot of questions about their dealings with management and not about their union. We're part of the workplace, too."

So we asked union members how satisfied they were with the influence they and their union coworkers had in union decisions in several areas. We worded this question similarly to the questions we had asked about worker satisfaction with influence on workplace decisions. This gave us a natural

EXHIBIT 4.5. Percentage of union members satisfied with their union.

	Very satisfied	Somewhat satisfied	Not too/ not satisfied	Don't know
Satisfied with say in local issues				
Choosing local leaders	35	44	17	4
Bargaining about wages and benefits	31	41	25	3
Less satisfied with national leaders				
Choosing national leaders in your union	20	49	35	6
Least satisfied with say in union political process				
Union positions on national political issues	15	53	25	7
Endorsements of candidates in political campaigns	13	50	29	8

Source: Based on this WRPS question: (W1.43a–e) (TO CURRENT UNION MEMBERS; N = 282) "How satisfied are you with the influence you and fellow union members have in union decisions about (VARIOUS ITEMS; ROTATE)?" (very satisfied, somewhat satisfied, not too satisfied, not satisfied at all).

measuring rod for comparing employee attitudes toward their say in union decisions and in their say in workplace decisions. The results, reported in Exhibit 4.5, show that union members are relatively satisfied with their influence on local leadership and on wage and benefit negotiations. Because unions are democratic organizations that elect local leaders, whose performance and their performance on wage and benefit negotiations is the key to their staying in office, union members can rightfully feel they have considerable influence in these areas. By contrast, union members are not particularly satisfied with their influence on national union operations, and are least satisfied with union endorsement of political candidates and the union position on national issues. One reason is that there is more division within the ranks of labor on political issues than is reflected in national union behavior. Whereas national union leadership almost invariably supports Democrats, only one-third of union members on the WRPS consider themselves Democrats. In the national election that immediately preceded the WRPS, 33 percent of union members in the survey reported having voted for Bill Clinton, as compared with 14 percent who voted for George Bush and 16 percent for Ross Perot. What happened to the rest? Like many other groups, a large number of union members simply did not vote.

That union members are happier with their influence on local leadership than national leadership is not a new finding. The result showed up in the 1973 Quality of Work Survey, which was one of the first national surveys to ask union members about their satisfaction with their union.[8] It also shows up in surveys that individual unions take of their members.[9] And it is consistent with American attitudes toward local versus national leadership in other areas. Voters usually express greater support for their House representative or local government than for the Congress or other Washington-based government bodies, and they like their local school more than the quality of education in America.

The different evaluation by union members of local and national unions might also suggest another factor behind the difference in the attitudes toward unions by union members and nonmembers. When union members are asked whether they would vote to maintain the union at their workplace, they probably think about the local union. When nonunion workers are asked about whether they want a union, they might think more about the national union, about whom even members express less satisfaction. We did not ask the questions that would test this story. We did, however, ask workers to tell us what they thought unions do for members. Exhibit 4.6 shows that while many workers cite the bread-and-butter issues of better pay/working conditions as the first thing, many also cite the voice issues of respect/fair treatment on the job and some cite giving workers a greater say in workplace decisions. Around 1 in 11 nonunion workers and 1 in 16 union members don't believe that unions offer anything for their members. The biggest difference in the opinions between union members

EXHIBIT 4.6. What do unions do for members?

	Union members	Nonunion employees
Better pay/working conditions	48	39
More say in workplace issues	11	14
More respect/fair treatment on job	31	22
Unions don't do anything	6	9
Don't know	3	13

Source: Based on this WRPS question: (W2.37) "What is the *most* important thing a union does for its members?"

EXHIBIT 4.7. Percentage of union members satisfied with influence on local union and on workplace decisions.

Degree of satisfaction with influence in choosing local union leadership

Very	35%	Of these workers
		    27% were very satisfied with their
		        influence on workplace decisions
		    25% were not satisfied with their
		        influence on workplace decisions

Not	17%	Of these workers
		    7% were very satisfied with their
		        influence on workplace decisions
		    44% were not satisfied with their
		        influence on workplace decisions

Degree of satisfaction with influence on workplace decisions

Very	20%	Of these workers
		    47% were very satisfied with their
		        influence on workplace decisions
		    6% were not satisfied with their
		        influence on workplace decisions

Not	29%	Of these workers
		    29% were very satisfied with their
		        influence on workplace decisions
		    26% were not satisfied with their
		        influence on workplace decisions

Source: Satisfaction with influence on union is based on this WRPS question: (W1.43a) "How satisfied are you with the influence you and fellow union members have in union decisions about choosing local leaders?" Satisfaction with influence on workplace is based on this WRPS question: (W1.14_1,2,3,4) "Overall, how satisfied are you with the influence you have in company decisions that affect your job or work life?"

and nonmembers is that nonmembers were more likely to say they didn't know what unions did.

How do employees' satisfaction with their say at their workplace stack up against their satisfaction with their influence on their local union?

Exhibit 4.7 shows that union members are more satisfied with their influence on their local union than they are with their influence on company decisions affecting their job. But this does not mean that satisfaction with the union competes with satisfaction with the firm in employee feelings. To the contrary, the exhibit shows a positive relationship between satisfaction with the union and satisfaction with say at the firm. Twenty-seven percent of union members who are satisfied with their influence on the union report that they are satisfied with their influence at the workplace. By contrast, just 7 percent of members who are dissatisfied with their say at the union are satisfied with their say at the workplace. Our data cannot determine whether satisfaction with say at the firm or say at the local union comes first, or whether (as we suspect) a positive labor-management relationship requires openness from both the firm and the union. But the correlation is consistent with the notion that good labor relations produce workers satisfied with both the firm and the union. In any case, at the local level, unions seem to be doing all right, and when they do all right, so does the firm in giving workers influence at the workplace.

The One-Third Who Want Union Representation

Thus far, we have focused on the 14 percent of the WRPS who are union members. But more than twice as many workers are nonunion members who say they want union representation. Who are these workers? What explains their desire for unionization? Why are workers who want to be unionized not represented by unions?

Two factors should determine worker desire for unions: the personal characteristics of workers and the way management treats workers at their workplace. Exhibit 4.2 showed that the personal characteristics of people affect their desire for unions, but not overwhelmingly so (except for race). In Exhibit 4.8 we look at the other part of the workplace equation: how management treats workers. This exhibit shows that employee desires for a union do in fact depend greatly on how management treats workers. Workers who report poor labor-management relations at their firm or who give management low grades in concern for workers and willingness to share power or who find management not trustworthy or who report that they do not look forward to work (presumably because their workplace is an unpleasant environment) are all especially likely to say that they would vote for a union.

To see whether the characteristics of workplaces or the characteristics of workers most affect the desire of nonunion workers to vote union, we estimated how well we would predict the votes of workers who differed in these two dimensions separately and together. Again, we used a linear

EXHIBIT 4.8. Percentage of nonunion employees who want unions.

When workplace relations are bad

Excellent 21, Good 31, Fair 40, Poor 50

Relations between employees and management

When management is not trustworthy

A lot 20, Somewhat 31, A little 36, Not at all 57

Trust management

When management shows little concern for employees

A 27, B 29, C 39, D 35, F 71

Grade management on concern

When workers dislike jobs

Look forward 27, Don't care 24, Wish didn't have to go 43

Feeling about going to work

When workers are dissatisfied with influence

Very 23, Somewhat 28, Not too 44, Not at all 54

Satisfaction with influence at workplace

When management is unwilling to share power

A 18, B 21, C 35, D 47, F 69

Grade management on sharing power

Source: Based on the following WRPS questions: (W1.10b) "Overall, how would you rate relations between employees and management at your (company/organization)?"; (W1.10a) "In general, how much do you trust your (company/organization) to keep its promises to you and other employees?"; (W2.16ab) "If you were to rate the performance of management in your company on a scale similar to school grades — A for excellent, B for good, C for fair, D for poor, and F for failure — what grade would you give *management* in its concern for employees?"; (W1.8) "On an average day, what best describes your feeling about going to work?" (W1.14_1,2,3,4) "Overall, how satisfied are you with the influence you have in company decisions that affect your job and work life?"; (W2.16ae) "If you were to rate the performance of management in your company on a scale similar to school grades — A for excellent, B for good, C for fair, D for poor, and F for failure — what grade would you give *management* in its willingness to share power and authority?"

probability model to predict how workers would vote. We classify workers with the highest estimated probabilities as "vote union" and those with the lowest estimated probabilities as "vote nonunion" (here "highest" and "lowest" are defined so that the model accurately predicts the proportion who actually voted union). If the model perfectly accounted for worker votes, it would assign a higher probability for voting union to all those workers who in fact said they would vote union than to workers who said they would vote against the union. If, by contrast, we randomly assigned workers to a "vote union" group in proportion to the actual proportion who voted union, we would correctly classify around one-third.[10] So the success of our model can be judged by the extent to which it exceeds the 0.31 percent correct classification from the random model and the closer it is to giving a 100 percent correct classification.

The results, summarized in Exhibit 4.9, show that personal factors (age, education, race, and gender) and the nature of the workplace (employees influence on workplace decisions, their pay, and whether their firm has EI committees) determine the probability of voting union roughly equally. By themselves, measures of personal characteristics correctly classify 67 percent of the sample, while measures of workplace characteristics by themselves correctly classify 68 percent of the sample.

The most powerful personal characteristic[11] that affects the vote for union is race. Conditional on other factors, nonunion black workers are 27 percent more likely to favor a union than are white nonunion workers. This is nearly the same as the unconditional black/white difference shown in Exhibit 4.2. That blacks favor unions more than whites with the same characteristics and workplace experiences might reflect the exceptional vulnerability of blacks in the job market, their need for protection against discrimination, or their historical reliance on collective action, such as through the civil rights movement, to improve their situation.

On the workplace side, employees dissatisfied with their influence are more likely to support unions than other workers. By contrast, workers in firms with EI committees are less likely to support a union.[12]

Taken together, the two factors correctly classify 69 percent of the sample. In the analysis with both sets of variables, the measures of workplace characteristics are more statistically important, save for the huge effect of race on the desire to vote union.

There is yet another way in which the WRPS allows us to examine the preferences of nonunion workers toward unions. We can compare the characteristics of a workplace organization that nonunion workers want with the charac-

EXHIBIT 4.9. Predicting which nonunion employees would vote union.

Model used for prediction	Percent of workers whose vote was correctly predicted
Random model	31
Personal characteristics of workers	67
Workplace characteristics	68
Both personal and workplace characteristics	70
Perfect model	100

Source: Based on linear probability models, with 1 for employees who said that they would vote union and 0 for employees who said they would vote against the union or didn't know/refused on the WRPS question (W1.41b), "If an election were held today to decide whether employees like you should be represented by a union, would you vote for the union or against the union?"

The sample size for the regression was 1,666. Personal characteristics were a set of dummy variables for five age groups (18–24, 25–34, 35–44, and 45–54), for two race groups (black and nonblack), for sex, and for five education groups (less than 11 years, high school graduate, technical school post-high school/some college, college graduate, and postcollege graduate). Workplace characteristics were a set of three dummy variables for whether workers were very, somewhat, or not satisfied with their influence on workplace decisions; two dummy variables for whether they participated in an employee-involvement program or were in a company with a program; three dummy variables for the quartile of their weekly earnings; and one dummy variable for those who did not report earnings. To estimate the proportion of workers whose vote was correctly predicted, we ranked workers by the estimated probability they would vote union and determined a cut-off point that divided the sample, so that the number of workers with a probability greater than or equal to the cutoff was equal to the number who said they would vote union. We then gave all workers a predicted 0/1 for voting union, depending on how their predicted probability compared with the cutoff. The percent of workers whose support is correctly predicted is the sum of those for whom the model correctly predicted a 1 or 0 relative to the entire sample.

teristics that union workers want. If nonunion workers who would vote union are being deprived of the representation they want, they should have similar preferences for an organization as union members. By contrast, nonunion workers opposed to unionization should want workplace organizations that operate much as management wants. Exhibit 4.10 provides such a comparison.

In sum, there is thus nothing odd about the one-third of the nonunion workforce who say they want unions. They cannot readily rely on the job market outside their firm to give them bargaining power, and the management at their workplaces seems to show little respect for them. Their preferences for an independent organization are similar to those of workers who are represented by a union.

EXHIBIT 4.10. Percentage of workers who want a strongly independent workplace organization (electing representatives and using arbitration to settle issues).

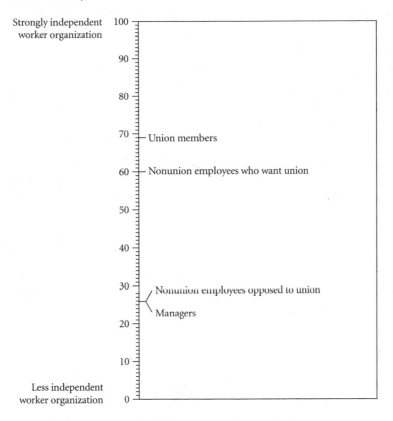

Source: Calculated from this WRPS question: (W1.48) "Thinking now about any kind of employee organization, not just unions, how would you like it to work? If it was your decision alone to make, and everybody went along with it, would you prefer (W1.48a) an organization that can use an *outside* referee or arbitrator to settle issues, or one in which management makes the final decisions about issues? (W1.48c) An organization in which the key participants are *volunteers*, are *elected*, or are *appointed* by management?" We have omitted workers who said they don't know/refused or did not want any kind of organization. Strongly independent organization is defined as one wanting to elect representatives and to use arbitration to settle issues.

What about the majority of workers who do not want union representation or who reported that most workers at their workplace would vote against a union? Because unions raise wages and benefits, are they being irrational? What reasons do these workers give for opposing union representation?

Management often argues that the reason unions are declining is that unions are not providing adequate services to members. Enlightened firms, governmental protections, and a flexible labor market provide the services that workers once needed unions to give them. Unions blame much of their decline on management resistance to workers' efforts to unionize. They stress that anti-union managements bring in high-powered consultants, run expensive campaigns that impugn union supporters, and create a literal war at the workplace when workers try to organize.

The responses to the WRPS suggest that both claims have some validity. Many workers who said most employees at their workplace did not want a union said that collective representation was inferior to taking care of workplace problems on their own (27 percent); that having a union would create too much tension in the company (25 percent); that they didn't like the way unions operate (22 percent); and that unions were too weak to help workers (10 percent). The 27 percent who favored dealing with workplace problems on their own and 22 percent who said they didn't like how unions operate would seem to fit management's view. The 25 percent who cited tension with management fit the view of unionists. The 10 percent who considered unions too weak could be cited by other side: With less management resistance, unions would be stronger and thus might win the support of these workers, but perhaps the perceived weakness of unions relates more to their organizational deficiencies than to management.

What about the workers who reported that a majority of employees at their workplace would vote union? Why are they not organized when they want to be? We asked employees who said that a majority of their coworkers favored a union why their workplace was not organized. The biggest single explanation was management resistance to unions (55 percent), as opposed to unions not being interested in organizing employees like them (22 percent) or unidentified other reasons.

How much weight should we attach to this answer? Voting in NLRB elections about unionization is done through secret ballot administered by the government. We Americans like to think of ourselves as tough independent folk, pioneers of sorts, not easily cowed in our decisions. Can management resistance really be that important? While most analysts, including us, attribute a significant role to management opposition in the decline in unionization, there are skeptics.[13] For instance, in its analysis of the reasons for union decline, the management-oriented Employment Policy Foundation estimated that managerial opposition had very little effect on the trend in union density.[14] In fact, it is not easy to take limited quantitative data and parse the precise decomposition of the factors that underlie the decline in union density, any more than it is easy to determine the reasons for slowdowns or accelerations in productivity, the increase in U.S. income inequality, the low level of inflation despite surging employment and tight labor markets, or rises or falls in the stock market.

How, then, might we better resolve this argument? One approach is to call on commonsense economic theory, which provides an unequivocal answer. As one of our conservative colleagues said, "Of course, management resistance is important. If it didn't matter, why does management put so much of its resources into fighting unions? And why is management so opposed to any labor-law reform that might restrict its ability to run anti-union campaigns? Shareholders don't pay managers millions to blow money on something that doesn't matter."

But our approach is not to rely on theory but on empirical evidence. We asked workers on the WRPS if their vote on unionizing their workplace would change if management signaled a different attitude on unionization. Although we initially doubted that very many workers would admit that their vote would depend on management, even if that was the case, a sufficiently large proportion said, "Yes, I would switch, depending on management's views" to swing many NLRB elections. Some 12 percent of workers who said that they would vote anti-union told us that they would vote pro-union if management was not hostile to the union; some 8 percent of pro-union voters said that they would change their vote and oppose the union if management was opposed to the union. Because NLRB representation elections are often won or lost by swings of 5–10 percent of the vote, these numbers are enough to change the outcomes of many such NLRB elections. The fact, noted earlier, that workers value management cooperation so highly in assessing the form of labor organization they would want at their workplace strengthens this conclusion.

How Management Sees Unions

Given that worker attitudes toward unions are influenced by management's position, it is important to find out how management views unions. In U.S. labor law, workers are supposed to decide by themselves without management interference whether they want to be unionized. But while management doesn't vote in the election, it tries to influence results, and in the view of workers, competitive theorists, and most empirical analysts, it does in fact do so. Management can influence whether workers want a union and how they vote in an NLRB election by treating workers well or poorly. And management can influence results by using its free-speech rights to try to convince workers to vote one way or the other. In fact, in the vast majority of NLRB representation elections, management not only gives its opinion that unionization is not in the workers' interest but also conducts an aggressive expensive campaign to convince workers that they should vote against the union. In many cases, management pays lawyers and consultants who specialize in union prevention to run their anti-union campaigns and convince workers that a union is not in their interest. Nor is illegal "campaigning" — for example, firing workers for supporting the union — uncommon.

We asked the managers on the WRPS their views about unionization at their workplace: "Mr. or Ms. Nonunion Manager, how would you and your firm respond to worker efforts to unionize?" Fifty-three percent of the managers in nonunion firms said they would oppose any effort by their employees to form a union; 27 percent said they wouldn't care; and 15 percent said that they would welcome the effort. When we presented these results to AFL-CIO leaders, they salivated to know the names of the 15 percent of managers who were pro-union, "so we can send out some organizers today." When we presented the results to business leaders, they were equally interested in the 15 percent of managers who were pro-union, "so we can get them fired immediately." In fact, nearly one-third (32 percent) of nonunion managers thought it would hurt their career if the employees they managed succeeded in forming a union, with more than half of those thinking it would hurt their career a great deal.[15]

Are most managers in union firms also opposed to unions? Mr. or Ms. Union Manager, are unions good or bad for workers at your firm? Are they good or bad for the firm itself?

Some 64 percent of managers in firms with unions thought unions made the lives of workers in their firm better.[16] Twice as many managers in unionized companies also reported that in recent years unions were more cooperative rather than more confrontational with the firm.[17] The vast majority of managers in union firms reported that top management in their firm accepted the union as a partner in workplace decisions. But nearly one-quarter said that management wanted to get rid of the union. Most managers in union companies said that the union did not affect their day-to-day work, but of those who said that the union did affect them, more reported that the union made their job harder than reported that the union made their job easier.[18] Eight percent of managers in union firms thought the union hurt the performance of the firm "a lot"; 25 percent thought the union hurt the firm "a little." On the other side of the spectrum, 19 percent of managers in union firms thought the union helped the firm "a lot"; 8 percent thought it helped "a little." The remaining managers thought the union had no effect on firm performance.

So what's the one-paragraph sound-bite that summarizes how workers judge American unions? Taking union and nonunion workers together, the bottom line for this chapter is that *looking upon unionization as a good produced by the market, the United States is producing too little.* Despite the widely publicized flaws of unions and the unease that many members feel about the role of unions on the national scene, 44 percent of private-sector American workers would like to be represented by a union, more than three times the 14 percent share of our sample who reported union membership. The workers who want a union but do not have one receive lower wages, are disproportionately black, report particularly poor labor-management relations at their workplace, and have similar attitudes toward the independence of any workplace organization as union members. In short, they seem to be just the sort of folks who could truly benefit from union representation. As far as our evidence goes, the main reason these workers are not unionized is that the managements of their firms does not want them to be represented by a union.

CHAPTER 5

How Workers Judge Management

With the decline in collective bargaining as a means of governing work-places and a forum for discussion between labor and management, management-led human-resource policies have become the chief deter-minant of how most employees fare at their workplace and how much say they have about their job. Virtually all large firms have sizable and sophis-ticated human-resource or personnel departments. Many have intro-duced innovative labor practices — employee involvement (EI) commit-tees and worker teams — to harness employee skills and effort to improve firm performance.

The business press offers much advice about how to manage employees. Some consultants advise management to operate "lean and mean"; to run things like Attila the Hun or to follow the strategic precepts of Musashi, the famous Samurai swordsman; or to master Sun Tze's *Art of War*.[1] Others tell management to listen more closely to what employees say and to involve workers in the firm's decision making;[2] to support EI programs of different kinds; and to let workers have real responsibility in self-managed work teams. Some argue for gain-sharing or other profit-sharing schemes, while others advocate stock-ownership plans to align the interests of employees with those of the firm. The goal is to give workers control over the decisions about which they have the most information and to develop incentive systems so that the workers make decisions that produce the most value for the firm. At the end of this rainbow of competitive democ-ratization is the high-performance workplace — a near mythical organiza-tion in which workers make continuous improvements in product quality or productivity for the mutual advantage of themselves and the firm, with-out much supervision.

How Common Are Advanced Human-Resource Systems?

The question of how many advanced human-resource practices exist in the job market occupied the initial deliberations of the Commission on the Future of Worker-Management Relations. The chair of the commission, former labor secretary and Harvard Professor Emeritus John Dunlop thought the high-performance stuff was vastly exaggerated. He recalled wave upon wave of revolutionary "new" ways of managing — from the workplace cooperation movement of the 1920s through the quality circles of the 1970s and 1980s. Taking a long-term perspective, he was less impressed with the new kid on the block than were others. CEOs might tell his commission or Congress that their firm had the latest employee-empowerment programs, but that didn't mean middle management had implemented the program on the shop floor, much less that any worker saw the firm as operating differently.

Still, the business people who testified before the commission swore that their companies could not compete in global markets without employee involvement, teamwork, total quality management, decentralized decision-making, the whole shebang. And they said everybody was doing it.

There are three ways to discover what firms are doing in human-resource management: ask knowledgeable managers at particular sites about practices at that workplace, visit workplaces and observe how they operate, or ask employees themselves — the human resources that management is managing — what is going on at their workplace. We, of course, did the third.

Exhibit 5.1 shows that a large proportion of American workers report that their firm has a given advanced human-resource practice or policy. More than two-thirds report that their firm has a personnel/human-resource department. Nearly as many say the firm holds town meetings in which management discusses issues with the whole workforce.

Most workers report that their firm has an open-door policy for individual employees to talk directly to top management, and nearly half say that their firm has an open-door policy for groups of employees who want to do the same. One-third report that their management meets with committees of employees to discuss problems. One-third have a grievance system to resolve individual problems that involve an outside referee. Most important to us, 56 percent of respondents reported that their firm has some form of EI system, and nearly one-third reported that they themselves participated in it.

On the pay front, U.S. firms reward workers in ways that go far beyond traditional hourly or monthly wage and salary checks. Many employees report that they receive bonuses based on profit sharing or based on meeting workplace goals. Some 22 percent of nonmanagerial employees report

EXHIBIT 5.1. Modern human-resource policies are widespread.

Personnel practices	Percentage of employees with given practice
Personnel or human-resource department	68
Open door to management	
For individual problems	85
For group problems	63
Regular "town" meetings	47
Committee of employees that discusses problems with management on a regular basis	37
Employee-involvement program at firm	52
Participated in program	31
Grievance system with outside arbitrator	32
Modes of pay/share participation	
Bonuses through profit sharing	30
Bonuses based on workplace goals	27
Participates in employee stock-ownership plan	23
Employee-owned	11

Source: Tabulated from background questions and from these WRPS questions:
(W1.36) "Which of the following, if any, does your (company/organization) have to deal
with issues that affect employees as a group? (W1.36a) Regular 'town' meetings with
employees, called by management, (W1.36b) An open-door policy for groups of employees to raise issues about policies with upper management, (W1.36c) A committee of
employees that discusses problems with management on a regular basis, (W1.36d) A
union that negotiates with management on a regular basis."; (W1.29) "Which of the following, if any, does your (company/organization) have? (W1.29a) A *personnel* or human
resource department, (W1.29b) *An open-door policy* so employees can tell upper management about problems with their immediate supervisors, (W1.29c) A *grievance* procedure that uses an outside referee or arbitrator to settle disputes between an employee
and management."; (W1.d16) On your (main) job, do you (W1.d16a) Receive any
bonuses based on profit sharing? (W1.d16b) Receive any bonuses based on meeting
workplace goals? (W1.d16c) Participate in an employee stock-ownership plan?
(W1.d16d) Work in an employee-owned (company/organization)? "The percentages are
for the entire sample, including that small percentage who responded "don't know" or
refused to answer.

that they participate in some form of employee stock-ownership plan, and
12 percent describe their firm as employee-owned.[3]

    Advanced human-resource practices are found to some degree through-
out the U.S. labor market.[4] As Dunlop suspected, these programs are more
prevalent in large firms and in manufacturing, but they are not limited to
those high-profile enterprises.[5]

Do Human-Resource Programs Work?

The programs work tolerably well, although not perfectly, according to employees. Some 28 percent of our respondents said that their firm's policies toward the problems faced by *individuals* at the workplace were "very effective"; 49 percent rated the policies as "somewhat effective"; 21 percent rated them as "not too effective" or "not effective at all."

Asked separately about each policy that deals with problems that face workers as a *group*, most employees gave a comparable assessment. Thirty-three percent judged open-door policies as "very effective" in dealing with group problems, as compared with 17 percent who saw their firm's open-door policies as "not too effective" or "not effective." Twenty-nine percent judged employee committees as "very effective," as compared with 10 percent who saw them as "not too effective" or "not effective." Twenty-four percent judged town meetings as "very effective," as compared with 17 percent who judged them as "not too effective" or "not effective."

To get some perspective on these numbers, compare them to workers' assessment of unionization as a means of dealing with workplace problems. Some 30 percent of unionized employees report that their union is "very effective" in resolving group problems, as compared with 15 percent who report it as ineffective. This puts the most highly rated firm-based policy — the open-door policy — in the same range of effectiveness as unions. Nonunion workers in unionized firms, however, rate the effectiveness of the union less favorably than do union members: 18 percent judge the union as effective, and 20 percent judge the union as ineffective. But union members judge firm-based policies as less effective than do nonunion members, so that on average union members view the union as the most effective way of resolving group problems. We see the endowment effect at work once again.

High-Performance Workplaces?

There is no single definition of a high-performance work organization. Business analysts often identify these organizations as those that apply many advanced human-resource practices to a large portion of their workforce. The argument is that no single practice does much for productivity or worker well-being, much less transforms a workplace into the high-performance mode. It is the combination of practices as complementary synergistic parts of a new work system that produces high performance. In this view, the high-performance workplace is a bit of an all-or-nothing proposition — qualitatively different from other workplaces.

The idea that these workplaces are something special is intuitively appealing. It tracks what workers told us in the focus groups. Recall that in most groups, only one or two workers reported that their firm involved employees in decisions, and that the other workers looked enviously on them as inhabiting a different universe than themselves.

If high-performance workplaces differ qualitatively from others, how might this show up in our data? By the existence of a distinct cluster of firms having many effective advanced practices; this should separate them from the pack. High-performance firms should have many effective practices, whereas other firms should have very few, with few organizations in between. To examine this issue, we needed to form some sort of scale from the various human-resource practices about which workers reported. But how should we group the practices, and how should we treat worker reports on their effectiveness?

Our first thought was to use the Guttman scaling technique developed in the 1940s. A Guttman scale assumes that responses to yes/no questions have a cumulative property that allows the analyst to rank them on a scale from highest to lowest, and that people answer these questions so that they themselves can be similarly ordered. Think of 20 questions on a test, ranked from easiest to hardest. If the ranking is valid and you answer 10 questions correctly, you should answer Questions 1 through 10 correctly, not the harder ones that follow or some mixture of hard and easy questions. If you can correctly answer Question 20, which is the hardest, you should answer all the questions correctly. Knowing how many questions you answered thus tells us exactly where you fit on a scale of 1 to 20.[6] But the system does this only if the responses fit the model perfectly, which is rare in practice. Maybe you answered the hardest question because you got lucky. Maybe you missed some easy ones because your mind wandered. Maybe the single scale does not truly capture the variation of difficulty among questions.

For questions with multiple responses — say, 1 is the lowest answer and 4 the highest — there is natural analogue to the Guttman scale. This is the same summated rating technique that we used in Chapter 3, which is simply the sum of the answers to the relevant questions, all ordered in the same direction. Say we ask you to assess fairness at your workplace with four related questions. Each question has three possible answers, with 1 being the least fair and 3 the most fair. If you answer 1, 3, 1, 2, the summated rating for your workplace would be 7. If you answer 3, 2, 3, 2, the summated rating for your workplace would be 10 — higher in the fairness scale. Summated rating works perfectly when variables are measured in common units, so that each item contributes equally to overall fairness and when the differences among responses (for instance, between "not important," "somewhat important," and very important") across items have the same meaning. Neither of these is likely in questions that ask people for subjective judgments. The answer "somewhat important" might be closer to "very important" on one question but closer to "not at all important" on another question.

As psychologists at a seminar pointed out to us, however, educational psychologists had developed measures that allowed for responses to diverge from the rigid Guttman or summated rating pattern. The key was to assume that an individual has a probability of answering questions in a particular way depending on his or her characteristics and the item. They told us that the Rasch scale (invented by a Danish researcher of that name) was the appropriate measurement tool for what we wanted. This procedure effectively orders responses from high to low, adds them up, and then rescales the sum of responses depending on where the score fits in the distribution of outcomes. Instead of giving you a 7 when you answer 3, 1, 1, 2 on four questions, the Rasch scale gives you a score that depends on how many people scored higher or lower than you.[7]

The Rasch procedure treats the least frequent practices as the most advanced (that is, as the hardest questions on the exam). If a firm has the most advanced practice, it should have all the less advanced practices, and thus have more practices than a less-advanced firm. If the firm has few practices, these should be the most common and thus the least advanced practices. And as with practices, so, too, with effectiveness. Given two firms with the same practice, the scaling places the one in which the practice is judged most effective as more advanced. We proceeded to develop a Rasch scale for human-resource practices reported on the WRPS. The data supported this formulation, indicating that this scaling captures the major interrelations among the practices.

As noted earlier, if "high-performance" firms are truly separate from other firms, we would anticipate finding a sharp divergence in the position of firms on the scale of advanced practices: the high-performance firms at one end and the rest at the other. But when we made a histogram of practices and their effectiveness, we obtained the results in Exhibit 5.2.

The distribution does not fit the expected pattern. It resembles more the bell-shaped normal curve, with a central tendency around which firms cluster. There are firms having more practices and more effective practices at the upper tail and firms with fewer and less effective practices at the lower tail. But there are many firms in the middle.

EXHIBIT 5.2. Distribution of advanced human-resource practices.

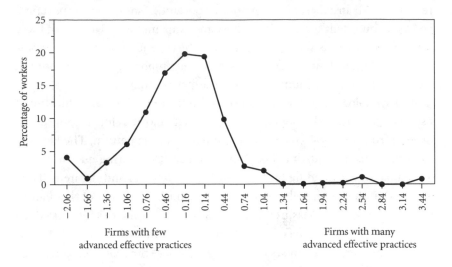

Source: Calculated by forming a latent variable for advanced human-resource practices
from ten WRPS questions regarding the presence and effectiveness of practices.

Six of the questions related to how firms deal with problems that affect workers as
a group: (W1.36) "Which of the following, if any, does your company/organization have
to deal with issues that affect employees as a group? (W1.36a) Regular 'town' meetings with employees, called by management, (W1.36b) An open-door policy for *groups*
of employees to raise issues about policy with upper management, (W1.36c) A committee of employees that discusses problems with management on a regular basis.";
(W1.37) "How effective were (THE PRECEDING ITEMS a, b, AND c) in resolving group problems
or concerns?" (very effective, somewhat effective, not too effective, not effective at all).

Four of the questions related to how firms deal with problems faced by individuals:
(W1.29) "Which of the following, if any, does your company/organization have?
(W1.29a) A personnel or human resources department, (W1.29b) An open-door policy
so employees can tell management about problems with their immediate supervisor,
(W1.29c) A grievance procedure that uses an outside referee or arbitrator to settle disputes between employees and management."; (W1.32) "Overall, how effective is your
company's/organization's system for resolving the problems *individual* employees have
at work?"

Two of the questions related to employee-involvement programs: (W1.23) "Some
companies are organizing workplace decision-making in new ways to get employees
more involved — using things like self-directed work teams, total quality management,
quality circles, or other employee-involvement programs. Is anything like this now being
done in your company/organization?"; (W1.27) "How effective would you say these programs have been in improving productivity or quality?"

The latent variable was formed in two steps. First, we gave a value of 0 to 4 to each
of the seven practices based on its existence and effectiveness: A 0 meant the firm did
not have the practice; a 1 meant it had the practice and that the practice was not effective at all; a 2 meant that the practice was not too effective; a 3 meant that it was
somewhat effective; and a 4 meant that it was very effective. We summed these variables to get a single number and then transformed that number into a Rasch score, as
discussed in the text.

Are high-performance workplaces not magically transformed firms but the upper tail of a continuous population of all firms? This interpretation is enough at odds with popular business discussion that we decided to examine the distribution of human-resource practices in two other data sets and found that the distribution of firms by number of advanced practices looks more like a normal distribution than a discontinuous one in those data sets also.[8] To say that the distribution of effective practices resembles a normal distribution does not mean that it is randomly generated, natural, or fixed in shape. Some kinds of workers and some kinds of firms have more human-resource management practices than others. The mean practice in a normal distribution of practices can change, and firms can be clustered closer to or farther from the average. What is important is that firms do not appear to cluster neatly into "high-performance firms" and "all others" in the way that the popular understanding suggests.

Who Has Advanced Practices?

Exhibit 5.3 shows the proportion of workers with differing characteristics who are in firms with many effective advanced human-resource practices (those in the upper decile of our measure) and those in firms with few effective advanced human-resource practices (those in the lowest decile).

Worker characteristics have only a modest effect on the prevalence of advanced human-resource management. There are no race or sex differences to speak of, relatively modest variation by education, and, save for the youngest workers, who are less likely than others to be in a firm with advanced practices, relatively little variation by age. What matters significantly are (1) the worker's position in the earnings distribution, with higher-paid workers more likely to be in firms with advanced human-resource management; (2) union status, with unionized firms having more advanced practices;[9] and (3) size of firm or workplace, with more advanced practices in larger firms and workplaces.[10]

Do Advanced Human-Resource Practices Improve Worker Well-Being?

One way to judge the effectiveness of advanced human-resource policies is to compare how workers in firms with differing practices rate labor-management relations at their company and their own job satisfaction. If the policies are effective, employees should be happier at their

EXHIBIT 5.3. Percentage of workers in the upper decile of firms with advanced human-resource practices.

Sex		
	Male	10
	Female	10
Age		
	24 or Less	5
	25–34	9
	35–44	10
	45–54	14
	55–64	12
Race		
	Black	9
	Nonblack	10
Education		
	College graduates	10
	Some college	12
	High school	9
	Less than high school	8
Earnings		
	Upper quartile	13
	Second quartile	9
	Third quartile	9
	Bottom quartile	6
Union status		
	Member	17
	Nonunion employee	9
Number of employees in firm		
	Less than or equal to 99	3
	100–499	10
	500–999	9
	1,000 or more	14
Number of employees in workplace		
	Less than 25	7
	25–29	7
	100–499	11
	500–999	13
	1,000 or more	20

Source: Calculated using the human resource practices measure described in Exhibit 5.2 and in the text. This measure takes seven human resource practices and workers' assessment of their effectiveness to form a single "latent variable." The top decile consists of workers in firms that score in the upper 10 percent. Workers in groups that score below 10 percent are thus underrepresented in firms with advanced human resource practices. Workers in groups that score above 10 percent are disproportionately in firms with advanced practices.

EXHIBIT 5.4. Effective advanced human-resource practices and worker satisfaction go together.

	Position of firms in distribution of advanced practices	
	Upper decile	Lower decile
Attitude toward work		
Look forward	78	44
Wish didn't have to go	15	46
Labor-management relations		
Excellent	21	5
Good	62	30
Fair	15	33
Poor	2	32
Labor-management relations compared with average		
Better	59	12
Average	40	50
Worse	1	37

Source: Calculated using the human resource practices measure described in Exhibit 5.2 and in the text. This measure takes seven human resource practices and workers' assessment of their effectiveness to form a single "latent variable." The top decile consists of workers in firms that score in the upper 10 percent; the bottom decile consists of workers in firms that score in the lowest 10 percent.

job and report more pleasant labor-management relations at firms with those policies than at firms lacking those policies. Exhibit 5.4 shows that, in fact, workers in firms with more advanced and effective human-resource practices are more likely than workers at less-advanced firms to say they look forward to going to work, to report that labor-management relations are excellent, and to believe that management shows concern for workers.

This association of employee satisfaction with advanced human-resource practices does not prove that the practices themselves create better workplace relations, or even better worker perceptions thereof. Good firms with relatively worker-friendly cultures might treat workers well even in the absence of such practices, with the practices simply being the least-costly or the au courant way of doing the right thing. Correlation does not mean causality. Still, even if the link between advanced human-resource practices and worker satisfaction simply means that advanced practices are a good indicator of a more worker-friendly culture, we will have identified a measurable indicator of the often fuzzy notion of corporate culture.

The Open-Door Policy

You think your firm is doing something wrong. It does not respond properly to customer complaints; it fails to take advantage of a new technology or market opportunity; it fails to deal with an employee whose coughing might make the entire workforce sick. Or perhaps the firm is not paying you the salary you deserve, or your supervisor is picking on you or sexually harassing you.

A direct way to deal with these or any other problem is to march into top management's office, explain the problem, and ask management to rectify it. Firms with open-door policies encourage such individual expression of voice. Initially we viewed open doors skeptically. We thought that few workers or groups of workers would bring serious problems to higher-ups for fear of antagonizing their immediate superior or being labeled a malcontent. In the focus groups, workers did not volunteer "open door" as a policy that meant all that much to them.

But so many workers on the WRPS reported that their firm had an open-door policy and said that this policy was effective that we thought we ought to find out something more about it. In our follow-up survey we asked employees how much they used the open-door policy and what issues they brought to the open-door manager.

About one-fifth of employees said they went to high-level management with problems three or more times in the previous twelve months.[11] About one-fourth reported using the policy once or twice a year. The majority reported that they had not used it at all in the past year. Workers with individual market power are more likely to use an open-door policy than are workers in a weaker position in the job market. A large number of managers and college-educated workers used the policy during the year.[12] The workers *least* likely to walk through the open door are those with the least market power: younger workers (ages 18 to 24), those 55 and older, and those who are semi-skilled or manual laborers.[13] Just 40 percent of black workers reported that they had used the open door.

In addition, the workers who described their firm's open-door system as relatively effective used it more frequently.[14] For instance, 42 percent of workers who said that their system was very effective used it three or more times in the past year, and just 9 percent said that they had not used it in the last year. By contrast, of the workers who judged the open door as ineffective, 17 percent did not use it at all, while 33 percent used it three or more times over the year. The implication is that when the policy is real, it creates a steady flow of complainants to management.

We asked workers to tell us about the problem they raised *the last time* they used the open door. The majority of problems were in the areas of production/procedures/operations and general working conditions.[15] Very few workers used the open door to discuss problems with their immediate supervisors or wages or benefits. Managers and union members are most likely to bring up money problems.[16] Workers who used the open door for problems with operations or general working conditions reported most favorably on its effectiveness.[17]

Open doors increase communication between workers and higher management in regard to day-to-day production problems or working conditions. They are not widely used, however, to deal with issues that have more potential to cause conflict — for instance, employee-supervisor difficulties and wages and benefits — or for larger questions regarding company governance or policy.

Employee Involvement

The firm-based policies or programs of greatest interest to us are EI programs, as such programs are specifically designed to increase worker influence on workplace decisions. EI programs come in various flavors: quality circles and discussion groups, total quality management, self-directed work teams, safety committees, production committees, Christmas party committees, and diverse small groups that work on sundry other issues. What places these disparate programs under a single rubric is their goal of giving workers more say in decision making. Consider them the firm's response to the representation/participation gap.

More Is Better

The extent to which EI resolves the representation/participation gap depends on the types of committees management sets up and on how these committees function. Despite occasional business claims that committees are primarily short-term groups that deal exclusively with specific problems, many EI participants report that their firm's program includes long-term committees that deal with different problems. Sixty percent of workers said that their firm had both long-term and short-term EI committees, and of those workers who said that their firm had only one type of committee, nearly the same proportion reported it as being long term (18 percent) as those who reported it as being short term (19 percent). Adding the 60 percent of workers who said their firm had long-term and short-term EI committees and the 18 percent who said their firm had only long-term committees, we see that 78 percent of firms with EI have committees that discuss different problems over a long period of time. Even when management limits EI to short-term committees, moreover, the range of issues covered by all of the short-term committees taken together might be quite wide.

Most EI committees of whatever duration focus on issues relating to production. Approximately half of workers participating in long-term committees and half of those on short-term committees reported discussion of quality assurance, safety, and technology/new products. By contrast, only 14 percent of workers on long-term committees and only 8 percent on short-term ones reported discussing issues relating to job advancement/performance.

This does not mean, however, that there is no substantive distinction between EI committees that are short term and those that are long term. Twenty-four percent of workers on the long-term committees said that the committee discussed *issues of corporate direction*, as compared with 8 percent of workers on short-term committees. Firms with the longer-term EI committees seem to give workers greater say in the broader operation of the firm, and thus to come closer to the ideal high-performance workplace than those firms whose committees are short term.

U.S. labor law limits, in theory, what an employer-controlled EI committee can do. Under Section 8(a)(2) of the NLRA, firms cannot set up groups of workers to help set policy on issues such as wages, benefits, and working conditions covered by collective bargaining. The intent of this section was to outlaw company unions of the type that firms established in the 1930s and 1940s to subvert workers who wanted to form independent unions. Paradoxically, perhaps, this effort to protect workers allows EI committees to discuss productivity and other matters that might benefit the firm, but does not allow them legally to do much that might benefit workers.[18]

The extent to which EI committees step over the legal line and operate as illegal company unions is an area of contention between management and labor. Management's belief that the law is too restrictive has motivated the various teamwork bills that Congress has considered but has not enacted into law. To get some notion of how much illegal discussion goes on, we asked workers who participated on an EI committee whether the committee discussed wages and benefits. Twenty-eight percent of the participants reported discussing wage and benefit issues. We then asked those who discussed these issues if continuing such discussion was very important to the success of the program: 72 percent said it was. Initially, we also intended to ask workers whether they discussed working conditions in their EI committees, but our management and union advisors convinced us that this would be redundant. In reality, it is nearly impossible to talk about productivity without discussing working conditions.

Productivity Effects and Voice

Employee involvement supposedly raises productivity by encouraging workers to make more suggestions about how to improve their job environment and committing management to take those suggestions seriously and act on them. If EI works this way, EI participants should report that they make more suggestions and that management acts on them more frequently than do other employees.

Exhibit 5.5 shows that they do. Measured in percentages, nearly twice as many EI participants as nonparticipants say that they make suggestions often, and nearly twice as many EI participants as nonparticipants report that management takes the suggestions seriously. Managers tell the same story. One-third of managers involved in an EI program said that they almost always find worker suggestions useful, as compared with one-fourth of managers not involved in an EI program.

As a crude indicator of the greater flow of useful suggestions from EI participants than from other employees, we multiply the proportion of workers who say they make suggestions "often" by the proportion who say that management "almost always" takes their suggestion. This gives us a measure of the likelihood that employees regularly make suggestions that in fact improve their workplace. By this measure, EI participants are *three times* more likely to report being in this position than are nonparticipants.[19] Our data cannot determine, however, whether this in turn means that firms with EI programs are more likely to make continuous quality improvements than other firms, justifying the expense of an EI program. It is possible that managers in non-EI firms discover comparable improvements in their firms as workers do in EI firms, or that the value to the firm of employee suggestions generated by an EI program does not meet the

EXHIBIT 5.5. The value of employee involvement (EI) to the firm.

EI participants make more suggestions that management take seriously

	Percentage of workers who make suggestions		Percentage of managers who find suggestions useful		Chance that employees make potentially valuable suggestions (%)
	Often	Hardly ever/never	Almost always	Hardly ever/never	
EI participant	57	6	45	9	26
Nonparticipant in EI firm	30	22	27	19	9
No EI at firm	33	21	23	31	8

EI participants are more involved in the firm's success

	Percentage of workers who rate employees				Percentage of workers who say EI raises productivity/product quality	
	Willingness to work hard		Care about success of firm		Very effective	Not too effective
	A	D/F	A	D/F		
EI participant	38	2	30	3	32	11
Nonparticipant in EI firm	35	3	28	6	14	21
No EI at firm	33	5	20	12	—	—

Source: Based on these WRPS questions: (W1.17) (TO NONMANAGERS) "How often, if ever, *do you* make suggestions to your supervisor or to management about how to improve quality or productivity?"; (W1.17a) (TO MANAGERS) "How often, if ever, *do you* get suggestions from the people you manage about how to improve quality or productivity?"; (W1.22a) "Imagine that *more* decisions about production and operations were made by employees, instead of by managers. How do you think this would affect your (company/organization) in the following areas?"; (W1.22b) (BASED ON FORM B) "Would the *quality* of the (company's/organization's) products or services get *better or worse?*"; (W2.16b) "If you were to rate the performance of employees in your company on a scale similar to school grades — A for excellent, B for good, C for fair, D for poor, and F for failure — what grade would you give *employees* in their (W2.16ba) Willingness to work hard? (W2.16bb) Concern for the success of the company? (W2.16bc) Willingness to take on new responsibilities?"

program's costs. This is possible but unlikely — at least in our view and in that of management at companies with EI.

Employee involvement might also improve a firm's performance by inducing greater effort. If you are involved in making a decision, you might try harder to carry it out. We asked employees to grade the willingness of their coworkers to work hard, using the easily recognizable school grade scale. The lower panel of Exhibit 5.5 shows that proportionately more participants in EI programs than other workers gave high grades to the work effort of their coworkers and believe that their coworkers were concerned about the success of the company, although the differences are not large. As nearly half of EI participants report that they supervise other employees or tell others what to do (as compared with many fewer of nonparticipants in firms with EI and employees in other firms), these grades are presumably based on direct knowledge, not hearsay.[20]

Most employees who participate in EI programs believe that EI raises productivity, although with varying degrees of effectiveness. Nearly one-third of nonmanagerial EI participants rated the programs as very effective in improving productivity or quality; a majority viewed them as somewhat effective, while just one in nine people found them ineffective.[21] And although we did not ask about EI's direct effect on company success, a larger proportion of EI participants described their company as successful (79 percent) than did nonparticipants (65 percent).[22]

Several studies have compared productivity between firms or establishments with and without various forms of EI, ranging from formal programs to employee-ownership programs. Some researchers have examined the same firm before and after introduction of programs designed to increase worker participation in decision-making. As a broad summary, employee participation raises productivity modestly — say, by 2 percent to 5 percent. Studies based on small numbers of firms or observations sometimes find that these effects are not "statistically significant,"[23] but this appears to be more a problem of sample size than lack of an effect. Several small samples that give weak results in the same direction can cumulate into statistically significant results when considered as a whole.[24] Thus it appears that the moderately positive views that workers express on this issue are consistent with what economists and business experts find in their studies.

Why Doesn't Every Firm Do It?

Productivity increases of 2 percent to 5 percent may seem modest to some readers, but in fact they are not. Productivity growth of the United

States has been on the order of 1.5 percent per year, so that 2 percent to 5 percent translates into 1 to 3 years of growth. Productivity improvements of 2 percent to 5 percent can greatly increase the value of profits to the firm and its shareholders. In the U.S. economy as a whole, capital's share of output (value added) is around 25 percent. An increase in productivity that raises output by, say, 3 percent, *all* of which went into capital in the form of profits, would raise profits by 12 percent.[25] Multiply this by typical price-earnings ratios, and the value of shares could more than double.

If EI is generally found to raise productivity, why doesn't every firm do it? One explanation is a "market knows best" theory. Managers know what they are doing. EI works for some firms, and managers in those firms adopt it. In other firms, EI would not work, and managers there reject it. Different strokes for different folks. There must be some truth to this explanation. Even if management isn't all that bright, surely it is more likely to introduce EI where it works than where it doesn't. If this explanation is right, firms for whom EI pays off more ought to make greater use of EI than firms for whom EI pays off less.

Going beyond argumentation, there is some evidence for this. EI appears to be more effective in union settings than in nonunion settings,[26] and unionized firms are more likely to have an EI program than nonunion firms. But this explanation also has a Dr. Pangloss flavor. It suggests that everything management does is the best in this best of all possible worlds. Every firm knows what it should do, and it goes about doing it. This may fit an Economics 101 blackboard model of the economy, but not the dynamic world of modern capitalism.

Another explanation is that EI programs might give a firm a competitive edge when few firms institute them but lose their advantageous effects as more and more firms adopt them. If, say, 30 of 100 firms implement a successful EI program that gets them to the high-performance ideal, they might benefit; to the thirty-first firm, however, the rewards from adopting the strategy might be negligible. There are too many good employers in the market, and the thirty-first firm may find it wiser to go lean and mean. In a well-functioning market, the returns to different human-resource strategies ought to be the same for the firm on the margin between the alternatives, and possibly to all firms as well.

There is probably some truth to this explanation. Innovators in EI might garner most of the gains — for instance, by attracting the best workers or those most likely to be more productive when they participate in decisions. Imitators might find imitating an EI strategy to be less profitable for them. We know of no evidence for this sort of explanation, however.

The most important reason that EI is not universal is that it is not easy to implement. Management can't simply prance into the office or shop floor and announce, "Workers, we want you to be involved and participate in decisions," and expect results. EI succeeds by getting workers to look at their jobs differently, by getting managers to look at workers differently, and by getting managers and workers to interact differently. In many firms this requires change in corporate culture. If the company cannot transform the way people see themselves and behave in workplaces, then EI can fail.

Indeed, while the business press publicizes EI successes, there are also EI failures. We know one major firm that introduced EI and found that workers simply took advantage of less supervision to slack off. It had to kill the program to get back on track. In the mid-1990s, Levi Strauss introduced a teamwork system in its apparel plants, which seems to have created as many or more problems than success for the firm and its workers.[27] It can also take a long time to find the right EI program for a given firm at any given time. What works for Motorola or Xerox (two firms with highly publicized EI programs) in 1990 might not work at XYZ production or even at Motorola or Xerox in 2000. We visited one establishment in which a manager favored EI for moral reasons. For years he tried different types of involvement programs, but nothing worked until, finally, he found a way that struck a chord with workers and succeeded in getting them involved.

Do Employees Want It?

To determine worker attitudes toward EI, we first asked if workers personally benefited from involvement in their firm's EI program. If they benefited, they presumably would favor continuing the program. The vast majority of nonunion/nonmanagerial participants in EI programs reported that they had personally benefited from their involvement in the program by getting more influence about how they did their job.[28] Thirty-six percent said they benefited from an increase in pay (although EI committees are not supposed to discuss issues of pay).

Second, we asked EI participants how they would feel if the company dismantled the program. Although most EI participants told us that they thought that their management was committed to the firm's EI program,[29] there is always the risk that the firm might decide that some other way of managing is more profitable. Perhaps the CEO will read the new business best-seller *Managing the Queen Ant Way* and decide that success requires turning workers into drones rather than empowered EI participants.

We posed the issue to workers in terms of a takeover: "Imagine your company was taken over tomorrow by new managers who did not want to continue the employee involvement program. If your company got rid of these teams or committees, how would it affect you personally?" The vast majority of EI participants said that eliminating the EI program would make their work lives worse. Twenty-three percent said that closing the program would be very bad for them, and 48 percent said it would be bad, as compared with 22 percent who said it wouldn't affect them one way or the other. Just 5 percent thought this would be good for them.

If we assume that workers who say that eliminating EI is bad for them would vote for continuing their firm's EI program if the firm polled them on the decision, the level of support among EI participants for EI approaches the level of support among union workers for their union. Because voting on EI is not an option, in hindsight we should also have asked the workers who said the elimination of their firm's EI program would be bad or very bad for them what, if anything, they might try to do to save the program. But we didn't think that far ahead.

One other way of assessing employee attitudes toward EI is to compare overall attitudes toward workplaces between workers in EI programs with workers in firms without such programs or nonparticipating workers in firms with EI programs. If employees value EI as much as they claim, participants in EI programs should have more positive attitudes toward their firm, its management, and its labor relations policies than nonparticipants.

Exhibit 5.6 shows that this is the case. Compared to nonparticipants, workers in EI programs express more loyalty and trust toward the firm, rate employee management relations better, are more likely to think their firm has better than average labor relations, are more likely to look forward to going to work, and give their employer higher grades in concern for employees and giving fair pay increases/benefits.

Note, moreover, that the difference in attitudes is nearly as substantial between participants and nonparticipants in firms with EI programs as between participants and nonparticipants in firms without EI programs. This implies that the EI effect is not simply a difference between workers in firms with good labor practices and workers in firms with bad labor practices. Rather, it is an effect within firms associated specifically with EI.

Sixty-four percent of workers without an EI program said they wished that their firm had one. These workers have a mixed set of characteristics.

EXHIBIT 5.6. Employee-involvement (EI) participants have more positive attitudes toward their work and management.

	Percentage of workers loyal to firm		Percentage of workers who trust firm		Percentage of workers who report labor-management relations			
	A lot	Only a little/none	A lot	Only a little/none	Excellent	Fair/poor	Better than average	Worse than average
EI participant	63	8	49	12	21	25	50	5
Nonparticipant in EI firm	52	15	36	18	14	36	35	8
Firm has no EI program	49	17	30	28	17	36	31	13

	Percentage of workers who grade management on				Percentage of workers with attitude toward work	
	Concern for workers		Giving fair pay increase			
	A	D/F	A	D/F	Look forward to work	Wish didn't have to go
EI participant	26	9	23	12	74	19
Nonparticipant in EI firm	19	15	23	18	63	25
Firm has no EI program	22	25	12	29	61	30

Source: Based on these WRPS questions: (W1.9c) "How much loyalty would you say you feel toward your (company/organization) as a whole?" (a lot, some, only a little, no loyalty at all); (W1.10a) (BASED ON FORM A) "In general, how much do you trust your (company/organization) to keep its promises to you and other employees?"; (W1.10b) (BASED ON FORM B) "Overall, how would you rate relations between employees and management at your (company/organization)?"; (W1.8) "On an average day, what best describes your feeling about going to work?"; (W2.16A) "If you were to rate the performance of management in your company on a scale similar to school grades — A for excellent, B for good, C for fair, D for poor, and F for failure — what grade would you give *management* in (W2.16aa) Overall company leadership? (W2.16ab) Concern for employees? (W2.16ac) Giving fair pay increases and benefits? (W2.16ad) Understanding and knowledge of the business? (W2.16ae) Willingness to share power and authority?"

They are higher paid than the workers in non-EI firms who told us that they did not want a program at their firm. The workers who wanted an EI program are more likely to be hourly paid than salaried. They are disproportionately black and especially likely to be employed in manufacturing and in large firms and at large work sites.

What seems to unify this disparate group is their desire for more say at their job. The representation/participation gap for these workers is larger than it is for workers who said they did not want their firm to introduce an EI program. Similarly, 81 percent of workers without an EI program who were very dissatisfied with their influence on decisions at their workplace said they wanted an EI program, whereas just 50 percent of workers who were satisfied with their influence on workplace decisions said that they wanted an EI program. So among those most desirous of more say, EI is seen as part of the solution.

It Reduces But Doesn't Close the Representation/Participation Gap

As the major employer-initiated effort to give workers more say on the job, EI should increase worker participation in all sorts of decisions relating to their job. While we do not have a before-and-after research design to test this, we can compare EI participants with nonparticipants. Exhibit 5.7 shows that proportionately more EI participants say they have a lot of direct influence on a workplace decision than do nonparticipants in firms with EI and workers in firms without an EI program. More than one-third of EI participants report that they are "very satisfied" with the influence they have in company decisions that affect their job or work life, as compared with 12 percent who are "not too satisfied" or "not at all satisfied." By contrast, nonparticipants are more likely to report that they are "not too satisfied" or "not at all satisfied" with their influence than those who say they are "very satisfied." Because nonparticipants in firms with EI programs report similar say on the job and satisfaction with their influence on decisions as workers in firms with no EI program, we interpret these results as reflecting the impact of EI rather than of being employed in a good firm.

But EI does not eliminate the representation/participation gap. Exhibit 5.8 contrasts the representation/participation gap between workers with and without EI.[30] Item by item, EI participants have smaller gaps than nonparticipants in firms with EI programs and nonparticipants in firms without programs. But even among EI participants, a sizable representation/participation gap remains.

EXHIBIT 5.7. Employee-involvement (EI) participation gives workers more influence on the job.

| | EI participants have more influence on the job | |
	Lots of influence	Only a little/none
EI participant	46	24
Nonparticipant in EI firm	32	36
Firm has no EI program	29	38

| | Are more satisfied with their influence on decisions that affect their work life | |
	Very satisfied	Not too satisfied/ not at all satisfied
EI participant	34	12
Nonparticipant in EI firm	19	24
Firm has no EI program	19	29

| | Think that speaking up against company policy would help/hurt their career | |
	Help	Hurt
EI participant	39	23
Nonparticipant in EI firm	25	39
Firm has no EI program	27	47

Source: Respondents' involvement with decisions is based on WRPS question W1.12aa–ah, as described in Exhibit 3.5. We exclude responses on deciding on raises in pay or on kinds of benefits in this question, as these are legally proscribed issues for employee-involvement committees.

The satisfied-with-influence panel is from this WRPS question: (W1.14_1,2,3,4) "Overall, how satisfied are you with the influence you have in company decisions that affect your job and work life?" (very satisfied, somewhat satisfied, not too satisfied, not satisfied at all).

The speaking-up-against-company-policy panel is from this WRPS question: (W2.17) "If there was some company policy that you *spoke up against* in your company/organization, how would that affect your chances for advancement in the company/organization? Would it *help* you or *hurt* you in getting ahead?"

One possible reason that EI falls short of closing the gap is that having a say in decisions increases the desire for say. Workers who participate in EI programs are more likely to report that it is very important to have an influence on workplace decisions than are persons who do not participate in EI. This is most striking with respect to deciding how to do one's job: 86 percent of EI participants say that this is very important to them, as compared with just 70 percent of workers in non-EI firms and 73 percent of

EXHIBIT 5.8. Representation/participation gap (by employee-involvement [EI] status).

Workplace decision	Difference between percentage who say it is very important to have influence and percentage who have a lot of direct involvement on workplace decisions		
	EI participant	Nonparticipant in EI firm	Non-EI firm
Setting work *schedules*, including breaks, overtime, and time off	1	15	18
Setting safety standards	9	20	28
Deciding what *training* is needed for people in the work group	26	30	37
Deciding what kinds of *benefits* employees get	47	53	59
Deciding how to work with new *equipment* or *software*	19	21	28
Deciding how much of a *raise* in pay people in the work group get	32	29	39
Setting *goals* for group or department	17	22	23
Deciding *how* to do your job and organize the work	18	21	20
Average of all items	21	26	32

Source: Based on these WRPS questions: (W1.12a) "How much direct involvement and influence do *you* have in (ITEM)?" (a lot, some, only a little, no direct involvement at all); (W1.13a) "Suppose you *could* have a lot of influence in these areas at work, regardless of whether you do now or not. How important would it be for you to have *a lot* of influence on these decisions? First, how important would it be to you to have influence on (ITEM)?" (very important, somewhat important, not too important, not important at all).

nonparticipants in EI firms. EI raises the proportion of workers who have a lot of influence on deciding how to do their job, but it also raises the proportion of those to whom this is important, producing only a modest difference in the gap.

Another reason that EI leaves a sizable representation/participation gap might be that EI programs simply do not go far enough in empowering workers. Eighty-two percent of EI participants believe that giving employees a greater say would make their firm's EI program work better, and many EI managers tell much the same story: that their programs are not as advanced as they could be, or that they're not as advanced as top management would like.

It Reduces Worker Desire for Unionization

Many union activists are uneasy about EI programs because they believe that nonunion firms introduce them in part to reduce worker interest in unions and that unionized firms introduce them to undermine the union role in decision-making. Even if firms are less Machiavellian in introducing EI programs than the activists think (nonunion firms have more direct ways to keep a workplace nonunion if they so desire, and most union firms seek cooperative relations with their union), EI may still reduce interest in unions by giving workers more say at the workplace outside the union venue.

Exhibit 5.9 shows that union activists' concern about the effect of EI on nonunion workers' desire for unionization is well-placed. EI participants are much less likely to say that they would vote for a union in an NLRB election than are nonparticipants. But even nonparticipants in a company with an EI program are less likely to say that they would vote union than workers in companies without programs, perhaps because of the other good labor-relations practices in EI firms. And EI participants are less likely to think that the majority of workers at their workplace would vote union than are nonparticipants.

Consistent with these results, EI participants also show less desire for group decision-making than do nonparticipants. On our split questions that probed attitudes toward group or individual voice, EI participants did not want to deal with management through a group or employee association as much as nonparticipants did. And EI participants are more favorably inclined than nonparticipants to employee organizations that are management-dominated. For example, while a majority of EI participants prefer that disagreements between management and workers be settled by an arbitrator rather than by management, that majority is much less

EXHIBIT 5.9. Employee involvement (EI) reduces workers' desire for an independent organization.

	Support for union in NLRB election	
	For union	Against union
EI participant	23	66
Nonparticipant in EI firm	27	61
Firm has no EI program	39	47

	Belief that employee representatives would improve firms' system for solving employee problems	
	More effective	Less effective
EI participant	65	31
Nonparticipant in EI firm	75	19
Firm has no EI program	71	22

	Desire for arbitrator to reach final decision when committee of workers and management disagree on workplace issue	
	Arbitrator decides	Management decides
EI participant	49	43
Nonparticipant in EI firm	58	33
Firm has no EI program	61	33

(NLRB=National Labor Relations Board.)
Source: Based on these WRPS questions: (W1.41b) "If an election was held *today* to decide whether employees like you should be represented by a union, would you vote for or against a union?"; (W1.38c) "Imagine employees chose their own representatives to meet with management and discuss the problems employees have as a group. Do you think this would be *more* effective or *less* effective (as compared with your current system) to resolve employees' concerns?"; (W1.48a) "If it was *your* decision alone to make, and everybody went along with it, would you prefer an organization that can use an outside referee or arbitrator to settle issues or one in which management makes the final decisions about issues?"

among EI participants than among nonparticipants. Indicative of the more positive attitude that workers in EI firms have toward their management than workers in non-EI settings, just 11 percent of workers in firms with EI believed their management would break the law to bar the union, as compared with 21 percent of workers in non-EI firms.[31]

It Is More Likely with Unions, and Member Satisfaction Rises

While EI programs reduce the desire of nonunion workers for unions, they are found more frequently at union workplaces than at nonunion

EXHIBIT 5.10. Unionized workers with employee involvement (EI) are more satisfied with their union.

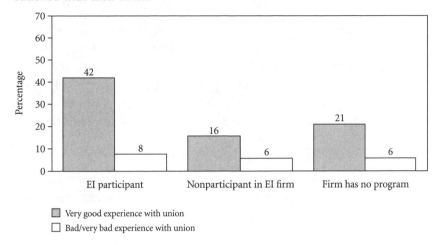

Source: Based on WRPS question (asked to union members only:) W1.40b "How would you describe your personal experience with the union at your company?"

workplaces. On our survey, 55 percent of unionized workers had an EI program at their workplace, and 33 percent participated in it, as compared with 49 percent of nonunion workers with an EI program and 28 percent participating in the program. Perhaps because unions give workers an independent source of authority or strength to deal with management, or perhaps because EI makes it easier for management to deal cooperatively with union workers, EI complements unionism.

Consistent with this, there is general agreement among managers that EI programs work well in unionized settings. Whereas managements from nonunion companies usually claim that they can run their business better without a union, when it comes to EI committees, nonunion managers who testified before the Commission on the Future of Worker-Management Relations claimed only that they could run an EI program as well as unionized managements, implicitly recognizing that unionized firms set the standard.[32] Econometric evidence[33] goes even further, suggesting that in fact EI produces greater gains in union settings.

Finally, contrary to the fears of some union activists, EI does not undermine worker support for unions at union workplaces. In fact, it has the opposite effect. As Exhibit 5.10 shows, workers in unionized workplaces who participate in EI programs describe their experiences with their union as markedly better than unionized workers who are not EI participants. A

How Workers Judge Management | 143

unionized workplace with EI makes workers more satisfied with both the union and management.

Employee-involvement programs make workers' lives better. Workers believe that EI improves company performance as well, and studies of worker participation in company decision-making suggest that, at a minimum, such programs do not harm productivity on average and, more likely than not, raise it. Most workers want these programs and want them to become more extensive, giving workers greater say. While workers in EI programs are less likely to want unions, EI is more prevalent under unionism, and unionized workers are happier with their union in EI settings. EI represents a road toward a new mode of labor-management relations that most workers want, but given competing managerial paradigms and fads, it is doubtful that management alone can travel far enough down that road to give workers what they want.

CHAPTER 6

How Workers Judge Government Regulations

Faster than a speeding bullet. Stronger than the strongest steel. Able to leap into your workplace to rescue you from an unfair supervisor, sexual harassment, discrimination, dangerous work conditions. Willing to battle million-dollar corporate lawyers to guarantee your employment rights in court. Is it a bird? Is it a plane? Is it Superman? Spiderman? The Incredible Hulk? The U.S. cavalry? No, it's your federal government regulator!

You haven't seen the advertisement? You wouldn't believe it if you did? It sends shivers up your spine?

At one time the United States had a largely unregulated labor market. American unions opposed laws that would protect workers on the notion that the government should not substitute for unions. American management opposed regulations requiring businesses to treat workers decently on the notion that the government should not substitute for voluntary business activities.

But this is no longer the case. The Great Depression and New Deal introduced labor legislation covering unionization, minimum wages, and hours worked, among other things. The civil rights revolution created a new corpus of individual rights at workplaces. Problems with pension funds, health and safety on the job, and other workplace-related issues ranging from family and medical leave to employer use of lie-detector tests generated additional labor-market regulations.[1] From the 1960s through the 1990s, under Republican as well as Democratic administrations, legislation governing the workplace has grown. Decisions and problems once dealt with at the workplace now often wind up before regulatory agencies or in court.

If regulatory agencies or courts remedied problems quickly and restored good working relations between employees and firms at low cost, legal regulation would be a fine way to treat workplace problems. But if regulatory agencies take years to reach decisions, if court suits are so expensive that only the well-heeled and their lawyers or the lucky few gain from them, and if regulations extract a huge cost on business, legal regulation is a poor way to govern workplace relations. Assuming, that is, that some alternative exists.

On this issue, as on most other aspects of labor regulations, business and labor are at odds about which of the "ifs" are valid. Business complains about a litigation explosion that is invading their bottom line and sapping American productivity. Unions and consumer groups point to areas in which workers need greater regulatory protection and complain that much critical workplace regulation is poorly enforced.

How do workers see growing legal protections at the workplace? How many regard regulatory agencies and the courts as their ultimate protector at the workplace? Do employees want more or less legal protection? What is their response to possible reforms in the system of legal protection?

Do Workers Know What Protections They Have?

Is it legal or illegal for your employer to

- Fire you for no reason?
- Move you to a lower-paying job because you wanted to form a union?
- Refuse to let you take time off from work to take care of your sick baby?
- Fire you for refusing to do hazardous work?
- Permanently replace you if you went on strike?
- Avoid hiring minorities for "good business reasons"?

Exhibit 6.1 summarizes the responses on the WRPS to these questions. It shows that employees vastly exaggerate their workplace rights. For instance, most workers believe that it is illegal for a manager to discharge an employee at will or for refusing to do hazardous work. But both forms of discharge are perfectly legal under U.S. labor law. More than half of employees believe that a firm cannot legally replace permanently striking workers. This, despite the fact that shortly before the survey Congress had rejected a bill that would have outlawed permanent replacement of strikers.

On the other hand, most employees correctly recognize that firms cannot legally discriminate against someone for trying to form a union, that "good business reasons" do not excuse racial discrimination in hiring, and that an employer cannot legally refuse unpaid family leave to an employee to care for a sick child (although workers might not have known that an

EXHIBIT 6.1. Employees believe the law protects them when it doesn't.

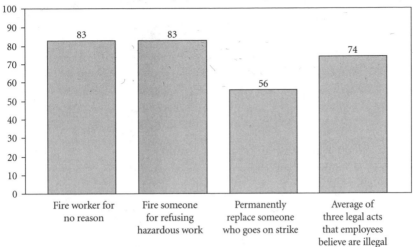

Percentage of employees who believe legal acts are illegal

83	83	56	74
Fire worker for no reason	Fire someone for refusing hazardous work	Permanently replace someone who goes on strike	Average of three legal acts that employees believe are illegal

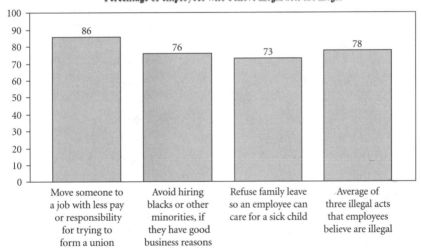

Percentage of employees who believe illegal acts are illegal

86	76	73	78
Move someone to a job with less pay or responsibility for trying to form a union	Avoid hiring blacks or other minorities, if they have good business reasons	Refuse family leave so an employee can care for a sick child	Average of three illegal acts that employees believe are illegal

Source: Based on this WRPS question: (W1.50) "Federal law guarantees employees certain protections in the workplace. To the best of your knowledge, please tell me if you think it is now legal or not legal for employees to do each of the following: (W1.50a) Fire an employee for no reason; (W1.50b) Move someone to a job with less pay or responsibility for trying to form a union; (W1.50c) Refuse family leave so an employee can care for a sick child; (W1.50d) Fire someone for refusing to do hazardous work; (W1.50e) Permanently replace someone who goes on strike; (W1.50f) Avoid hiring blacks or other minorities, if they have good business reasons for doing so."

employer could refuse unpaid family leave to a worker until August 1993, when the Family Leave Act took effect).

Indicative of employee misperception of labor law, a nearly identical proportion of employees believe, wrongly, that the three legally permissible unfair actions listed in the exhibit are illegal as do those who believe, rightly, that the three unlawful actions in the exhibit are illegal. Even more striking, a smaller proportion of workers answered the items correctly than would have answered them correctly had they simply guessed.[2]

Worse than chance in getting all items correct? What gives?

What gives is that people think that anything that is blatantly unfair at the workplace must be illegal — a kind of "there's got to be a law" syndrome. Surely it must be illegal for an employer to order a worker to stick his head in a furnace and then to fire the worker if he or she refuses to do this. Surely it must be illegal to walk into the worker's office and simply say, "You're gone," without giving a reason, with no due process, and with no chance for the worker to appeal.

In fact, the employment-at-will doctrine that dominates U.S. labor relations allows the employer to say "fired" without giving any reason.[3] Seventy-eight percent of the errors in the "quiz" were errors in which workers thought they were legally protected from ill treatment when in fact the law was silent on the issue.

Do more highly educated workers have better knowledge of the labor laws than other workers? Not much actually. Most college graduates think that all unfair acts are illegal, just as do most other workers, although college graduates do a bit better than nongraduates on the quiz.

Do union members have better knowledge of their rights as members of a union than other workers? No. The majority of union members think it is illegal to hire permanent replacements in a strike, just as do the majority of nonmembers.

Do managers have better knowledge of the laws that might restrict their power at workplaces than nonmanagers? Not much. Seventy-six percent of managers thought that firing someone for no cause was illegal, as compared with 88 percent of nonmanagers. Averaging across laws, 68 percent of managers believe erroneously that the legal "unfair" actions in Exhibit 6.1 are illegal, whereas 80 percent of managers believe correctly that the illegal actions in the exhibit are illegal. No bonus or bananas here.

There is nothing odd about our results, however. Researchers on law and society have long pointed out that people are generally ignorant of their rights and of the system that protects them. Ask citizens about the terms of U.S. senators or the difference between various types of courts or the division of the federal budget among various uses, and they will show similar lack of knowledge. Perhaps you would expect managers to know better, but your average manager is not a human-resource or personnel expert, much less a labor law expert. If you would never dream of firing someone for no reason, it's easy to think that such an act is unfair. If you discuss workplace problems with committees of your workers, it's hard to imagine that using those committees to help set policy about wages and benefits is illegal, at least until someone charges you with violating Section 8(a)(2) of the National Labor Relations Act.

That workers have incorrect perceptions of labor regulations and law creates a problem for this chapter. If workers don't know what they have in the form of legal protections, why should you, or we, take seriously their views about legal regulation? What value is there in finding out what workers think about "Washington" issues as opposed to the individual workplaces on which the rest of the book focuses? Maybe this is a situation in which it is better to leave things to the experts.

Our defense for asking workers their views of legal protections and possible reforms in the way the regulatory system works is threefold.

First, that workers overstate legal protections at the workplace can be viewed as a "blessing in disguise," if — as turns out to be the case — we find that workers say they want more regulatory protection than they currently have. Because workers think that they have greater legal protections than they have, we can be pretty sure that their desire for more regulations would be greater than they report to us if they were informed about the true state of the law. In social science, a bias that works against a result is much better than one that works for it.

Second, in this chapter as elsewhere in the book, we direct several questions only to workers who have in fact experienced the situation under examination — in this case, going to court or an agency to seek legal remedies for workplace problems. Workers' assessment of these personal experiences should be as valid as their assessment of how their workplace functions, even though the workers do not know the ins and outs of the law.

Third, when it comes to assessing *reforms* in labor regulations, we sought to reduce the lack of knowledge of workers by sending them written materials describing those reforms in some detail. Hence, in those parts of the chapter we report the views of relatively informed respondents, some of whom told us that they had discussed the issues with friends or relatives. To be sure, the material we gave to workers did not go into legal fine points or lay out the full spectrum of thought on the various reforms. It did, however, give them the basic facts from which they could form judgments.

In any case, here is what we found about how workers assess legal regulations.

See You in Court, Boss

Have you or anyone you know personally ever gone to court or to a government agency because of a possible violation of workplace rights? Six percent of Worker Representation and Participation Survey (WRPS) respondents answered "Yes" when asked whether they had gone to court or to an agency at least once in their lives because of a possible violation of workplace rights. An additional 17 percent said someone they knew had done so.

Because people have many acquaintances, and like to talk about their workplace and legal problems, the 17 percent figure did not surprise us. The 6 percent did. With a private-sector workforce of some 100 million people, this implies that around 6 million workers at one point in their lives felt sufficiently aggrieved about a workplace problem to go to an agency or court. That's an awful lot of people seeking legal redress for workplace problems. Given that the average worker has been employed for about 15 years, the 6 million court or agency "visits" implies roughly that workers make 400,000 *complaints* or so per year.[4] But because the number of complainants has risen over time with the increased regulation of the labor market, the number of complainants in the mid-1990s should exceed the 15-year average, whereas the number in earlier years should be smaller. Roughly, we estimate that the respondent reports of "ever" going to court or an agency are consistent with workers making around 600,000 *complaints* annually in the 1990s.[5]

Is 600,000 complaints to courts/agencies a plausible number? Given the many agencies and court jurisdictions involved in labor disputes, and the multiple administrative complaints or judicial actions arising from the same underlying dispute, it is not easy to find an answer. To see whether the WRPS respondents have the right "order of magnitude" answer, we had to piece together statistics from federal and state agencies, using Wisconsin for our state data.

Start at the top of the court and agency system. In 1995, some 290,000 complaints were made to federal agencies charged with workplace regulations, and some 20,000 federal district court filings were issued on labor-related matters. Because states are responsible for unemployment and worker-compensation claims, and most have state-specific antidiscrimination, occupational health and safety, or other labor regulations, they deal with many employment-related complaints from workers as well. Extrapolating from the 5,000 or so labor disputes that come to Wisconsin, we estimate that states deal with around 200,000 cases a year.[6] Two hundred thousand federal agency complaints, plus 20,000 court filings, plus 200,000 complaints to states brings us to 420,000 complaints — a *large number, although short of our estimated 600,000.*

But not all the complaints reported by workers on the WRPS will be counted in the official data. Workers might bring problems to agencies that the agency does not pursue because of lack of evidence, staffing, or legal basis, and thus does not list in its reports. The most popular complaint brought to field offices of the National Labor Relations Board (NLRB), for instance, is about being discharged for no particular reason (as we just saw, most workers believe this to be illegal). Such a complaint will not show up on the NLRB records as a formal complaint, as it is in fact invalid, but it might show up in a worker's mind as bringing a complaint to a government agency.

Again looking at Wisconsin, the state department of labor reports that its Milwaukee and Madison field offices alone receive some 90,000 inquiries annually. Extrapolated to other states, this turns into about 2.25 million inquiries per year. Field offices of the NLRB estimate comparable numbers of inquiries. Extrapolating to the entire nation and other agencies, government regulatory agencies receive on the order of 4 million to 5 million law-related inquiries a year about workplace problems. If only 10 percent to 15 percent of these are genuine attempts to take an issue to an agency, we are again in the ballpark of the 600,000 or so complaints per year that would validate what workers said on the WRPS.

Another way to judge whether our respondents overstate their reliance on courts and agencies to protect them at workplaces is to consider the situation from the employers side. According to the U.S. Society of Human Resource Management, a majority of firms have been sued by employees, and one-fourth of managers have been individually named in a lawsuit, largely in cases of alleged discrimination.[7] Every firm deals regularly with complaints about the myriad of government health and safety, pension and welfare benefits, and wage and hour regulations.

In short, the WRPS estimate that 6 percent of workers have tried to sue their firm in court or have brought the firm before a government agency for alleged violations in legal rights at the workplace is not excessive. See you in court, Mr. or Ms. Boss.

And Then What Happens?

Are workers satisfied with the outcomes of the legal process for dealing with alleged violations of workplace rights?

Exhibit 6.2 shows that a high proportion of employees who went to court or to a regulatory agency were dissatisfied with the outcome. One-third of workers said that they were very satisfied with these government processes. This figure is in the same range as the proportion of workers who find unions or employer modes of dealing with workplace problems "very effective." Relatively fewer workers, however, said that they were "somewhat satisfied" with their trip to court or a regulatory agency than said that union or firm-based systems of resolving problems were "somewhat effective."

Most striking, one-third of workers who went to courts/agencies reported that they were not satisfied with the outcome of their complaint. Contrast this to the 6 percent of workers who viewed their firm's system for dealing with the problems workers have as "not at all effective" or the 4 percent who viewed their union as "not at all effective" in dealing with problems.

Why are so many workers who take job-related problems to agencies or courts so dissatisfied with the outcomes?

One reason might be that many of these workers are disgruntled people in general — the kind who find all systems of dealing with workplace problems ineffective. In fact, 10 percent of workers who went to courts/agencies reported their firm's policies for resolving individual problems as being "not at all effective," and 10 percent reported their union as being "not at all effective." These proportions exceed those reported by other workers, but they do not approach the 23 percent who reported themselves "not at all satisfied" with courts/agencies. Workers who take problems to courts/agencies are more dissatisfied with that method than with other modes of resolving problems.

A second reason that so many workers are unhappy with the way courts or agencies resolve workplace problems might relate to the nature of administrative or judicial proceedings. Legal processes are often zero-sum games, with distinct winners and losers. Go to court and win, and you are very satisfied with the outcome; go to court and lose, and you are very dissatisfied. Equally important, taking your employer to court or an agency

EXHIBIT 6.2. Legal system produces many unsatisfied complainants compared with union and employer systems for solving problems.

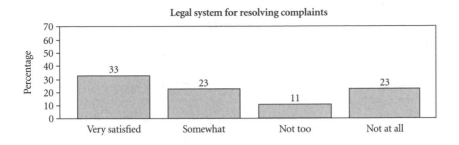

Legal system for resolving complaints

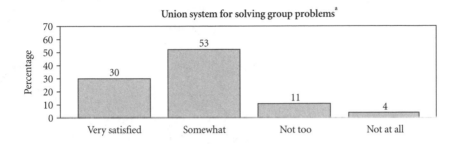

Union system for solving group problems[a]

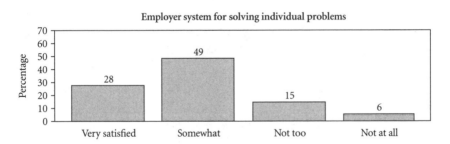

Employer system for solving individual problems

Source: Tabulated from these WRPS questions: (W1.53) (TO THOSE WITH WHO WENT TO COURT OVER WORKPLACE RIGHTS) "How satisfied were you with the outcome of your complaint?"; (W1.37d) (TO ALL WHOSE COMPANY HAS UNION) "How effective has union been in resolving group problems or concerns?" (very effective, somewhat effective, not too effective, not effective at all); (W1.32) "*Overall*, how effective is your (company's/organization's) system for resolving the problems *individual* employees have at work?"
[a] These percentages are based only on union workers.

usually involves a decisive break. Win or lose, your firm is going to hold it against you for having sued it in court or complaining about its practices to a government agency. The winner-take-all nature of court/agency proceedings explains why a relatively large number of workers report themselves as "not at all satisfied," and a relatively large number also report that they are "very satisfied" with outcomes, with few workers in between.

Finally, another reason for worker unhappiness with resolving disputes through courts or agencies is that the legal system can take a long time to reach a final resolution and might not recompense the worker for the time and pain of going through the legal process even if he or she wins. Huge backloads exist in many agencies. Court dockets are filled to capacity. And some legal remedies — say, for being fired for trying to form a union — hardly recompense workers for the pain and suffering incurred.[8]

That so many American go to courts or agencies with their workplace problems despite the costs and risks of doing so is a strong indicator that they have nowhere else to turn.

You might think that because many workers are dissatisfied with the outcomes of court or agency proceedings, firms would be satisfied. After all, they are on the other side of the dispute. But the reality is far from it. Firms regularly complain about the expense of regulations and are eager for new ways to adjudicate problems with workers. Many argue that the threat of lawsuits hampers the way they manage employees who are slacking off or whose competence has deteriorated. Everyone at the workplace might know that Q does nothing useful, but if Q fits into a protected group by reason of age, race, gender, or the like, Q can threaten an expensive lawsuit if the firm demotes or fires him or her on the grounds of discrimination. Wishing to avoid a court battle, the firm may decide that there is nothing to do about Q or might "bribe" Q to leave with some early-retirement bonus.[9] Other firms say that they have settled cases out of court even when they believe they were completely in the right because the cost of defending themselves in court is so high.

Thinking about It

Have you or anyone you know ever *thought about* going to court or to a government agency because of a possible violation of workplace rights but then decided *not* to go? Nine percent of workers on the WRPS told us that they had thought about going to court or to a government agency but decided not to; 19 percent said that someone they knew had considered complaining to a court or agency about their workplace rights. Adding the number of employees who have gone to the government and the number who have thought about going but didn't (adjusted for the overlap in responses), 14 percent of American workers have used or considered using legal remedies for workplace problems. Adding the number of employees who know people who have gone to the government and the number who know people who have thought about going but didn't go (adjusted for the overlap in responses), some 30 percent of American workers know others who have gone to or considered seeking legal remedies. Consequently, many workers in the putatively deregulated U.S. job market have lawsuits or regulatory appeals on their mind.

Why do some workers choose to go to court or to an agency while others do not?

One reason workers go is because they have a serious problem at their workplace. Exhibit 6.3 shows that the probability of taking a problem to court/an agency is higher for workers who report that employee-management relations at their workplace are poor or who do not trust their management — which suggests that they have a serious problem at work.[10] But having a problem is not by itself enough to bring a case to an agency or court. Unionized workers and high wage workers are more likely to go to an agency or court than are other workers, presumably because they have greater access to the resources needed to bring a case forward or protect them during the process.[11] Consistent with this interpretation, roughly 40 percent of workers said that they did not bring forth a complaint because the regulatory/court system was too expensive in various ways. One in ten could not find or afford a lawyer. Nearly one in five was frightened by what their employer would do in reprisal. One in eight was intimidated by the process of making a complaint.[12]

On the other side, workers in firms with effective systems for resolving individual problems are less likely to bring a workplace problem to court or a government agency. These are "good" firms that generate few serious labor problems and in which aggrieved workers can get a fair resolution of their problem at their workplace.

Employees Want More Legal Protection

Before we undertook our survey, the Employment Policy Foundation (EPF), a business-supported group in Washington, D.C., sponsored an opinion survey designed in part to determine if workers wanted more or less protective legislation. This survey asked a question of the form "Gov-

EXHIBIT 6.3. Percentage of employees who go to the courts/agencies.

By employee-management relations

By trust in employer

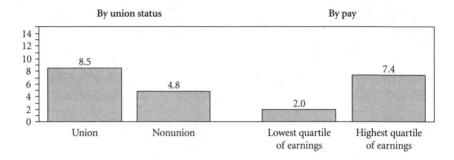

By union status

By pay

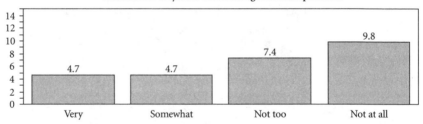

Effectiveness of systems for resolving individual problems

Source: Tabulated from this WRPS question: (W1.52) "Have you or anyone you know personally ever gone to court or to a government agency because of a possible violation of workplace rights?"

ernment regulation imposes severe costs on business. Do you think that there should be more government regulation of the workplace?"

You probably can guess how most people answered this question: "No more regulations!" When we saw these results, we thought we could increase the credibility of our study by asking the EPF question, followed by a more even-handed question. But Princeton Research Associates refused to ask the leading question. To do this went against their professional integrity and might lead some respondents to wonder whether our survey was the academic research instrument we told them it was. So we decided to ask a single "correct" question that recognized that regulations protect people at the workplace as well as restrict business in ways that could be costly.

This, we learned, is easier said than done on a telephone interview. If you phrase the question so that the costs of regulations are foremost in respondents' minds, they are likely to oppose regulations. If you phrase the question so that the protections are foremost in their minds, they are likely to favor protections. If you fill in all the "on the one hands" and "on the other hands," you have lost the respondent. Maybe you can come up with a short question that does the trick, but we could not.

To the rescue came the split-question design. We asked half of the sample, "Do you think current laws give employees too little legal protection or more protection than is necessary?" This wording stressed the protection given workers by the laws. We asked the other half, "Do you think current laws put too few legal restrictions on management or more restrictions than are necessary?" This wording stressed the restriction on business under the laws. We expected that the differing stress on protection or restrictions in the two questions would tilt answers in different directions.[13]

Exhibit 6.4 shows that posing the issue in these ways did indeed produce differences in the proportions wanting more or less legal protection in six different areas. Use the word "protections" and many people want more; use the word "restrictions" and fewer people want more. On average, 59 percent of workers believe that current laws provide too little protection, as compared with 45 percent who believe that current laws put too few restrictions on management — a difference of 14 percentage points.

On both designs more employees said that there is too little labor regulations than too much or about the right amount in all areas but one. The exception is employment discrimination. Phrased in terms of protecting workers, the majority see protections as too little; phrased in terms of restricting management, the majority sees too much restriction.

In three of the areas covered in Exhibit 6.4, there is in fact little or no protection: "firing without cause," "layoffs and plant closings," and the "use of temporary or part-time employees to replace full-time employees." In three areas, there is some legal protection: "conflicts between work responsibilities and family responsibilities," "rights to form unions and employee associations," and "job discrimination based on race, sex, or age." If workers' views have some basis in reality, we would expect more to

EXHIBIT 6.4. Workers want more legal protection.

	Percentage of workers who believe protection in area is			Percentage of workers who believe restrictions on managers are		
	Too little	About right	Excessive	Too few	About right	Excessive
Average of all areas	59	11	19	45	8	35
Without legal protection						
Being fired without cause	67	9	16	55	7	31
Use of temporary or part-time employees to replace full-time employees	64	8	18	46	5	36
Layoffs and plant closings	63	7	17	50	8	29
With legal protection						
Conflicts between work responsibilities and family responsibilities	60	13	18	41	8	40
Rights to form unions and employee associations	53	11	24	39	7	37
Job discrimination based on race, sex, or age	45	16	33	41	15	38

Source: Based on these WRPS questions: (W1.51a) "In the following areas, do you think current laws give employees *too little* legal protection or *more protection than is necessary*?"; (W1.51b) "In the following areas, do you think that current laws put *too few* legal restrictions on management or *more restrictions than are necessary*?"

Exhibit 6.5. Percentage of workers who say laws give too little protection to employees or put too few restrictions on management (by worker characteristics and workplace characteristics).

Worker Characteristics

Female	30
Male	26
Black	43
Nonblack	26
Less than high school education	35
College graduates	21

Workplace characteristics

Satisfaction with influence on job	
Not at all satisfied	43
Very satisfied	19
Feelings toward job	
Wish you didn't have to go	37
Look forward to it	25
No EI at firm	34
Nonparticipant at EI firm	25
EI participant	23
Union member	33
Nonunion employee	28

Workers who've brought complaints to court/agency want more laws

Went to court/agency	38
Know someone who went to court/agency	30
Never went to court/agency	27

(EI = employee involvement.)
Source: Based on the following WRPS questions: (W1.51a) "In the following areas, do you think current laws give employees *too little* legal protection or *more protection than is necessary?*"; (W1.51b) "In the following areas, do you think current laws put *too few* legal restrictions on management or *more restrictions than are necessary?*" These questions were cross-tabulated with other relevant questions.

say protection/restrictions are too little/few when laws are nonexistent than when they are. This is in fact the case. Workers overstate the extent to which the law protects them, but they want more laws in precisely the areas where legal protection is lacking.

What kinds of workers want more legal protection?

Exhibit 6.5 shows that workers who have troubles at their workplace and who have little influence are more likely to want more laws than other workers while, by contrast, workers in firms with EI see less need for additional protections. Workers in relatively weak positions in the job market — blacks, women, and the less educated — also want more laws. More surprising, union workers, who have independent protection at the workplace, also want more legal protections than other workers. We interpret this as reflecting the fact that the union gives workers greater ability to make use of legal protections than other workers.

Finally, despite the fact that many workers who went to court/an agency were not happy with the outcomes from the legal or regulatory system, these workers want more legal protections than those who never went. If you felt sufficiently mistreated at work to bring a complaint to court or an agency, you feel a need for greater state protection, even though the system of enforcement might not have served you well.

All told, the desire of workers for more protection at the workplace fits a sensible pattern.

But Not If There Is Something Else

When you have a problem at your workplace, would you prefer to go to court or an administrative agency or to resolve the dispute through an alternative dispute-resolution system based at your workplace?

What, you ask, is "an alternative dispute-resolution system"? It is a system in which a third party — a neutral arbitrator — has the final word in determining the outcome. Many firms use arbitration to resolve arguments about interpretation of commercial contracts. Almost all collective-bargaining contracts use arbitration to resolve disputes about the application of the contract. Professional sports use arbitrators to deal with the complaints of athletes that they have been mistreated by leagues. Alternative dispute-resolution systems of various forms are a growing mode of resolving problems outside the judicial system.

In Wave 1 of the WRPS, we asked employees their views of arbitration at their workplace: "Going to court or to a government agency can be expensive and time-consuming. Here is an alternative system . . ."; then we gave a one-sentence description of arbitration. Most respondents said they thought arbitration could effectively resolve disputes between workers and management. About one-fourth thought arbitration would be "very effective" in resolving disputes over legal rights, a bit more than half thought it would be "somewhat effective," and about 20 percent thought it would be "not too effective" or "not effective at all."[14] Asked to choose between this sort of a system and courts or agencies, more than half of the workforce preferred going to an arbitrator. Workers who had in fact been to court or to an agency favored arbitration as well, but they differed in their views from other workers in one important way. Many of them told us that arbitration would be "very effective" *if an elected committee of workers was involved in selecting the arbitrator*; they said they would choose this option if this were the case more so than if management selected the arbitrator. Other workers did not make such a distinction.[15]

But how much credence, you ask, should we give to these responses? We did not describe how the alternative system would work in any detail. We did not ask workers what type of problem they would bring to the system or the type of arbitration system they would prefer. We introduced arbitration in a leading way, reminding workers that going to courts or agencies could be expensive or time-consuming. Arguably, we had done here what we had tried so hard to avoid throughout the WRPS — posing an issue in a leading manner. Perhaps if workers heard arguments for and against arbitration, they might find the arguments against more compelling.

Concerned about these problems, we mailed a six-page description of an arbitration system (see Appendix D) to half of the population in our follow-up survey. We detailed the problems the system would cover, gave arguments for and against the system, and asked workers to think about how effective such a system would be at their workplace. Several days later we called and asked workers if they had read the material, if they understood how arbitration worked, and finally what they thought about arbitration of disputes over workplace rights.

The majority reported that they had taken the material seriously: 57 percent said they had read *all* of the material; 24 percent said they had read *most* of it. More than one-fifth said they had an excellent understanding of the arbitration system, and most said they had a good understanding.[16] One-third said they had discussed the system with someone else. Although workers might have exaggerated the attention they paid to our material, they surely were more informed than otherwise. And, most important, they were sufficiently interested in the issue to bear with another telephone interview.

As in the main survey, the majority of workers reacted favorably to the idea of arbitrating disputes at their workplace (see Exhibit 6.6). Most viewed arbitration to be a "very good idea" or a "good idea," as compared with just 8 percent who viewed it as a "bad idea" or a "very bad idea." Most thought arbitration would work well at their firm, although the percentage who said it would work well fell short of the percentage who said it was a

EXHIBIT 6.6. Workers' views on using arbitration to settle legal disputes.

	Percentage of workers who think committees would
Overall use of arbitration	
Very good idea	17
Good idea	66
Bad/very bad idea	8
Mixed feeling/don't know	9
Would work at their company	
Well	62
Not well	27
Depends/don't know	11
Complaints against employer	
More	59
Fewer	17
Stay the same	19
Fairness in dispute settlement	
More fairly	62
Less fairly	13
Stay the same	17
Ease of workers getting fair hearing	
Easier	71
Harder	15
Stay the same	11
Effect on workers	
Better off	73
Worse off	13
Stay the same	10
Effect on management	
Better off	71
Worse off	15
Stay the same	10

Note: Numbers do not add to 100 percent for items 3–7 because some respondents answered "Don't know" or refused to answer.

Source: Based on these WRPS questions: (W2.5) "Overall, what do you think about using arbitration to settle legal disputes? Do you think it is a very good idea, a good idea, a bad idea, or a very bad idea?"; (W2.6a) "Suppose [an arbitration] system was set up in your (company/organization). That is, employees who felt their legal rights had been violated would take the case to a neutral arbitrator to be decided, rather than to court. Do you think this system would work well, or not well, at your (company/organization)?"; (W2.7A) "If arbitrators replaced the courts in solving most employee disputes about legal rights, (W2.7aa) Would more employees or fewer employees bring complaints against their employers? (W2.7ab) Would disputes be settle more fairly or less fairly? (W2.7ac) Would it be easier or harder for ordinary workers to get a fair hearing of their complaints? (W2.7ad) Would workers overall be better off or worse off with this kind of system? (W2.7ae) Would management overall be better off or worse off with this kind of system?"

very good or good idea in general. Most thought that more employees would bring complaints to an arbitrator than to court, that disputes would be settled more fairly, and that arbitration would make both management and workers better off and save them money.

Comparing the arguments for and against arbitration, the majority of workers found arguments for arbitration more convincing than those who did so for arguments against arbitration. We do not think that this reflects any tilt in the pro and con arguments that we offered, but you can judge that for yourself by looking at Appendix D.

Employees do not favor arbitration blindly, however. Workers rejected the practice of some firms that insist on employees relinquishing their right to go to court and agreeing to use a management-appointed arbitrator for disputes over legal rights as a precondition for getting a job. Three-fourths said that such a practice should be illegal.

Finally, we asked workers to choose the features of an arbitration system themselves: "Suppose Congress passed a law that encouraged companies to use arbitration to settle employment disputes about legal rights. If it were your decision to make, and everyone went along with it, what type of system would you like Congress to encourage?" Exhibit 6.7 shows that the majority of workers favor an arbitration system in which

- the procedures for using it are set up by management and employees together;
- expenses are paid by management and employees or by them with a government contribution;
- workers receive expert advice and assistance preparing their case; and
- arbitrators' decisions are not subject to government review.

What surprised us is that workers want to contribute to the costs of an arbitration system. Where is the economists' "free rider" principle of letting the other guy pay the costs of a public good? Why didn't workers simply say, "Let the firm pay from the savings it will get from avoiding expensive lawsuits?" The most likely reason is that workers recognize that if the firm pays arbitrators' fees, even the most fair-minded arbitrator will probably tilt decisions toward the firm.

Does an alternative dispute-resolution system based on what workers want constitute a feasible way to deal with disputes over workplace rights? Absolutely. Is this the type of system firms are introducing at workplaces? Not entirely. Most firms do not involve workers in the design and administration of their dispute-resolution system. And some firms hire em-

EXHIBIT 6.7. The "ideal" arbitration system to settle employee disputes about legal rights.

Percentage of workers selecting systems with given characteristics

Set up jointly by employees and management	95
Set up by employees or management alone	5
Allows employees to use arbitration or court	78
Must use arbitration alone	18
Provides expert advice/assistance to employees	82
Makes employees responsible for own case	17
Expenses paid by management and employees	43
Expenses paid by management, employees, and government	39
Expenses paid by management alone	15
Operates without government review	56
Decisions reviewed by government	42

Source: Based on this WRPS question: (W2.10A) "Suppose Congress passed a law that encouraged companies to use arbitration to settle employment disputes about legal rights. If it was your decision to make and everyone went along with it, what type of system would you like Congress to encourage?"

ployees only if they sign away their right to go to court for violations of labor laws.

Workplace Committees to Monitor Labor Regulations?

We asked workers about one other explicit workplace reform: the use of workplace committees of employees and managers to enforce compliance with legal workplace standards, such as occupational health and safety regulations, antidiscrimination laws, and the like. While the idea of devolving regulatory authority to workplace committees was not on the national policy agenda, it is not a far-out idea.[17] In the area of occupational health and safety, ten states mandates joint committees as of 1994;[18] Canada mandates such health and safety committees nationwide; and most European Union countries have similar workplace-based committees in health and safety and other areas.

We mailed a four-page description of how workplace committees might function to the one-half of the follow-up survey who had not received our arbitration module. We gave arguments for and against the system; we asked workers to think about whether a workplace-committee system would be better or worse than the current system of enforcing legal stan-

EXHIBIT 6.8. Employees' views of workplace committees for workplace standards.

	Percentage of employees who think workplace committees would
Overall view of committees	
Very good idea	21
Good idea	64
Bad/very bad idea	7
Mixed feelings/don't know	8
Would work at their company	
Well	64
Not well	29
Depends/don't know	7
Standards enforced compared to government regulators	
More often	64
Less often	12
Stay the same	19
Ease for companies to meet standards	
Easier	58
Harder	23
Stay the same	14
Standards of enforcement	
Stricter	57
Weaker	19
Stay the same	16
Effect on workers	
Better off	80
Worse off	7
Stay the same	9
Effect on management	
Better off	73
Worse off	15
Stay the same	8

Note: Numbers do not add to 100 percent because some answered "don't know" or refused to answer.
Source: Based on these WRPS questions: (W2.7B) "What do you think would happen if workplace committees were given some responsibility for enforcing workplace standards? (W2.7ba) Would standards be enforced *more often* or *less often* than they are now? (W2.7bb) Would it be *easier* or *harder* for companies to meet standards in a way that fits well with how they operate? (W2.7bc) Would enforcement be *more strict* or *less strict*? (W2.7bd) Overall, would *workers* be *better off* or *worse off* with this kind of system? (W2.7be) Overall, would *management* be *better off* or *worse off* with this kind of system?"

dards; and, finally, we asked how workers would like such a committee to operate. Several days later we called the workers. As with the workers who received the arbitration module, most said they had read the material and had a good to excellent understanding of how committees for workplace standards would function.

Overall, employees were favorably inclined toward workplace committees to enforce labor standards (see Exhibit 6.8). As a general policy matter, 85 percent of workers thought workplace committees were a "very good idea" or a "good idea." When it came to their own workplace, however, the percentage favoring committees fell to 64 percent, as a significant minority of 29 percent thought standards committees would not work well. That more workers viewed the committees unfavorably at their workplace than in the abstract suggests that we made the right choice in directing most WRPS questions at employees' views of their workplace rather than of the American labor scene in general. People might favor something in the abstract that they reject as unworkable in their particular situation.

Exhibit 6.8 also shows that the majority of workers thought committees would enforce standards more often and more strictly than regulators, would make it easier for companies to meet standards, and would make both workers and management better off. The pro-committee argument that resonated most with workers was that committees would give workers more say in workplace decisions, followed by the argument that committees would give companies more choices about how to meet standards. Most workers found less convincing the arguments against committees for workplace standards. The anti-committee argument that carried the most weight was the cost of training committee members and giving them time off to attend meetings. The idea that committee members would be less knowledgeable than government inspectors or that committee members might not enforce standards as strictly as government inspectors carried less weight.

Finally, we asked workers their ideal design for a system of workplace committees: "Suppose Congress passed a law encouraging companies to set up workplace standards committees. If it were your decision to make and everyone went along with it, what type of committee would you like Congress to encourage?" The responses, given in Exhibit 6.9, show that workers want to resolve workplace problems cooperatively with management but that they want some independent standing as they do so. The majority favor committees in which (1) employee members are elected by employees, (2) outside experts give advice and help to the committee, and (3) the committee is responsible for all types of workplace standards.

EXHIBIT 6.9. The "ideal" workplace committee system to enforce workplace standards.

	Percentage of workers selecting committee with given characteristics
Commitees with elected employee members	85
Commitees with members chosen by management	11
Committees responsible for all workplace standards	63
Committees cover only a few standards	35
Committees get advice/help from outside experts	83
Committees operate on their own	14
Committees that have power to enforce regulations	49
Committees that only give advice to management	47

Source: Based on this WRPS question: (W2.10B) "Suppose Congress passed a law encouraging companies to set up workplace standards committees. If it was your decision to make and everyone went along with it, what type of committee would you like Congress to encourage?"

By contrast, workers are roughly evenly divided between committees that have the power to enforce regulations and committees that only advise management.[19] Determining the powers that a standards committee should have is critical to any reform, so more needs to be explored here. Still, there is no gainsaying that workers prefer a more decentralized mode of regulating workplaces than the United States currently has — conditional on their having a significant input into the process.

The bottom line is that these responses show that, given a bit of information, workers can assess possible new workplace institutions and design what seems to be a reasonable supplement to government regulators enforcing standards.

CHAPTER 7

If Workers Could Choose

If, more generally, workers were free to choose the institutions that would give them their desired representation and say in workplace decisions, as well as settle disputes about legal rights and to enforce workplace standards, what kind of institutions would they pick? What sort of labor-relations system would they like to see in the United States?

This chapter moves from reporting how workers view existing workplace institutions to examining what they want in the form of new or expanded institutions of representation and participation. It gives what are arguably the most conjectural but important results in *What Workers Want*. Conjectural, because determining preferences for institutions or policies that workers have not experienced pushes survey methodology to its limits. Important, because we cannot imagine how private or public policy-makers could improve the U.S. labor system without taking account of the design features that workers want.

To discover the institutions that workers believe would best increase their workplace representation and participation, we used two different types of questions. First, as we did in the questions about arbitration systems and workplace committees in Chapter 6, we asked about the attributes or characteristics that workers would like to see in a workplace organization. Here, however, rather than specifying the particular institutions among which workers could choose, we gave them a checklist and simply asked if they preferred an organization with attribute X or Y. Second, we presented them with three alternative institutions: increased legal protection, unions or a workplace organization that negotiated with management, and a potentially new institution — an employee-management committee that discussed workplace problems but did not collectively bargain. We asked workers to select one of the three institutions, even though it might not be their ideal.

Both approaches have strengths and weaknesses. The first approach identifies the functions and attributes that workers want in a workplace organization without reference to any particular existing institutions. Ideally, it captures their preferences without any distortions that might come from their associating particular attributes with existing institutions. The downside of this is that it doesn't tell us how workers would react to a choice between different institutions with different clusters of attributes. Preferences on individual items might not add up to a valid composite organization. You like pepper and you like ice cream, but you probably don't like pepper on your ice cream.

The second approach forces respondents to look at a workplace institution in its entirety and to make something that approaches a real choice between potentially imperfect institutions. The disadvantage of this approach is that different workers might have different ideas of how the three institutions we gave them would actually function. This is particularly the case for the option of a joint workplace committee, which some employees may see as a near-union in which they have considerable independence from management, whereas other employees might see it as a more management-run operation.

By asking both sorts of questions, and working back and forth between their responses, we are able to fill in some of the gaps in each. The result is a coherent picture of the new or expanded workplace institutions that different groups of workers want.

Desired Organizational Attributes

To determine the attributes of an ideal workplace organization we asked employees, "Thinking now about any kind of employee organization, not just unions, how would *you* like it to work? If it was your decision alone to make, and everybody went along with it, would you prefer . . . ?" We listed six items[1] and asked workers if they thought employees who participated in an organization with the attributes they chose would need legal protection from discrimination or harassment, and whether they would volunteer time to the organization. Column 1 of Exhibit 7.1 gives the average response for all nonmanagerial employees to the six items. Column 2 shows how union workers answered the question. Column 3 shows how managers answered the question. Ignore Column 3 for the moment and focus on the preferences of workers in Columns 1 and 2.

The most striking fact in the exhibit — sufficiently striking that we raised it in Chapter 3 — is that the vast majority of workers want an organization run jointly by employees and management. This overwhelming preference reflects employees' desire for cooperative labor relations with

EXHIBIT 7.1. Percentage of employees choosing attributes of an ideal organization.

The "ideal" employee organization should . . .	Nonmanagerial employees	Union members	Managers
Be run jointly by employees and management	85	83	90
Be run by employees alone	10	14	3
Have elected employee representatives	59	76	47
Have volunteer representatives	25	16	25
Have management select representatives	10	6	20
Include similarly situated workers	55	57	48
Include everyone but top management	31	30	32
Have arbitrator make final decisions in cases of conflict	59	86	37
Have management make final decisions in cases of conflict	34	10	55
Have access to confidential company information	47	50	38
Rely on public records	39	38	48
Draw on company budget and staff	52	37	57
Rely on own budget and staff	34	48	31

Source: Tabulated from these WRPS questions: (W1.48a–f) "Thinking now about any kind of employee organization, not just unions, how would *you* like it to work? If it was your decision alone to make, and everybody went along with it, would you prefer (ITEMS)?"

their firm and their recognition that management must be deeply involved in any workplace institution if workers' say is to affect decisions. That most union members — whom, as we have seen, would vote overwhelmingly to maintain their union — support such joint governance tells us that workers' preference for a jointly run organization does not imply that they favor a management-dominated organization. The key phrase is *jointly run*.

The responses to the other items makes this point clearly. They show that the majority of workers favor an organization with more independent rather than less independent authority. The majority want to elect employee representatives to the group and to use outside arbitrators to make final decisions when management and workers disagree. In addition, they want the organization to have access to confidential company information, to be limited to employees doing the same kind of work, and to receive company budget and staff for the organization. They are almost exactly evenly split on whether workers involved in the organization would need legal protection.

On all these questions, union members favor an organization that is more independent of management in greater numbers than do nonunion workers. More than three-fourths of union members want to elect employee representatives, and 86 percent want an arbitrator to make final decisions when management and labor disagree. The majority of union members who responded to the question want the organization to rely on its own budget and staff (as unions do), rather than to draw on company resources.

The "Just Say No" Respondents

When we asked workers the attributes of their preferred organization, we did not offer them the option of saying they wanted no organization of any kind. In fact, a number of respondents volunteered that they were opposed to any workplace organization, and we recorded their answer as a kind of write-in response. Depending on the attribute, as many as 7 percent volunteered that they did not want any organization. In addition, up to 9 percent of workers either "didn't know" what they wanted or refused to answer various questions. If, to be conservative, we assume that those who "didn't know" or refused to answer actually oppose any workplace institution, we would conclude that about 16 percent of American workers reject any workplace organization.

But even these figures might understate the proportion of workers who want no workplace organization. Some respondents opposed to any organization might have answered the attributes question out of politeness to the interviewer. We can get a fix on that number by looking at responses to a succeeding question: "How willing would *you* be to volunteer two or three hours a month to participate in an employee organization to discuss workplace issues with your management?" Seventy-seven percent said they would "definitely" or "probably" be willing to do so; 10 percent said they were "probably not willing," 5 percent said that they would "definitely not participate," and 7 percent said that they did not want any kind of employee organization. If, again to be conservative, we assume that anyone who was not "definitely" or "probably" willing to volunteer two or three hours a month to participate in an employee organization was truly against it, we get an upper bound of 23 percent on the "just say no" proportion of the workforce. Put positively, American workers want some sort of organization to represent them at their workplace by a better than three-to-one ratio.[2]

Management Preferences

Imagine that workers came to management asking for an organization with the characteristics of the composite given in Exhibit 7.1 How might management respond? Does management have a similar or dissimilar notion of the ideal workplace organization as do workers? The right-hand column records the type of employee organization managers prefer to deal with, given that the workplace has some organization. Managers favor an organization that differs in some critical respects from that chosen by workers. The majority of managers want to make a final decision when employees and management disagree, and they do not want an organization to have access to confidential company information. These are bottom-line issues of who has power and authority at workplaces. Because management has power, and people do not relinquish power readily, we do not find this pattern of preferences surprising.

What is perhaps surprising, though, is that nearly half of managers report that they would prefer to deal with elected employees if their firm had an employee organization, and 37 percent say they would prefer an outside arbitrator to resolve disagreements with employees in such an organization. One reason these managers favored electing workers to committees is that they think it would increase the effectiveness of labor relations. Sixty-nine percent of the managers who favored employees electing representatives thought that their firms' method for resolving workplace problems would be more effective if employees chose their own representatives to meet with management, as compared with 21 percent of managers whose ideal workplace organization depended on management selecting workers or on volunteers. Managers from union firms, which regularly negotiate with elected representatives of workers, were moderately more favorable to electing employee representatives than managers from nonunion firms.[3]

The managers who wanted employees to elect representatives to joint workplace committees also seem to be reacting to the way their firm manages employees. They expressed less satisfaction with their influence on workplace decisions than did those managers who opposed the election of worker representatives; they trusted their firm less than others to carry out its promises to workers;[4] and they were more likely to rate labor-management relations at their firm as fair or poor or as below average than were other managers.[5] The message from these managers seems to be that their firm (and maybe they themselves) needed an independent workplace organization to improve working conditions and give workers a say in decisions.

Variation in Preferences

The composite workplace organization in Exhibit 7.1 is based on average responses, item by item. But averages can be misleading. That a majority of workers say that they want to elect workers to an organization on one item and that a majority say that they want the company to fund the organization on a second item does *not* imply that a majority favors the two attributes together. Perhaps the two majorities barely overlap, so that only a minority favor the composite.[6] In fact, workers who desire elected representatives are less likely to want the company to fund a workplace organization than other workers. By contrast those who favor company funding are less favorable to electing representatives than are other employees.[7] What is true for two attributes holds even more so for a composite of six attributes.

To determine the actual configuration of workplace features that individual workers want, we tabulated the distribution of worker preferences for combinations of workplace characteristics. Because each respondent has selected one of two choices for five features and one of three for one feature, ninety-six outcome configurations are possible.[8] With this large number of possibilities, it would be remarkable indeed if the majority selected the composite. In fact, only 8 percent of workers selected the majority items on the composite, but many chose something close to the composite: 23 percent chose an ideal institution that differs in just one feature from the composite, and 38 percent chose an institution that differs in two features, so that 61 percent of workers selected an institution in the neighborhood of the composite. By contrast, less than 4 percent had an ideal organization that had only one feature in common with the composite, and 13 percent had an ideal organization that had only two features in common with composite.[9]

The six attributes listed in the exhibit are not, however, equally important in determining the character of a workplace organization. The independence and relative power of workers and management depends fundamentally on two attributes of an organization: the mechanism for selecting worker representatives and the way the organization resolves disputes between management and labor. Whether all employees below top management or only similarly situated employees are members of the group, access to confidential company documents, and even the mechanism for funding the organization, are less central to guaranteeing workers an independent say in decisions. If workers have a coherent view of the authority a workplace organization ought to have, we would expect their opinions on selection of representatives and resolving disputes to overlap. Indeed, 71 percent of workers who want to elect employee representatives also want an arbitrator to decide disputes, whereas just 29 percent of those who want management to select representatives favor an arbitrator resolving disagreements.

Exhibit 7.2 shows the distribution of workers according to their preferences on the two items together. Forty-four percent of workers want an organization that both elects worker members and uses an outside arbitrator to resolve disputes — which we will call a "strongly independent" worker organization. (Had worker preference on these two items been unrelated, the proportion choosing this organization would have been less: 35 percent.) Under current U.S. labor regulations, the only organization that has both of these desires is a trade union. That the percentage of workers who want a strongly independent workplace organization is exactly the same as the 44 percent who said they would vote union in an NLRB election if given the opportunity is an accident, but that the two statistics are of the same magnitude is not. Many more U.S. workers want some independent organization at their workplace than currently have it.

At the opposite end of the spectrum, 7 percent of workers want management to select representatives to any workplace organization and to decide on issues of disagreement. We will label this a "not independent" workplace organization. Most in this group said that they also wanted management to make final decisions when the management-selected representatives disagreed with management, but one-third said they wanted an outside arbitrator to make the final decision.[10] Still, as long as they want management to select worker representatives, they belong in the "not independent" group. An additional 7 percent of workers said that they did not want any organization to either of these items, or to some other question about their preferred organizational form.

Somewhere between these two clearly defined groups are the remaining workers who want something more than to be completely dependent on management and something less than a strongly independent organization.

EXHIBIT 7.2. Proportions of workers favoring a workplace organization with different degrees of independence from management.

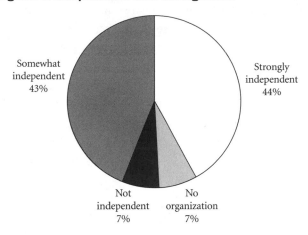

Somewhat independent 43%

Strongly independent 44%

Not independent 7%

No organization 7%

Note: "Strongly independent" means that respondents want elected representatives and arbitration of disagreements; "somewhat independent" refers to all other combinations (volunteer representatives with or without arbitration, elected representatives without arbitration, management-selected representatives with arbitration); "not independent" means that management selects worker representatives and decides issues of disagreement; "no organization" refers to those who want no organization on any item on the WRPS questions that are the source of this pie chart.

Source: Tabulated only for nonmanagers from this WRPS question: (W1.48) "Thinking now about any kind of employee organization, not just unions, how would *you* like it to work? If it was your decision alone to make, and everybody went along with it, would you prefer (W1.48a) An organization that can use an *outside* referee or arbitrator to settle issues? (W1.48b) An organization in which *management* makes the final decisions about issues? (W1.48c) An organization in which the key participants are *volunteers*? (W1.48d) An organization in which the key participants are *elected*? (W1.48e) An organization in which the key participants are *appointed* by management?"

Seventeen percent want an organization in which workers elect representatives but in which management makes final decisions when workers and management disagree. A strongly independent group? Not by our criterion, as they give management the final word. But any organization to which workers elect representatives will have some independent standing at the workplace.

Twenty-six percent of workers want an organization in which worker members are volunteers. Nearly sixty percent of these want disputes with management to go to an outside arbitrator, which would give their ideal organization some independent power to affect decisions at the workplace. The other 40 or so percent want to leave the final decision to management, which makes their organization closer to the "not independent" group.

While recognizing the range of desire for an independent organization among these workers, for ease of analysis, we shall combine them into a single category: as workers who want an organization with "some independence."

Summarizing, the largest single group of workers (by a hair) want a strongly independent organization, as we have defined it, a minority want an organization that depends entirely on management or no organization at all, and a large group fall somewhere in between.

Who are these people? What sort of workers want an organization with strong independence, with some independence, or with no independent standing or no organization at all?

Exhibit 7.3 compares the dependence of worker preferences for workplace committees with greater or lesser independence from management — indeed, for any organization at all according to the characteristics of the worker and his or her workplace. The upper part of the exhibit shows that preferences for different types of organizations varies relatively modestly by workers' personal characteristics. College graduates are less likely to want an independent organization and more likely to want no organization than are persons with high school or less schooling. Black workers are more likely to want an independent organization than are whites. Blue-collar workers have a greater preference for an independent organization than white-collar workers. But there are essentially no differences between men and women or between workers with different levels of pay, and the biggest difference among groups — between blacks and whites — is not all that large.

By contrast, the differences in preferences by the condition of the workplace, shown in the bottom part of the exhibit, are huge. The biggest single factor that determines people's desire for a more independent workplace organization is the quality of labor-management relations. Workers with poor employee-management relations are much more likely to want an independent organization as workers with good employee-management relations. Seventeen percent of employees who report excellent employee-management relations want no organization or one that is highly dependent on management. Unionized workers and nonunion workers who say they would vote union in an NLRB election also greatly favor an organization with independent authority. By contrast, only 37 percent of workers who participate in employee-involvement (EI) committees at their work-

EXHIBIT 7.3. Employee-management relations dominate workers' desire for independence of the employee organization.

Worker characteristics	Percentage of workers who want organization to be			
	Strongly independent	Somewhat independent	Not independent	No organization
Sex				
Male	42	43	7	8
Female	45	43	7	6
Race				
Black	49	39	7	5
White	43	43	7	7
Education				
College graduate	38	47	7	9
High school or less	44	41	8	6
Occupation				
Professional	41	43	6	10
Other nonmanagerial white collar	39	47	8	7
Blue collar (craft, operatives, service, laborers	49	39	6	6
Level of pay				
Upper quartile of wages	45	43	7	0
Lower quartile of wages	44	41	11	4
Workplace characteristics				
Employee-management relations				
Excellent	37	46	9	8
Good	45	41	6	7
Only fair	53	36	4	7
Poor	65	25	5	5
Union status				
Union member	69	25	2	5
Nonunion employee favorable to union	60	32	5	3
Nonunion employee opposed to union	26	55	9	10
Employee involvement (EI)				
Participant in EI committee	37	46	8	8
Nonparticipant in EI firm	45	43	7	6
Firm has no EI	47	41	6	7

Note: "Strongly independent" means that respondents want elected representatives and arbitration of disagreements; "somewhat independent" means that respondents want any of the following combinations: (volunteer representatives with or without arbitration, elected representatives without arbitration, or management-selected representatives with arbitration); "not independent" means that management selects worker representatives and decides issues of disagreement; "no organization" refers to those who want no organization on any item on the WRPS questions that are the source of this table.
Source: Tabulated from WRPS question as described in Exhibit 7.2; cross-tabulated with other relevant questions. The wage quartile data are based on the wages in the entire sample, including managers.

place want a strongly independent organization. Mr. or Ms. Manager, if you provide your employees with say at their workplace and an excellent labor-relations environment, they see less need for an independent worker organization than otherwise.

The conclusion seems inescapable: The variation in the attributes of the ideal workplace organization that workers want is largely grounded in their diverse experiences on the job.

Choosing a Single Option

Our second way of determining the workplace institution that employees want was to ask workers to choose a single best way to improve their situation at the workplace. Having found that workers wanted more unionization, expanded EI programs, and more legal protection, we asked, "During this interview we've talked about a few different ways to increase employees' say in workplace matters and make sure they are treated fairly. Which *one* of the following three ways do *you* think would be most effective? (1) *Laws* that protect the rights of individual employees, (2) joint employee and management *committees* that *discuss* problems, or (3) unions (employee organizations) that *negotiate* or bargain with management over issues?"

Using the split-question design, we asked half of the sample if they wanted a *union* that "negotiates or bargains" and the other half if they wanted an *employee organization* that "negotiates or bargains." Because an "employee organization that negotiates or bargains" with management over issues is essentially a union, this verbal distinction might seem silly. But one of our union advisors said that if we asked about "unions," we would be biasing responses against organizations that negotiated for workers. He cited AFL-CIO polls that showed that workers respond less favorably to "the U word" than to other nomenclature and respond least favorably to AFL-CIO–affiliated unions. (In fact, the National Education Association, the Association of University Professors, and various police organizations often defeat AFL-CIO affiliates in elections for union representation because these groups are seen as something different from a union, although in fact they bargain collectively just as do AFL-CIO affiliates.)

Exhibit 7.4 shows the results. Twenty-three percent chose a union as their preferred option. This is much greater than the 14 percent in our sample who currently belong to unions. But 31 percent chose an employee organization that negotiates with employers, a union in all but name. Our

EXHIBIT 7.4. Most workers want joint committees; more want unions than are unionized.

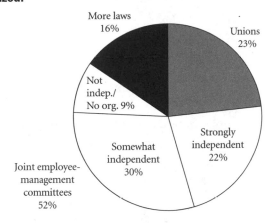

More laws
16%

Unions
23%

Not indep./ No org. 9%

Strongly independent 22%

Somewhat independent 30%

Joint employee-management committees 52%

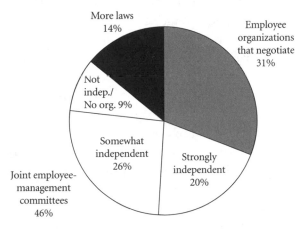

More laws
14%

Employee organizations that negotiate 31%

Not indep./ No org. 9%

Somewhat independent 26%

Strongly independent 20%

Joint employee-management committees 46%

(Not indep./no org. = Not independent/no organization.)
Source: Based on this WRPS question: (W1.58) "During this interview, we've talked about a few different ways to increase employees' say in workplace matters and to make sure they are treated fairly. Which *one* of the following three ways do *you* think would be most effective?: *Laws* that protect the rights of individual employees; Joint employee and management *committees* that *discuss* problems; (FOR FIRST HALVES OF FORMS A AND B) Employee organizations; (FOR SECOND HALVES OF FORMS A AND B) Employee organizations that *negotiate* or bargain with management over issues."

union adviser was right: Simply dropping "the U word" made a big difference in how many workers wanted an organization that would negotiate for them with management. By contrast, only a small proportion of workers selected additional laws as the most effective way to increase their say at the workplace and make sure they are fairly treated. Consistent with the findings in Chapter 6, employees prefer workplace-based organizations and arrangements for dealing with workplace problems over additional legal protections.

The majority of workers, roughly 58 percent (the average of the 61 percent in the upper panel and 55 percent in the lower panel of Exhibit 7.4) of the population, want an institutional form that does not effectively exist in the United States: joint employee-management committees that discuss and resolve workplace problems. At least in practice, U.S. labor law nowhere encourages an organization of this form, and many believe that if such an organization discussed issues that fall into the domain of collective bargaining, it would be illegal.[11]

What do workers who seek this new form of organization have in mind? The questions we asked about the attributes that workers would choose in a workplace organization gives us an answer. Thirty-six percent of those who said they favored joint committees and told us about their organizational preferences reported that their ideal organization was one in which workers elected their own representatives and disputes between their representatives and management were resolved by an outside arbitrator — a strongly independent organization. Fifty-six percent of those favoring joint committees wanted an organization in which workers volunteered for the committee (usually with an arbitrator to resolve disputes) or elected representatives but which did not rely on an outside arbitrator to resolve disputes or — a less independent group. Eight percent of those favoring a joint committee wanted an organization with effectively no independence from management.[12]

Combining these responses with the other answers to our "ultimate" question gives the distribution of worker desires for different ways to increase employees' say and make sure they are fairly treated (see Exhibit 7.4). Exhibit 7.4 shows that almost half of American workers want an organization that has considerable independence at the workplace — 45 percent want a union or a strongly independent joint committee; 51 percent want an employee organization that negotiates or a strongly independent joint committee. Between 26 percent and 30 percent of workers want a somewhat independent organization. Nine percent want either no organization or an organization with no independence.[13]

The Consistency of Choices

When we began this study, our labor and management advisors warned us that worker responses to hypothetical questions concerning labor reforms could be unreliable, dependent on the wording and context of questions rather than on more deeply rooted attitudes. If this is a serious problem, we would expect to see little consistency between the objective situation of workers or how they judge existing institutions and their choice of a single most effective way to increase their say in workplace matters and assure fair treatment. Alternatively, if what workers told us about unions, management policies, and government regulations in earlier chapters are closely related to their bottom-line assessment of how to improve workplaces, we can put aside the worry that workers' views of reforms are unreliable.

Exhibit 7.5 shows that, contrary to the fears of our advisors, employees' choices seem well-grounded in their experiences in the job market and fit with their attitudes toward unions and the state of worker-management relations at their firm.

Consider first the responses of workers according to their union status or desire to join a union. Union and nonunion workers who would vote union in an NLRB election are much more likely to say that their first-choice institution is a union or other employee group that negotiates with management than are nonunion workers opposed to unions. More union workers want a union than a joint committee, and nonunion workers favorable to a union are evenly split. A larger proportion of union members want a union than want an employee group that negotiates, perhaps because union members fear that such a group would be weaker than a traditional union. By contrast, a large majority of nonunion workers opposed to a union want joint committees.

Given that workers with experience on EI committees report generally good experiences with them, we would expect those workers to be *more* favorable to joint management-worker committees than other workers. Exhibit 7.5 shows that, faced with the option of a union, laws, or a joint committee, 68 percent of EI participants choose a joint committee, as compared with 61 percent of nonparticipants in firms with EI and 58 percent of workers in firms without EI. The proportion of EI participants favoring a joint committee falls when the option is an employee organization to negotiate with management but remains above the comparable proportions for other workers.

Finally, the exhibit shows that workers who said that they would prefer to go to court or a government agency if their workplace rights had been violated are more likely to view increased laws as the most effective way of improving their situation than workers who said that they would prefer

EXHIBIT 7.5. Percentage of workers who choose different ways to increase workers' say

	Union option			Employee organization option		
	Union to negotiate	Joint committee	Laws	Employee organization to negotiate	Joint committee	Laws
By union status						
Union member	54	39	7	44	45	11
Nonunion employee favoring union	40	42	18	44	43	13
Nonunion employee opposing union	5	78	17	20	66	14
By employee involvement (EI) status						
Participant in EI committee	19	68	12	30	59	11
Nonparticipant in EI firm	21	61	18	32	55	13
No EI at firm	26	58	17	32	52	16
By attitude toward government solutions to workplace problems						
Prefer to take problems to court/government agency	23	58	19	36	47	16
Prefer arbitration system	24	63	13	29	60	11

Source: Based on WRPS question (W1.58) as described in Exhibit 7.4; cross-tabulated with questions on union status, employee-involvement status, and intention to vote union, and also with question (W1.57), "If you felt your own legal workplace rights had been violated, would you prefer to use this alternative system, or would you prefer to go to court or to a government agency?"

going to an arbitrator to resolve their workplace problem. Even here, however, increased legal protection is the least preferred first option.

Conclusion: Toward Improving U.S. Workplaces

Our central finding in *What Workers Want* is that, given a choice, workers want "more" — more say in the workplace decisions that affect their lives, more employee involvement at their firms, more legal protection at the workplace, and more union representation. Most workers reported that existing institutions — from unions to EI committees to government regulations — are either insufficiently available to them or do not go far enough to provide the workplace voice they want. A substantial number of nonunion workers want the benefits of unionization. An even larger number would like to see some sort of employee-management committee, with varying degrees of independence from management, at their workplace. Irrespective of the workplace organization they desire, however, most workers do not believe that, under current U.S. policies, they can get the additional input into workplace decisions that they want. They believe that management is unwilling to share power or authority with them. And management generally agrees. Left alone, this system promises continued frustration of worker desire for more say.

Perhaps surprisingly, *What Workers Want* has shown that employees can specify with some precision new forms and attributes of workplace organization and ways to enforce regulations. Employee desire for additional voice and input into workplace decisions is not inchoate but well-formed and practical enough that it could readily guide business, union, and political leaders in modernizing our labor-relations system. Workers want a more decentralized and varied system of workplace organization than the one now offered them — a system that admits new institutions as well as extension of current ones. And throughout, they want more cooperative and equal relations with management in making workplace decisions.

The basic message to decision-makers in business, labor, and government is clear: A huge opportunity exists for America to increase the representation and participation of workers at their jobs and thereby to improve the quality of working life. Political leaders will find potential votes for such reforms; unions will find scores of potential members; business will find a better and more loyal workforce. Of course, whether any of these groups take full advantage of this opportunity is their choice. But the right choice for private action and public policy would be to help workers gain the voice and representation in workplace decisions that they so clearly want.

CHAPTER 8

Toward a New Labor Relations System

Let us stipulate, as lawyers do, that the major findings of this book are valid. There is a major gap in America between what workers want by way of democratic say at their workplace and what they have. From one-third to over one-half of private-sector nonunion workers want trade unions to represent them in collective bargaining with employers. Much larger numbers of workers, up to 80 percent, want a workplace organization of their own, stopping short of collective bargaining but with some fair adjudication of disputes, to consult with management regularly about workplace issues. This type of organization does not exist at present.

That so many workers do not have the voice at the workplace that they want bespeaks a remarkable institutional failure in the country's labor laws and labor relations system. No other advanced market democracy has anything like America's level of unfilled demand for workplace representation and participation. The proportion of workers in the United States who cannot obtain the voice they want is higher than in other major English-speaking economies.[1] It is also higher than in the countries of the European Union, where proportionately more workers are unionized; where collective bargaining agreements are extended to nonunion employers; and where labor laws mandate that firms meet and consult with works councils elected by workers at workplaces.

The reason for the huge gap between what workers want and what they have in labor relations in the United States is that the legal core of the U.S. labor relations system, crafted during the Great Depression and immediately after World War II, has not been changed since to meet the changing needs of workers and employers.[2] Indeed, despite all that has happened to the U.S. economy since — America's move from a manufacturing to service economy, the rise of giant multinational firms, world economic integration, the increased proportion of women in the labor force, and industry deregulation — the core law determining worker rights to voice and representation has barely changed. The basic private-sector labor law, the

Labor Management Relations Act (LMRA), has not been amended in sixty years.[3]

This law worked passably at one time. From the Depression through the Korean War, it succeeded in channeling issues of union recognition into a secret ballot election process, overseen by the National Labor Relations Board (NLRB), that both unions and management generally accepted. But it has outlived its usefulness. Rather than helping workers establish voice, the LMRA wraps them and employers in a straitjacket of declining traditional unionism, while discouraging experimentation with alternative modes of worker representation and participation in workplace decisions.

As traditionally interpreted, U.S. labor law has four flaws that make it an impediment for dealing with the labor problems of the twenty-first century. First, it privileges collective bargaining by exclusive union representatives as the focal point of employee representation, to the effective elimination of other forms. Second, it gives management near-veto power over whether workers can achieve such union representation, through their critical role in NLRB-supervised elections on union representation. Third, it forbids management from offering alternative institutions of representation to workers, and does not recognize alternative worker-initiated forms. Fourth, it gives the sole right to regulate and enforce private-sector labor law to the federal government, precluding states or localities from experimenting with alternative labor codes, alternative forms of representation, or modes of enforcing the laws.

The result is an ossified system, limited to a shrinking union core, out of step with current economic practice, and increasingly irrelevant to the bulk of workers and employers.

The disconnect of the labor law from business is apparent in discussions of labor issues with managers of the high tech companies that are the leading edge of the U.S. economy. Human resource managers in the big Silicon Valley firms have only vague knowledge of "labor law." The disputes over LMRA provisions that exercise the AFL-CIO and Washington-based business lobbyists are almost irrelevant to these and many other employers. Leading firms seek labor practices and modes of compensation that will motivate workers to contribute to company goals and attract and retain workers. They want worker voice to the extent that this contributes to these goals. They want to share information with workers, involve them in decisions, and motivate them by linking compensation to performance without engaging in collective bargaining with an elected trade union.

The disconnect of the labor law from workers is apparent in the WRPS.

The survey shows that workers seek cooperative relations with management and want employee organizations to meet and discuss workplace issues with management. Some want unions. More want joint committees, of varying power. The majority of those who want unions and nearly all of those who want workplace committees are unable to have the type of representation or participation that they want. This unmet demand for representation is prima facie evidence that the U.S. labor relations system is broken.

Minor Patch or New Beginning?

Unions and business have sought legal patches to fix the system, but their search for reforms has failed to produce meaningful change.

From the 1970s through the mid-1990s, the AFL-CIO tried to convince Congress to enact "labor law reform," by which the Federation meant legal provisions to restrict the ways management oppose unions; to increase penalties on management for violating the labor law; and to enforce mediation and arbitration of first-contract disputes between a new union and a newly organized employer. None of the proposals succeeded. In 2005, unions again initiated a campaign for labor law reform through the Employer Free Choice Act (EFCA). This would require employers to recognize a union if a majority of workers signed cards authorizing the union to represent them, rather than requiring that the union win majority support in a secret-ballot election. It would also provide access to binding arbitration in disputes over first contracts, impose real penalties for employer violations of the LRMA, and offer injunctive relief for gross employer violations during an election or first-contract campaign.[4] But a Republican Congress and president are certain to block the EFCA. And even if the Democrats controlled Congress and the presidency, it seems unlikely that unions would succeed with this initiative in its present form, since it would fundamentally alter the balance of power between them and employers.[5] Labor's influence on Congress has declined as union density has fallen. Contributions from corporations and the wealthy have become critical to the campaigns of Democrats as well as Republicans, making both highly sensitive to business interests. There are also problems with public support for the EFCA. A majority of the public favors increased penalties against employers who break the law,[6] but a much larger majority, including most union members, favor elections for representatives over card checks.[7]

On the business side, the Republican Congress passed the Teamwork for Employees and Management Act (TEAM) in 1996. This would have relaxed restrictions on employer-sponsored "company unions" and promoted employer-sponsored employee involvement programs. But unions bitterly opposed TEAM, and President Clinton vetoed it. Reintroduced since, it has never become law. Rather than seeking to reform the LMRA, the Bush administration has used its NLRB appointments and other executive powers to chip away at union strength — for instance, by excluding large groups of employees from collective bargaining rights on national security grounds, banning project labor agreement for federally financed construction, restricting LMRA coverage of employees, and imposing new reporting requirements on unions. Given the downward trajectory of unionism, business does not view TEAM as a critical element in its long-term strategy for obtaining the labor relations system it would ideally like.

Thus it seems reasonable to expect that the federal government will not enact either an all union-favoring or an all business-favoring reform of the LMRA in the foreseeable future.

The Union Response: Don't Mourn, Organize!

Following the failure of the Clinton administration to enact pro-union legislation, unions looked inward to reverse their decline. In 1995, the AFL-CIO, in the first contested leadership election in its history, elected (Service Employees International Union) SEIU president John Sweeney to head the federation with a "New Voices" team of other leaders dedicated to convince affiliates to increase their organizing resources to at least 20 percent of their budgets. With total union dues of about $5 billion, this would amount to a huge $1 billion annual organizing fund.

Some unions met this challenge. UNITE, which chiefly organizes textile, apparel, and laundry workers, raised organizing from 20 percent of its budget to 40 percent between 1995 and 2002. SEIU went on a huge campaign to organize workers in hospitals and home health care. The United Automobile Workers invested resources in organizing graduate students around the country. The Communications Workers of America stepped up their organizing budget in the rapidly shifting and deregulated telecommunications industry. Four major unions also chose organizing directors to lead their union: UNITE, Here (which represents hotel and restaurant workers, and which later amalgamated with UNITE to form a single union, HERE-UNITE); SEIU; and the Communications Workers of America. But most unions did not come close to spending the 20 percent of dues money on organizing that the AFL-CIO wanted them to spend. The Teamsters cut their organizing budget. Others, like the Steelworkers, increased their budget but had trouble finding campaigns where large expenditures would pay off.

Still, aggregate union organizing budgets surely rose (though in the absence of a national survey of union organizing activity it is difficult to know by how much). As of early 2005, about 25 of the 58 unions affiliated to the AFL-CIO reported devoting 10–50 percent of their annual budgets to organizing.[8] But this increased effort notwithstanding, private-sector union density fell from 10.4 percent in 1999 to 7.5 percent in 2005 — a 2.9 percentage point, or 28 percent, decline. Whatever the precise magnitude of the increase in organizing, it didn't reverse union decline, though it does appear, at least momentarily, to have stabilized it. In 2005, SEIU, Teamsters, United Food and Commercial Workers, and United Farm Workers left the AFL-CIO, joining with the Carpenters (who had already left the AFL-CIO) and HERE-UNITE and the Laborers (who remained in the AFL-CIO) to form the Change To Win (CTW) coalition. The formation of CTW signals the biggest split in labor's ranks since the 1930s. It is effectively a rival federation, with a collective membership of 5.4 million workers, or nearly half that of the old AFL-CIO. The declared reason for the split was the failure of the AFL-CIO to undertake the radical changes that would increase the ability of unions to organize workers, ranging from increased funding for organizing to the amalgamation of unions into larger entities that would concentrate on particular sectors. The CTW argued that too many unions competing over the same industrial space, or turning themselves into general membership unions without a clear sectoral focus, stymied organizing. Only by forming larger, more focused unions could labor organize at a scale sufficient to reverse its decline.

Spending additional resources to organize workers and increasing the efficiency with which those resources are deployed is almost certainly *necessary* to labor's revival. But without changes in union form, and the meaning of union membership, it is just as certainly *insufficient*. If the sole "product" unions offer to U.S. workers is majority-based collective bargaining, they will neither satisfy worker desire for increased workplace power nor raise union density enough to once again make labor a major force in the labor market.

Exhibit 8.1 gives the statistics behind this argument. The key to gaining workers the voice they seek at the workplace lies in the private sector, which holds 85 percent of the U.S. work force and where just 7.5 percent are in unions. The natural ebb and flow of business means that thousands of workplaces close every year. Since new firms and establishments are born nonunion, maintaining union membership requires unions to organize the same number of workers as they lose through the normal turnover of firms.

Exhibit 8.1. The arithmetic and costs of organizing

Organizing workers via NLRB Elections and campaigns for collective bargaining

Number of workers unions must organize to
maintain density of 7.5%	~ 400,000
increase density by 1 percentage point	~1,400,000

Cost of maintaining density
@$1,000 per member	$400 million
@$2,250 per member	$0.9 billion
@$3,500 per member	$1.4 billion

Cost of increasing density by 1 percentage point
@$1,000 per member	$1.40 billion
@$2,250 per member	$3.20 billion
@$3,500 per member	$4.50 billion

Recruiting workers via canvassing by Working America

Cost of 1 million additional members	@6.00 per member	$6 million
Cost of 10 million additional members	@6.00 per member	$60 million

Source: Organizing workers via NLRB Elections, estimated as described in text, recruiting workers via canvassing estimate of $6.00 provided by Working America.

When employment grows, to maintain density unions must organize the same proportion of the increase in employment that they hold of existing workers. With about 105 million wage and salary workers in the private sector in 2005, the problem of organizing enough members to maintain the union share presents a daunting challenge. To maintain the 7.5 percent share unions had in 2005, they would need to organize about 400,000 new members annually.[9] To increase that share by one percentage point, they would need to organize still another one million plus new members.

How close do unions come to these numbers? NLRB election statistics show that unions win less than 100,000 new workers annually, of whom at most two-thirds eventually end up with collective bargaining contracts. These NLRB figures on "traditional" election organizing miss organizing outside that process, but they are the only official record of organizing effort and results, and probably provide a reasonable order of magnitude estimate of both.[10] The AFL-CIO's *Work in Progress* gives a larger number by including new affiliations of independent unions with the AFL-CIO, new unionization of public sector workers, and new unionization of workers in areas like health care, where government funds much of the services.[11] As a result, of the 230,000 new members reported in 2002, for example, only 67,000 came from private industries exclusive of health care. In any case, the numbers of newly organized workers reported in *Work in Progress* have fallen far short of the number needed to stabilize density in all but one year. The exception was 2001, when *Work in Progress* reported 446,000 new members. But the jump in 2001 was largely due to the affiliation of existing non-AFL-CIO unions — the California State Employees Association (175,000) and the United American Nurses (100,000) to the Federation — not to organization of previously nonunion workers.[12]

To fund an organizing campaign that might reverse the downward trend in density would take huge resources in organizing effort and costs. Estimates of the cost of organizing new members vary widely. Some union activists use $1,000 per new member as a rule of thumb for organizing. But this figure seems low. Updating estimates from the one scientific study of the cost of organizing, which was conducted in the 1980s, we estimate that the marginal cost of adding a member in 2005 to range between $1,000 and $3,500, which averages to $2,250.[13] But the failure of the increased union organizing effort in the late 1990s/early 2000s to enroll many new members suggests that the average cost is higher than $2,250. If unions devoted 10 percent of their $5 billion dollar revenues to organizing and if two-thirds of this went to organizing private-sector workers, they would have spent about $335 million on organizing the private sector. But they gained less than 100,000 workers per year. This implies that the cost of obtaining a new member is on the order of $3,500.

All of these estimates — from the $1,000 to the $3,500 figure — imply that it would take massive funds for unions to raise union density, assuming again that the funds went to "traditional" organizing as defined above. To add 400,000 members annually at $2,250 per member would require unions to spend $0.9 billion — 18 percent of total annual union dues. Adding the additional 1,000,000 members necessary to raise union density by one percentage point would take an additional $2.3 billion of dues money. With this estimated cost of organizing, it would take $3.2 billion to raise union density from 7.5 percent to 8.5 percent — 64 percent of the dues of unions! No union in America has raised the organizing share of its budget near that amount.

But even these figures may underestimate the expense of organizing members through the collective bargaining channel. First, the cost of organizing is likely to rise as unions devote more resources to organizing. With huge organizing budgets, unions would quickly exhaust easier targets and would then increasingly devote their organizing resources to more difficult ones — for example, Wal-Mart or giant insurance, banking, or other financial services firms — where the cost of organizing would be considerably higher. Second, more aggressive organizing campaigns would likely stimulate management to increase anti-union activities. The result would be an arms race in organizing resources that unions are unlikely to win. Of course, it is *possible* that a huge expenditure of union resources on organizing a particular firm, sector, or region would pay off in terms of large gains in members. The demonstration effect of such success might convince other workers to seek unionization and thus reduce the costs of new organizing.

But it is also possible that huge expenditures would produce only a modest uptick in membership. Absent more scientific evidence in the form of a "controlled experiment," where unions increased spending on a particular employer, sector, or area and gained or failed to gain large numbers of members compared to a control area where they did not increase spending massively, there is great uncertainty about whether huge increases of spending on organizing would or not pay off in the immediate future.[14] What is certain is that as union membership falls, the expense to existing union members of organizing new workers rises, since the cost has to be shared among fewer members. A 10 percent drop in membership makes it 10 percent more costly to members to fund an organizing campaign of any given size. With the union share of the workforce falling, this produces a downward spiral in the organizing process: fewer members ⇒ increased cost of organizing per member ⇒ less resources spent on organizing ⇒ less organizing success ⇒ fewer members. The result is that a declining union movement increasingly finds it difficult to raise the resources needed for the sort of mass organizing that might bring success.

In sum, the economics of organizing shows that the prospect of growing union membership by spending massively on traditional member organizing, albeit with greater scale and focus, proceeds more on a "a wing and a prayer" than on a well-justified strategic plan. There is little hard evidence that it will succeed, and many reasons to doubt that it can be sustained.[15]

Prepare the Casket . . . or a New Spurt?

Analyses like ours have led most scholars who study unions to predict that private-sector unionism is heading to the grave and have turned meetings of experts on unionism into wakes. Sound the death knell. Prepare the casket. Out of respect and decency, find some unionized grave diggers to dig the hole and order the gravestone from some unionized stone masonry firm. "Alas, poor ~~Yorick~~ unionist, I knew him."[16]

And yet . . . projections of the death of unions have gone awry in the past. In 1933, just before the Depression-era growth of unionism, the president of the American Economic Association and labor expert, George Barnett, declared that unions had no future. Most, if not all, experts accepted this assessment. But Barnett and the other experts were wrong, as unions experienced the largest gain in membership in the late 1930s and early 1940s. A generation later, near the height of private-sector U.S. unionism in the 1950s, the new president of the merged AFL-CIO, George Meany, predicted that organizing public-sector workers was impossible. He too was wrong, as the explosion in public-sector organizing in the next decade showed.

The reason analysts have failed to predict union growth is that unions grow in sudden sharp "spurts" in periods of social crisis.[17] Union density grew in nearly all advanced countries during World War I when governments needed labor cooperation to prosecute the war. Density grew in advanced countries in the Great Depression because workers lost faith in business leadership and the market system. Density grew in World War II in advanced countries as part of national survival and solidarity. During the 1970s, density grew in most EU countries and in the U.S. public sector. Projections and analyses based on extrapolation of the recent past miss these spurts.

The configurations of social and economic factors associated with past union spurts do not produce any easy generalization about what could bring about any future spurt. Union growth during World Wars I and II occurred during a tight wartime labor market that shifted the balance of power from business to workers and that induced governments to help unions in order to avoid disruption in wartime production. Union growth during the Depression reflected a different dynamic: loss of faith in the business leadership and economic desperation. The 1970s oil shock crisis led to union growth in Western Europe, as workers sought protection against inflation through collective bargaining, but not in the United States, where the decline in private-sector unionism continued unabated and dominated an increase in public-sector organization. Perhaps U.S. division over the Vietnam War, which pitted many natural supporters of unionism against the AFL-CIO's support of the war, diverted activists from organizing in response to the oil price-induced inflation.

Difficult to predict though union growth spurts are, spurts have identifiable characteristics that provide some guide to the features of any future spurt. Spurts in the United States have been associated with *changes in union form* that attract previously nonorganizable groups of workers or with *institutional or legal changes* that greatly weaken employer opposition. In the 1880s, the new form was the geographic lodges associated with the Knights of Labor. In the Depression, the new form was the industrial union, which the CIO pushed and which the AFL eventually adopted as well. In the World War I and World War II periods, the new institutional form/legal change was the formation of war labor boards and compulsory arbitration to deal with disputes. The public-sector spurt transformed existing associations, such as the National Education Association, from nonunion groups into collective bargaining organizations. The associated legal change was the enactment of public-sector collective bargaining laws that forced public-sector employers to bargain collectively.

The evidence in the WRPS and in the ensuing surveys summarized in the Introduction suggest the form that any new union organization would have to take to meet worker desires for representation and participation and create a new spurt in membership. It also suggests the form that any nonunion firm-sponsored organization might take to help fill the representation and participation gap. In both cases, the key is that new organizations go beyond the *majority union, exclusive representation, collective bargaining model* to which the LMRA has de facto reduced the US labor relations system.[18]

Toward a New Union Form: Open-Source Unionism

Open-source unionism is the term we use to describe the new union form.[19] We have borrowed the term from software development, where "open source" refers to software created and improved by a diverse community of programmers working with source code available to all, rather than a single vendor or proprietary code. In the same way, open-source unions would be open to any employee who wanted to join with others in improving work conditions and opportunity, and would operate through networks of members rather than traditional union bureaucracies. Instead of limiting unionization to those workers who could get past the 50+ percent threshold to majority status and gain a collective bargaining contract, the open-source union would welcome any and all workers who wanted to be members, including those who had little chance of achieving majority-status unionism or collective contracts under the present system. These new members would invariably have to pay lower dues than members covered by collective bargaining but would otherwise be normal union members.

How would an open-source union support its members? It could help them navigate the job market by providing information about how their workplace compared to others, how workers at other workplaces had responded to like challenges and problems, and about their legal rights as employees. It could also give members advice about their own careers — how to get access to training and skills credentialing, how to handle their own retirement savings, how to protect their existing pension. Most of these information services, moreover, could be provided at very low cost over the Internet.

But open-source unions would go beyond cyberspace to provide their members with in-person support for the resolution of workplace problems, for example, by offering the services of an experienced lawyer or negotiator or advice from a worker in another firm knowledgeable about the problem. It would also bring together members in a local community to talk about, and act on, common labor market problems. In any given city or metropolitan areas, there are tens or hundreds of thousands of nonunionized workers in need of help to improve conditions at their workplace or in their careers or in their community. Open-source unionism would try to unite them in diverse ways beyond collective bargaining.

Historically, unions have eschewed recruiting members outside the bargaining relationship because the expense of providing services and communicating with members would far exceed the dues they could charge these workers. That was a reasonable assessment of the labor market in your mom or dad's time, but not today. The Internet has changed this cost calculus by making it feasible to service more varied and dispersed members at low cost, and thus at low dues charges. At firm-based locals, the union could inexpensively gather information about the firm from members as well as from business and economic news services. At locals in a given occupation or industry, the union could similarly inexpensively gather information about wage and employment developments in the specified job markets.

As experience in recent political campaigns has shown, the Internet is an inexpensive tool for an organization to coordinate offline as well as online activity, for assembling people as well as information and money. With enough activist members, meetings can be self-organizing through the Internet. The open-source union can decide on the logistics of particular meetings, post their location, and rely on interested members to select and sign up depending on their interests and schedule. And since the open-source union would not rely on its contractual power in particular workplaces, it would naturally engage in action, oriented toward broad labor market issues and public policy more than traditional unions. The example here is the political activity public-sector unions undertook when they were governed by meet-and-confer legislation and did not yet collectively bargain with their employers. In this way, labor would begin to bridge its role in employer-specific negotiations and servicing and its national program for improving labor market outcomes for all workers.

In short, open-source unions would expand the labor movement by offering membership and support to the millions of workers that the WRPS and ensuing surveys have shown want unions to represent them but who are unlikely to gain traditional collective bargaining contracts. Because membership in the new form would be based on workers, not some particular union-employer contract, the open source form would more easily keep its members as they changed employers over their working lifetimes. Most important, under an open source approach to membership the individual worker and union would decide who was "organized" and who was not. Employers would no longer have effective control of union membership through their power to block majority certification or by failing to reach contractual agreement. An open-source union with 10 percent, 20 percent, or 30 percent of the workforce in a given workplace would be able to act on behalf of its members and show the value of collective organization, without collective bargaining to make that demonstration.

How would an open-source union operate in disputes with management? It would use tactics that differ from those associated with traditional labor-management disputes, such as strikes. By providing accurate information about workplace problems to workers, management, and the general public, the open-source union could influence worker and management decisions and shape public discourse about workplace issues. Information may not be sufficient to improve worker well-being but it is arguably necessary.

Consider this example. In 1998, a group of young law firm associates wanted to pressure law firms to increase their pay. They set up the web site www.greedyassociates.com, which provided detailed information to potential recruits about salaries and working conditions at firms. Fearful that complaints on the site could adversely affect recruitment, the law firms quickly improved conditions, raising pay massively in some cities to remedy one of the problems — differential rates of pay between associates working in Silicon Valley and those working in other locales. In the space of one year, the law associates won larger gains in pay than almost any union has won through any single collective bargaining contract.[20]

The example of law associates might seem irrelevant to workers without such professional training, but it is not. In almost every sector of the economy, workers have skills that are important to employers. There is also wide variation across employers in their responsiveness to worker desires about workplace conditions. Collecting this information and putting it into the hands of workers can be a powerful tool for improvement. Since job seekers often use the Internet to find out about a prospective employer, open-source unions could provide the venue for current workers to inform potential new employees about working conditions and problems at the workplace, and about the way that other firms have resolved those problems better than they. This could harm the laggard firm's recruitment, pressuring it to bring its practices more in line with its better rivals.

More generally, open-source unionism could establish a link between workers in nonunionized parts of industry with those in unionized ones, a link that barely exists at present. By using information from relatively small groups of workers but covering many firms, open-source unionism could organize one of labor's key potential strengths in the economy relative to business, viz. its greater reach. Coordination among workers at different points in a firm's value chain of suppliers would help leverage its distant parts. Coordination among people working for different employers in a community would help in their political action in the community. There is strength in weak ties, if they are organized. Open-source unionism would show that strength.

In short, open-source unionism would operate differently from the majority-status collective bargaining unions that the LMRA has institutionalized as the sole union form in the United States. Exhibit 8.2 summarizes some of the key differences that we envisage between the proposed new form and the current union forms.

Exhibit 8.2. Open-source unionism versus traditional unionism

	"Traditional" collective bargaining-centered-majority unionism	Open-source unionism
Primary business	Collective bargaining	Individual representation and advice; political mobilization, collective bargaining where possible
Mode of gaining members	50%+1 vote in NLRB election at particular sites	Members everywhere in the economy
Primary organizational linkages	Locals integrated to national unions, organized on loosely industrial lines; weak regional bodies	"High tech" cyberspace, coupled with "high touch" geographic coordination and political action
Delivery of services	Workplaces	Workplaces, Web, communities
Who/what delivers	Services delivered by business agents, stewards	Services delivered by in-plant activists, web, local area groups
Content of services	Outcomes depend on collective bargain with employer; wages, hours, working conditions, insurance of various kinds	Outcomes depend on worker interest and local political power and workplace strength; wages, hours, working conditions, insurance of various kinds, advice and counseling about labor market
Method of dispute resolution and/or tactics	Arbitration, strikes, slowdowns and job resistance, public campaigns, pension money pressure	Cyber picketing, direct action, slowdowns and job resistance, public campaigns, pension money pressure, "members only" arbitration
Type of member	One, in majority settings, generally inactive	Potentially many, with graduated power and dues proportionate to commitment, and services offered
Duration of membership	As long as the CBA holds	As long as possible
Union democracy	Qualified, with unions heavily bureaucratic, "top down," and unresponsive	Stronger, with members able to force greater accountability by leaders, and in better communication with each other; more decentralized political governance

Historical Precedents and Legal Standing

Defining union membership outside a majority collective bargaining relation has historical precedents. In the 1880s, the Knights of Labor established "mixed lodges" that included workers from many occupations and firms in the same geographic area. This form underlies the 1880s spurt in unionization. The first constitution of the AFL, adopted at its founding in 1886, stated that membership was open to any "seven wage workers of good character and favorable to Trade Unions, and not members of any body affiliated with this Federation." Many groups received direct affiliation with the national federation, migrating later to an international union. This is part of the tradition that open-source unionism would bring back.[21]

Direct affiliation and membership in "minority" or "members only" unions was also important in the 1930s, when workers who did not fit well into established forms sought to join unions. In the early organizing of the mineworkers and steelworkers, such nonmajority unions provided a union presence in the workplace well before an employer recognized a collective-bargaining unit. Most public-sector unions in the 1960s and 1970s developed from minority associations that did not have the legal right to bargain collectively. Teachers unions, for example, first grew through agreements negotiated only with members of nonmajority associations. Over one million employees in the federal government have joined unions even though the federal government does not bargain over wages and working conditions. In 2005, union density among federal workers was over three times higher than among private-sector workers (29.9 versus 7.5 percent).

Many union and business leaders believe that organized workers without a workplace majority union exist in a sort of legal black hole devoid of the protections that U.S. labor laws give to concerted activity. Such is not the case. All the basic rights and protections of the LMRA apply to workers acting together in nonmajority situations: protection from discrimination against union activity, the right to strike without being discharged, the right to present demands and request negotiations with management, the right to designate union stewards, and the right to bargain and make a collective agreement for members, among others.[22]

Traditionalists in the union movement fear that the new workers brought in through open-source unionism will not look like or have the same concerns as many "traditional" members. They would be right. How could new members from throughout the American economy and society and drawn together by different means be replicas of current members? All spurts in organizing have been preceded by fears that the new members will be different from the old and by confusion as to the right form of unions — craft versus industrial, general versus narrow jurisdictions, public sector associations versus "real unions." What we know from this history is that forms must adjust to workers and the broader economy, and that workers, unions, and firms must experiment to develop the form that fits the job market.

Pie in the Sky . . . or Real?

Does an open-source union sound like "pie in the sky"? If we had offered this vision of a new union form in the first edition of this book, the chair of the Commission on the Future of Labor/Management Relations, John Dunlop, would have called for the white coats to cart us away. Most readers would have dismissed such a view as ivory-tower nonsense. Labor relations is a highly practical world, which disdains blue sky speculations.

But the pie is real. The sky is blue.

From the mid-1990s through the mid-2000s, innovative unions and other worker-based organizations have used modern technology and enlarged the meaning of membership along the lines of the open source form.[23] The AFL-CIO's new initiatives prove that nonunion workers will flock to a new union form and that the open source form can help workers outside the collective bargaining box.

Company, Occupation, and Area Innovations

Exhibit 8.3 summarizes the most important open source innovations designed to help workers in particular firms, occupations, and areas.

The Communication Workers of America (CWA) local union at IBM, www.alliance@ibm.org, is the archetype open-source union in a large firm. The CWA has a small number of voting members at IBM, most of whom joined online; a larger number of subscribers to e-mail messages; and a still larger number of IBM visitors to its Web site, which provides company specific information and where employees can discuss job-related issues. IBM employees developed the CWA after IBM's arbitrary change in pension benefits in 2000 greatly harmed some employees.[24] The publicity generated by the employees forced the company to modify its reduction in pensions.

The CWA also supports other open source initiatives. One is WashTech (www.washtech.org/wt), a virtual union to represent the interests of Silicon Valley and related high tech industry workers. This organization raised the issue of overtime pay for contract employees at Microsoft and other

Exhibit 8.3. Open-source union experiments: Company, occupation, area

Communications Workers

IBM Union (www.allianceatibm.org) is a company-based Internet union for IBM employees. It is a regular CWA local.

WashTech Union (www.washtech.org/at) an occupation/area union for high tech workers at Microsoft and other firms in the Northwest.

TechsUnite (www.techsunite.org) with organizing groups in 7 different geographic areas. Oregon IT workers set up their own organization, www.ortech.org, with $24/year dues payable through the CWA Local 7901 Associate Member program.

United Automobile Workers

National Writers Union (NWU, www.nwu.org) provides information and generic assistance via the Web to some 7,000 freelance writers. Describes website as the "cyberspace equivalent of the union hall where members (and prospective members) can find the information they need and conduct union business

International Association of Machinists

CyberLodge: An Open Source Union Project (www.cyberlodge.org). Organized over the Web: a guild-like structure where workers retain traditional employee-employer relationship while enjoying benefits normally reserved for employees with collective bargaining agreements: "the most important benefit is power—the ability to influence the movers and shakers who affect our working lives."

United SteelWorkers

(www.uswa.org/am)—associate membership—"open to anyone regardless of where they work . . . intended to revolutionize the American union movement and alter how the American people think about unions and belonging to them."

high tech firms that hire many software engineers as contractors. However, much of the discontent that developed among Microsoft workers when the firm reduced benefits and increased bureaucratic controls in the 2000s surfaced outside WashTech, in the form of blogs and discussion groups critical of the firm's policies on other Web sites.[25] Outside of Silicon Valley, the Communication Workers has developed a five-city organizing campaign to connect IT workers (www.techsunite.org) and set up Workers at GE, www.geworkersunited.org), for workers not covered by collective bargaining at General Electric.

Other unions also have begun Internet-based organizations. The National Writers Union, an affiliate of the United Automobile Workers, organizes freelance writers around the country (www.nwu.org). It describes its Web site as its union hall. The Machinists established Cyberlodge (www.cyberlodge.org,) an Internet-based union for IT workers. The IAM describes the organization as having a guild-like structure where workers retain their traditional employee-employer relationship while enjoying benefits normally reserved for employees with collective bargaining agreements. The Steelworkers also initiated a "new form of individual membership — open to anyone regardless of employment" that gave some services at modest dues, but the Steelworkers have not yet developed a separate Web site for this group of workers, although it has online enrollment.

Nonunion groups have set up worker centers to help temporary workers, particularly immigrants, with their workplace problems (www.fair jobs.org/fairjobs/reports/wcs_intro.php). The centers provide information and assistance and make use of the Internet to inform workers about issues but do not themselves negotiate collective contracts.

In 2005, with the support of unions and community groups seeking to improve the way Wal-Mart treats its workers, employees and former employees at Wal-Mart formed an association to represent them. The organizer described it as "not the traditional unit we have now in terms of collective bargaining or having an election. This is about what sort of problems Wal-Mart employees are having at work and what they can do to make their lives better at work."[26] Since Wal-Mart has employees around the country, the next natural step will be to connect them through the Internet.

Some, perhaps most, of these innovations will fail. But some will succeed, giving workers independent voice at their firm outside the traditional collective bargaining model.

National Initiatives

The AFL-CIO is a central federation, whose members are national unions, not workers. The only collective bargaining it does is as management when it bargains with its staff union. A large share of AFL-CIO resources and effort are centered on Washington politics, rather than in support of the "regional" bodies affiliated to the AFL-CIO: state AFL-CIO federations and central labor councils largely based in cities. Despite this, the Federation has developed three initiatives that are the cutting edge toward the new union form (Exhibit 8.4).

The first is the Working Families Network (WFN) (www.union voice.org), a massive e-mail list of union members and activists. To put together the list, the Federation had to convince member unions that they would not be surrendering their power as gateways to members of the cen-

Exhibit 8.4. Toward a general open-source form

Working Families Network (www.unionvoice.org)
>   E-mail list of 2+ million union members and activists. Used to organize Internet campaigns on labor issues.

Supporting Enron and WorldCom workers
>   The AFL-CIO lawyers gain severance package for laid off nonunion workers in bankruptcy court. Federation uses Working Families Network in Internet campaign to pressure the court. Campaign succeeds.

Working America (www.workingamerica.org)
>   Organizers recruit members in ten cities in five states into "community affiliate." Asks for $5 in voluntary dues. Enrolls one million members by Oct 2005. Provides information over web, informs members about broad labor issues

SEIU Purple Ocean (www.purpleocean.org)
>   Web site for discussion of labor issues—from outsourcing and offshoring to health care and pensions—focused on campaigns to improve worker well-being.

tral federation. The AFL-CIO did this by giving individual unions control over usage of their own e-mail list. If a union disagreed with a WFN campaign or feared that WFN messages would create online campaign fatigue for its members, the union could simply refuse to allow the AFL-CIO to e-mail its members. By 2004, the AFL-CIO had over 28 participating national unions, 84 geographically defined State Federations and City Labor Councils, and over 400 local unions and other union organizations involved with its Working Family Network, with more than 600 local administrators taking responsibility for particular lists. The network included over 2 million union "eActivists."

This large number gives the AFL-CIO the option of e-mailing small proportions of the list while still engaging large numbers of persons in particular disputes, and of localizing its appeals. During the 2003 Safeway strike in California, the AFL-CIO raised money for the Safeway grocery workers via its main activist list. To pressure management, the AFL-CIO e-mailed persons in the District of Columbia and asked them to join teams that would confront their local Safeway stores, even though those stores were not on strike. Responders were organized by their address to create local teams, and each person on the team then got the e-mail address and phone number of all the other people on their team (their neighbors), plus the local store information.

The second AFL-CIO initiative shows how unions can marshal support from a broad community to represent and win economic benefits for nonunion workers. This is the Federation's successful campaign to gain severance pay for Enron's and WorldCom's nonunion workers following the collapse of those companies due to executive malfeasance. The Enron scandal galvanized the AFL-CIO in 2002 to spend money and staff resources on behalf of Enron workers in the courts and in direct aid. Supported by the Federation, the Harris County (Houston, Texas, the headquarters of Enron) central labor council provided direct support to former Enron employees. The AFL-CIO lawyers fought for a larger severance package for the workers, while the Federation organized a public campaign to support this action and pressured other companies to remove members from the Enron board from their boards. The Federation lobbied Congress to change its laws to protect employees with 401K moneys.

Since no AFL-CIO union had a collective bargaining contract for more than a few laid-off workers, the union campaign was based on providing information, galvanizing community action, and giving legal support. The Federation provided an informative Web site on the Enron situation.[27] It called on its membership countrywide to support the Enron workers by leafleting creditor banks in cities throughout the country. Using the Working Families Network, it encouraged activists to send some 55,000 faxes and phone calls to creditor committees and Enron executives. Its legal staff submitted petitions to the SEC to tighten its rules and investigate diverse aspects of the Enron disaster. In June 2002, former Enron employees and their court-appointed Employee Committee reached an agreement with the firm that increased the amount of severance pay going to the workers by $32 million. In addition, the AFL-CIO pressured other companies to remove from their board directors who served on the Enron board. The Federation parlayed this success into pressures that forced WorldCom to pay its workers their full severance pay and other benefits, which the firm would have otherwise avoided.

But, having done all this for the nonunion workers, the AFL-CIO did not enlist any of the beneficiaries of its campaign as members. It had no place for workers outside of majority-status collective bargaining unions.

The third AFL-CIO initiative described in Exhibit 8.4 remedies this weakness. In 2003, the Federation developed Working America (www.workingamerica.org), a membership-based organization that it describes as a community affiliate to enroll nonunion workers and others favorable to worker interests into a new noncollective bargaining organization. Working America set up offices in ten cities in five states in the summer of 2004 and had 400 canvassers knocking on doors daily asking residents to join the group.[28] It targeted neighborhoods with many union members, on the notion that residents there would have pro-union attitudes. Even so, the Federation was stunned at the rate at which persons joined the organization: two-thirds of those canvassed signed up at a cost of recruiting of about $6.00 per member. This contrasts with the thousands of dollars to organize workers for collective bargaining (see Exhibit 8.1 again). In addition, the Federation reports that the recruits included many persons whose political and social orientation differs from that of most persons in the union movement: one-third were born-again Christians, 70 percent were conservatives or moderates in politics; and 32 percent supported the National Rifle Association. One-quarter of the members gave their e-mail addresses, which allows Working America to communicate with them weekly.

When the Bush administration changed the administrative rules governing overtime in August 2004, Working America added a page "Is Your Overtime Pay at Risk?" to its Web site, with a FAQ about the new regulations. The site hosted a young lawyer who answered questions about the new ruling, an indication of possible future services that workers could not obtain elsewhere. As a result of this, Working America recruited over 2,000 members per week via the Internet — a conversion rate of 7 percent of visitors to the site, about as high as any site can do. In October 2005, Working America announced that it had reached the one million mark on members and planned to reach two million over the next year.

The success of Working America proves the fundamental finding of the WRPS that there is a vast untapped market for voice among workers. Some critics of the first edition of *What Workers Want* rejected our analysis on the grounds that workers answer survey questions loosely, without giving them the serious deliberation that they would in an actual vote on unionization.[29] It is one thing to say to a telephone interviewer that you want greater say at your workplace through a union and another matter entirely to vote union in an organizing campaign after management has made clear its strong opposition. From this perspective, Working America put to a test the attitudes reported in this book. It gave workers an opportunity to join a union affiliate absent employer pressure. And, consistent with the survey results, workers signed up in huge numbers, even though the new organization offered uncertain benefits and had just begun to scratch the surface of the open source form. Given what Working America provides, the response to the new organization shows not only that workers want voice *at* work, they also want voice *about* work.

At this writing, Working America is grappling with how to respond to this great demand. When the AFL-CIO set up the organization, it viewed Working America largely as a way to reach out and influence nonunion workers in the 2004 election. It targeted recruitment at states likely to be pivotal in the election and devoted follow-up effort to influencing the votes of members, with some success. Conservatives have attacked the organization for electioneering as "part of an overall campaign to recruit more supporters for Big Labor's political agenda."[30] Some on the left have attacked the organization for making it too easy to join, for being controlled by AFL-CIO officials, and for not seeking collective bargaining.[31]

Will Working America become a new form of union organization or will it turn into a network for delivering political messages to members? Having successfully taken the first step toward recruiting workers outside of collective bargaining, the pressure will be for Working America to take the next step . . . and the next . . . toward the new open source form. If it succeeds in becoming an organization whose primary activity is to assist members in navigating the labor market and dealing with problems at work rather than one whose primary activity is to influence them in elections, it will change the face of U.S. unionism. If it doesn't do this, there is a reasonable chance that some other organization will fill this niche.

Indeed, as an indication of the growing attractiveness of the open source form in the summer of 2004 SEIU President Andy Stern called for the members to authorize the union to create Purple Ocean[32], which he called the worlds first open source union (www.purpleocean.org), "with a goal of uniting one million more people who want to join our campaigns for justice."[33] Since SEIU is one of the most successful and innovative unions in the United States and is the lead organization in the Change to Win rival labor center to the AFL-CIO, its decision to develop an open source form could have immense spillover effects on the entire U.S. labor movement.[34]

Workplace Committees versus "Company Unions"

The LMRA makes it illegal for firms to set up "company unions" — employer-sponsored organizations that engage in bogus collective bargaining with the firm (Section 8(a) 2 of the Act). In the Depression Era, many firms formed bogus unions to subvert union organizing efforts. The law ended this practice and forced firms to close down the vast bulk of company unions. But U.S. law goes further than outlawing collective bargaining between a firm-sponsored union and a firm. It makes *any* firm-initiated worker organization illegal, including noncollective bargaining organizations. This prevents firms from establishing committees of workers to discuss labor conditions, such as the elected workers councils that are a main pillar of the European Union's labor relations system.

The law says that a firm can set up "employee involvement" committees to improve productivity and profits but that these cannot discuss wages or conditions of work. Since firms recognize that workers are more likely to cooperate with the firm if they can see some gains to themselves, however, it is inevitable that such illegal discussions will occur. According to the WRPS, 28 percent of employee involvement committees consider the effects of changes at the workplace on worker well-being as well as on productivity and profits. By talking about matters that might benefit workers, these firms are breaking the law.

The U.S. policy of forbidding firms from establishing committees of workers to discuss workplace problems outside of collective bargaining is an aberration on the world labor scene. As noted, the EU has gone in the opposite direction. It requires firms to set up elected works councils for discussion of workplace issues, and gives workers the legal right to insist that their firm set up such committees if it does not do so of its own accord. Since most workers in EU countries are covered by collective bargaining agreements negotiated by unions directly or through the mandatory extension of agreements to all workers in a particular sector, most analysts have seen this "second channel" of worker voice as dependent on some form of national wage setting which removes conflict over wages and benefits from the local workplace. But advanced English-speaking countries outside the US — Canada, Australia, New Zealand, Ireland, and the United Kingdom — all of whom save for Ireland rely on decentralized wagesetting with many workers and employers not covered by collective bargaining, allow or encourage workplace-based nonunion channels of employee representation. As compared to these English-speaking economies, and those of the EU, the United States is unique in forcing workers and firms into the dichotomous choice of collective bargaining or no meaningful employee voice and representation at all.

Because Canada and the United States share much in common, the Canadian experience is particularly relevant to the United States. Canada developed its major labor law several years after the United States enacted the NLRA. Like the United States, Canada outlawed company unions that engaged in bogus collective bargaining. But Canada differentiated between unions and nonunion worker organizations, including those that a firm might initiate to facilitate discussion of workplace issues between management and labor. These nonunion organizations do not enjoy the same rights and protections as unions. Nor does their existence bar a union from organizing the workplace where they are present. Approximately 10 percent of Canadian workers are covered by nonunion voice arrangements. Canadian unions have little problem with these organizations. Canada has higher union density and less unfilled demand for unions than the United States.[35]

The other English-speaking countries also offer workers a wider range of modes of employee representation than the United States. New Zealand and Australia's historically centralized wage-setting systems oriented unions away from local bargaining, which encouraged firms to set up nonunion channels of representation. The United Kingdom has staff associations and joint committees and has adopted the EU works councils. Indeed, the British unions, which had initially opposed works councils as substitutes for unions, eventually decided that having a legally mandated mode of representation outside of collective bargaining would benefit workers and create new organizing opportunities for them.

How might the United States reform its labor system to enhance the range of choices that firms offer to workers?

One possible change would be to follow the Canadian example and remove the restrictions on company-initiated committees or groups that do not engage in collective bargaining. A more radical change would be to follow the European Union example and to give workers who want some elected body to meet with their employers the right to insist that the firm set up joint employee-employer committees to deal with workplace problems.[36] Either of these changes would reduce the representation/participation gap in the United States. They would give many of the workers who want something less than collective bargaining the type of consultative say at the company level that they want.

Opening the U.S. system to alternative forms of worker representation would require legal clarification of the rights of workers and of the rights and responsibilities of different sorts of worker associations. In Canada and the EU, the rights of unions and of nonunion consultative bodies are specified by law. This would presumably be necessary in the United States as well. In addition, given the United States' problem with unfair labor practices that make it hard for workers to attain union representation, the opening of the market in worker representation would also allow the country to improve enforcement of worker rights within that market.[37]

Devolving Labor Law

The federal government regulates private-sector labor relations through the NLRA and its successor legislation. State governments regulate state- and local-government labor relations. Unions and labor lawyers favorable to the purposes of the LMRA have traditionally preferred national labor legislation and NLRB administrative decision-making to state labor legislation and court interpretation of the LMRA. Given the history of judicial rulings in the United States unfavorable to unions, it is natural that proponents of collective bargaining would prefer power to reside with a dedicated national agency than with nonspecialized state or federal courts.

States' rights and federalism are usually associated with conservative political thinking, but the success of unions in the U.S. public sector and of unions in Canada, where provinces have the dominant role in labor law, suggests that unions would do better if states had greater leeway to adopt laws of their own choosing. Absent federal preemption, states that do not look favorably on unions might pass laws making union organizing harder, but states that look favorably on unions would provide stronger protection for workers seeking to unionize. The outcome would be wide diversity among states in laws regulating private-sector unionization, as currently exists in the public sector. Since union membership is slight in the states likely to enact legislation unfavorable to unions, unions would have little to lose in those areas, whereas they could gain considerable membership from favorable legislation in "pro-union" states. The competition between areas with more favorable union regulations and those with less favorable regulations would more likely benefit than harm worker desires for collective voice and unionization.

To free states to try different forms of regulating labor practices, it would be necessary to change the LMRA. This is because since the Supreme Court decision in *Garmon* (1959) courts have held that states cannot regulate activity that the LMRA protects or prohibits. The Warren Supreme Court ruled that the NLRB had exclusive jurisdiction over conduct regulated by the LRMA. In the early 1980s, Wisconsin tested this interpretation of the law. The state directed its Department of Industry, Labor, and Human Relations to list firms that violated the LMRA over a five-year period and to bar those firms from state procurement. In 1986, the Supreme Court unanimously ruled that by prohibiting state purchases from repeat labor-law violators, the state was acting as a regulator rather than as a purchaser and held that the LMRA preempted the Wisconsin statute. In 2000, California tried to get around this rule by enacting a law that prohibited employers from using funds received by the state to oppose union organizing.[38] The emphasis was on the state's rights as a purchaser rather than as an entity seeking to enforce the LMRA. In 2002, New York enacted similar legislation; and in 2003, the Hawaii AFL-CIO Federation proposed a similar statute for Hawaii. Employers challenged the California law on the grounds that it limited the legal rights of employers under the LMRA to speak against unionization. In 2002, the U.S. District Court for California decided in the employers' favor, interpreting employer free speech to include the right to use state contract moneys to fight unionization, even when state legislatures explicitly passed laws that said they do not want taxpayer money spent in that way.

Higher courts may find the reasoning behind the district court decision less convincing.[39] Much of the impetus for federal preemption came from liberal Supreme Court justices, influenced by pro-labor legal scholars such as Archibald Cox who argued for federal preemption although there is no explicit Congressional statement in this regard.[40] In employment law, which covers individual workers rather than groups, states have their own regulations and do much of the enforcement, though the Congress has passed strong antidiscrimination legislation. The 1993 unanimous decision by the Rehnquist Supreme Court that upheld the right of the state government to exclude nonunion contractors in the Boston Harbor construction case raises the possibility that the Court would favor more states rights and less federal preemption in the California case as well.[41] But *Boston Harbor* concerned the state's proprietary interest in avoiding labor unrest, whereas in the California case, the issue is how state contractors use the money awarded to them. The restriction on union busters promotes a state regulatory purpose, at odds with interpretation of the national one. Rather than relying on a change in court interpretation of the law, what is needed to free states to experiment in the labor area, as well as in others, is a national debate about the degree of federalism the country wants in this area and Congressional action to create that space for states to operate.[42]

Conclusion

The U.S. labor relations system is broken. It does not give workers what they want in representation and participation in their firms. Since the U.S. economy enjoyed relatively rapid economic growth, low unemployment, and productivity increases over the past decade, some might dismiss the failure of the labor relations system to deliver the voice to workers that they want as a minor blemish on the otherwise successful economy. But this failure is more than a minor blemish. While the economy has succeeded in some areas, it has failed to distribute the fruits of economic progress to employees. The real earnings of the majority of workers have fallen. The proportion of workers with health benefits has declined. Private pensions are endangered. The gains of economic growth have flowed to a small number of persons at the top of the income distribution — the upper 1 percent or so of income recipients. Within firms, the imbalance of power between labor and management has eased the way for the corporate criminality that brought down such companies as Enron and WorldCom. Globalization pressures from low-wage developing countries in the form of trade, competition for investments, and immigration, are near certain to create more problems for U.S. employees. A system in which employees do not have adequate channels for voice at their workplace is a system that will risk continued economic woes for workers. Increased worker representation and participation may not be the magic bullet to resolve this problem, but it surely will help.

To open the door to the participation and representation that workers want, the United States should break with the assumption that collective bargaining by a union that wins exclusive representation can alone provide workers with the say they want at their workplace. The analysis in this chapter has suggested four ways for the United States to deliver the diversity of representation and participation that workers want: (1) development of the open-source union form; (2) eliminating LMRA restrictions on firms forming nonunion employee groups as channels of collective voice, and giving workers rights to insist that their firm sets up such organizations; (3) perhaps in tandem with this, improving the protection of worker rights of association inside the firm — the basic promise of the Wagner Act; and (4) allowing states to sidestep the federal preemption doctrine and experiment with alternative ways of implementing labor regulations, including modes of enforcing worker rights. Reforms along these lines would begin to give American workers the choice of the diverse forms of representation and participation that *What Workers Want* shows they desire.

NOTES

INTRODUCTION TO THE UPDATED EDITION

1. A complete list of consulted post-WRPS surveys is provided, along with other materials on the WRPS itself, at www.nber.org/~freeman/wrps.html.

2. See Question 181 in James A. David, Tom W. Smith, and Peter V. Marsden, *General Social Surveys, 1972–2004*, 2nd ICPSR version (Chicago, Ill.: National Opinion Research Center, 2005).

3. Lynn Franco, *Take This Job and . . .* (New York: Conference Board, 2005). By age, declines were down 12 points (61–49) among workers aged 35–44, and 9 points (57–48) among those aged 45–54. By income, declines were down 15 points (56–41) among households earning $25–35K annually, and 13 points (60–47) among those earning $35–50K.

4. Harris Poll no. 38 (May 6, 2005), "Many U.S. Employees Have Negative Attitudes to Their Jobs, Employers, and Top Managers."

5. ws.cc.stonybrook.edu/surveys/index.html.

6. Les Christie, CNN/Money staff writer, "Bad Attitudes in the Workplace Survey Show that Employee Morale Has Taken a Hit Lately," August 24, 2005, 5:19 PM EDT.

7. TIPP/Investor's Business Daily/*Christian Science Monitor* Poll, October 2002.

8. Gallup Poll Social Series, Work and Education (www.gallup.com/poll/).

9. See Peter D. Hart Research Associates, Study no. 7518 (February 2005).

10. CBS News Poll: "Little Faith in Big Biz," July 10, 2002, "The Ethics of Big Business," www.cbsnews.com/htdocs/c2k/bizback.pdf.

11. Gallup Polls: "Mood of the Nation" (2005), for business influence; and November Wave 2 (2002) and November Wave 1 (2004) on business executive honesty. A Harris poll with different wording found that 83 percent wanted to reduce corporate influence.

12. See Peter D. Hart Research Associates, Study no. 7518 (February 2005).

13. Peter D. Hart Research Associates, Study no. 7704 (August 2005).

14. Peter D. Hart Research Associates, Study no. 7518 (February 2005).

15. Peter D. Hart Research Associates, Study no. 6924 (2003). The question asked: "I'm going to describe some ways that employers might express their opposition to union during union representation elections. For each one please tell me whether you think that employers do this all the time, fairly often, just sometimes, or not very often?" and listed eight tactics.

16. Kate Bronfenbrenner, *Uneasy Terrain: The Impact of Capital Mobility on Workers, Wages, and Union Organizing*, 2000 (www.citizenstrade.org/pdf/nafta_uneasy_terrain.pdf), reports that 92 percent of private-sector employers order employees to attend closed-door meetings to hear anti-union propaganda; 78 percent require that supervisors deliver anti-union messages to workers they oversee; half threaten to shut down if employees unionize; and a quarter fire union supporters.

17. According to Peter D. Hart Research Associates, Study no. 6924 (February 2003),

77 percent think employers should take no position in such campaigns and find "unacceptable" a number of common anti-union employer tactics: holding captive audience meetings (60 percent); sending anti-union letters to employees' homes (63 percent); warning of plant closings or layoffs from a pro-union vote (64 percent); distributing anti-union literature in pay envelopes (67 percent); predicting falls in pay or benefits from a pro-union vote (73 percent); holding one-on-one meetings with supervisors urging a vote against the union (78 percent); having security guards closely following pro-union employees at work (85 percent); and firing workers for being union supporters (92 percent).

18. Peter D. Hart Research Associates, Study no. 7518 (February 2005).

19. Peter D. Hart Research Associates, Study no. 6924 (February 2003).

20. Peter D. Hart Research Associates, Study no. 6221 (January 2001) and Study no. 6924 (February 2003).

21. Peter D. Hart Research Associates, Study no. 6924 (February 2003).

22. Zogby International, *The Attitudes and Opinions of Unionized and Non-Unionized Workers Employed in Various Sectors of the Economy toward Organized Labor*, report to the Public Service Research Foundation, August 2005.

23. We do not know why the 2005 Zogby estimate is so much lower than Hart's, or Zogby's own estimate the previous year. Then, on a slightly different question wording — "If you had a choice, how likely would you be to join a union?" — Zogby found that 45 percent of nonunion workers would likely join one. See Zogby International, *Nationwide Attitudes toward Unions*, report to the Public Service Research Foundation, February 2004.

24. See Gallup Poll, "Shift in Public Perceptions about Union Strength, Influence," August 23, 2005. The polling data vary quite a bit from year to year, so that it is possible the 53 percent is an aberration. On average over the period, 43 thought percent unions were going to get weaker compared to 22 percent who said they were going to get stronger.

25. Peter D. Hart Research Associates, Study no. 6221 (January 2001).

CHAPTER 1

1. Contrast this with another leading capitalist power, Germany, where 29 percent of the labor force is unionized but where 95 percent are covered by a collective agreement — through the process of "extension" of collective-bargaining terms from the union to the nonunion sector; or with France, where just 9 percent of workers are organized but where 95 percent are also covered. See OECD, *Employment Outlook*, July 1997 (Paris: OECD, 1997), Table 3.3.

2. Several books and articles address the disconnect between the U.S. labor-relations system to fit the modern economy. Among the major studies are Richard B. Freeman and Joel Rogers, "Who Speaks for Us? Employee Representation in a Non-Union Labor Market," in *Employee Representation: Alternatives and Future Directions*, ed. Bruce Kaufman and Morris Kleiner (Madison, Wis.: Industrial Relations Research Association, 1993); William B. Gould IV, *Agenda for Reform: The Future of Employment Rela-*

tionships and the Law (Cambridge, Mass.: MIT Press, 1993); Bruce Kaufman, "Company Unions: Sham Organizations or Victims of the New Deal?" *Industrial Relations Research Annual* (1997):166–80; Thomas Kochan, "Principles for a Post-New Deal Employment Policy," in *Labor Economics and Industrial Relations: Markets and Institutions*, ed. Clark Kerr and Paul Staudohar (Cambridge, Mass.: Harvard University Press, 1994), 646–71; Joel Rogers, "Reforming U.S. Labor Relations," in *The Legal Future of Employee Representation*, ed. Matthew W. Finkin (Ithaca, N.Y.: ILR Press, 1994), 95–125; David Levine, *Reinventing the Workplace: How Business and Employees Can Both Win* (Washington D.C.: Brookings Institute, 1995); Miles Raymond, "A New Industrial Relations System for the 21st Century," *California Management Review* 21 (Winter 1989): 9-28; Kim Moody, *Workers in a Lean World* (London: Verso, 1997); Michael Piore, "The Future of Unions," in *The State of the Unions*, ed. George Strauss, Daniel Gallagher, and Jack Fiorito (Madison, Wis.: Industrial Relations Research Association, 1991), 386–410; Joseph Reid, "Future Unions," *Industrial Relations* 31, no. 1 (1992): 122–36; George Strauss, "Is the New Deal System Collapsing? With What Might It Be Replaced?" *Industrial Relations* 34, no. 3 (1995): 329–49; Lowell Turner, *Democracy at Work: Changing World Markets and the Future of Labor Unions* (Ithaca, N.Y.: Cornell University Press, 1991); Paul C. Weiler, *Governing the Workplace: The Future of Labor and Employment* (Cambridge, Mass.: Harvard University Press, 1990); and Charles C. Heckscher, *The New Unionism: Employee Involvement in the Changing Corporation* (Ithaca, N.Y.: ILR Press, 1996).

3. The benchmark is the Quality of Employment Survey, conducted by the Department of Labor in 1977. Since then many opinion polls have been conducted on this or that aspect of worker attitudes, but none that focuses on workers' desires for participation or representation across a wide variety of forms or institutions.

4. The WRPS was limited to private-sector workers in firms or organizations with twenty-five or more employees. It excluded public-sector workers and workers in small firms who face different workplace governance issues than those in larger private firms. Since completing the WRPS, we have surveyed workers in Canada and in some parts of the U.S. public sector using essentially the same survey instrument. Other researchers have applied a version of our survey to workers in the United Kingdom, and others are using it in analyses in Australia and Japan.

5. All the data are available for further inspection at the NBER Web site listing for on-line data: http://www.nber.org/data_index.html

6. For discussions of the commission, see Thomas Kochan, "Using the Dunlop Report to Achieve Mutual Gains," *Industrial Relations* 34, no. 3 (1995); and John T. Addison, "The Dunlop Report: European Links and Other Odd Connections," *Journal of Labor Research* 17, no. 1 (Winter 1996): 77–99.

7. In the WRPS, the rate of unionization was 16 percent. This exceeds the national average for the private sector because we excluded workers from small firms who are less likely to be unionized than those in larger firms. If workers in small firms were included in the survey, the rate of unionization that workers want would probably be lower, but it would still be three or more times the national average for private-sector workers of around 10 percent to 11 percent in the late 1990s. The WRPS covered roughly three-fourths of the American workforce.

8. William Bridges, "The End of the Job," excerpt from "JobShift," *Fortune*, September 1994, 62–66.

9. Studies based on the standard monthly survey of American households — the Current Population Survey — as well as studies based on data sets that follow given groups of workers for many years of their lives, such as the Michigan Panel Survey of Income Dynamics, show that Americans stay with their firm for long periods. See Henry Farber, "Are Lifetime Jobs Disappearing? Job Duration in the United States," *NBER Working Paper No.* 5014, 1 February 1995; Francis X. Diebold, David Neumark, and Daniel Polsky, "Job Stability in the United States," *NBER Working Paper No.* 4859, 1 September 1994; David Neumark, Daniel Polsky, and Daniel Hansen, "Has Job Stability Declined Yet? New Evidence for the 1990's," *NBER Working Paper No.* 6330, 1 December 1997. It is true that Americans are more mobile than workers in most advanced countries, and that they also spend fewer years with the same firm than, say, the Japanese or Germans (Organization for Economic Cooperation and Development, *Employment Outlook, July* 1993 [Paris: OECD, 1993]). But the main reason for this is that Americans frequently shift jobs early in life as they search for the right match. And while years with a firm fell modestly for men in the 1990s, average employment duration has risen for women. Most important, the men whose tenure declined the most were younger and less educated. The phenomenon of lower male job tenure is thus best understood as part of the more general story of a worsened market for the less skilled, not as evidence of a sweeping trend away from traditional employee-employer relations.

10. In analyzing duration data, completed spells of tenure are roughly twice as long as incomplete spells.

11. These figures are from Exhibit 3.3.

12. Workers who leave have little or no incentive to tell employers what really bothers them, because if they complain, the employer might hold it against them and not give them a good recommendation for another job. Some firms have "exit" interviews to try to discover why workers are leaving, but these interviews often are noninformative. There is no benefit to giving your gripes when you are out the door.

13. Richard Freeman and James Medoff, *What Do Unions Do?* (New York: Basic Books, 1984). The importance of voice in society has been stressed by Albert Hirschman in his classic *Exit, Voice, and Loyalty* (Cambridge, Mass.: Harvard University Press, 1971).

14. This argument can be put formally. Let V be the total value of the relationship and let λ be Party I's share in that value. Then let W_I be what Party I gets from breaking the relationship and W_{II} be what Party II gets from breaking the relationship. Party I will stay with the relationship when $\lambda V > W_I$ and Party II will stay when $(1 - \lambda)V > W_{II}$. As long as $V > W_I + W_{II}$, it pays the two parties to resolve disagreements through bargaining rather than splitting. If $\lambda V < W_I$ it behooves them to increase Party I's share of the benefits, and conversely if $(1 - \lambda)V < W_{II}$. If $V < W_I + W_{II}$, no value of λ can make the relationship work for both parties.

15. This also can be demonstrated formally. See Richard B. Freeman and Edward P. Lazear, "An Economic Analysis of Works Councils," in *Works Councils*, ed. Joel Rogers and Wolfgang Streeck (Chicago: University of Chicago Press for NBER, 1995).

16. Many analysts have documented these facts. See, for example, Richard B. Free-

man, *When Earnings Diverge: Causes, Consequences, and Cures for the New Inequality in the U.S.*, National Policy Association Report #284 (Washington, D.C.: NPA, 1997); U.S. Department of Labor, *Report on the American Workforce* (Washington, D.C.: U.S. Government Printing Office, 1994); Lawrence Mishel, Jared Bernstein, and John Schmitt, *State of Working America* (Washington, D.C.: Economic Policy Institute, 1997).

17. Calculated from data in OECD, 1993.

18. The data on family incomes are taken from U.S. Bureau of the Census, *Historical Income Tables: Families*, Tables F-6 and F-3, U.S. Bureau of the Census Web site. The GDP figures are from *Economic Report of the President, February* 1998 (Washington, D.C.: U.S. Government Printing Office, 1998), Table B-2, adjusted for 1996 prices on the basis of Table B-3. The poverty rates are from Table B-33.

CHAPTER 2

1. Studs Terkel, *Working* (New York: Avon, 1975).

2. The reference is to Dennis Rivera, head of the hospital workers union in New York City.

3. The sample for the survey was a random-digit sample of telephone numbers selected from telephone exchanges in the continental United States. Many of the numbers called were not in service or were fax or business numbers, and some numbers called were never answered or picked up by an answering machine. A survey of this kind offers several possible ways to report response rates. Many households who talked with the interviewers did not have an eligible member. We identified 2,751 households with an eligible member and obtained a completed interview with 2,408 of these, an 88 percent response rate. But 3,423 households refused to answer our screening questions. If, conservatively, we assume that these households are divided between eligibles and noneligibles in the same proportion as households who did answer our survey, 20.5 percent (or 701 households) were in the group we were seeking to interview. This gives a response rate from our desired population of 70 percent. See Princeton Survey Research Associates, *Worker Representation and Participation Survey: Report on the Findings*, (Princeton, N.J.: PSRA, 1994), technical appendix.

4. This group should be distinguished from the Commission on the Future of Worker-Management Relations, which dealt with private-sector workers.

5. Richard Freeman discusses the public-sector survey results in "The Evolving Environment of Public Sector Labor Relations," in *Public Sector Employment in a Time of Transition*, ed. Dale Belman, Morley Gunderson, and Douglas Hyatt (Madison, Wis.: Industrial Relations Research Association, 1997).

CHAPTER 3

1. If you have problems that we have not considered or alternative interpretations you want to explore, contact us via e-mail or download the WRPS from our Web site (see Chapter 1, note 5) and perform your own analysis.

2. We use several questions to illuminate attitudes in an area, because all questions on a survey invariably have shortcomings. They could be phrased differently, located in different places, and so on. To find out what workers want at the workplace, we chose a particular set of questions. Someone else might choose a different set. We would choose a different set today. The best way to view particular items is as *indicators* of underlying attitudes or tendencies that subsume any single item. Technically, this underlying attitude/tendency is called "the latent variable." Various statistical models measure latent variables, essentially by identifying the common pattern or factor among particular items addressed to the same issue.

3. In this exhibit and throughout the book, we report tabulations that use the sample weights developed by Princeton Survey Research Associates for the study. But because the WRPS sample had such a good response rate, results that do not use the sample weights give virtually identical figures to those based on the sample weights in almost all cases.

4. Sixty-seven percent of workers with 10 or more years of tenure said that they wanted more influence, as compared with 52 percent of workers with less than one year of tenure; 67 percent of those working more than 45 hours wanted more influence, as compared with 55 percent of those working less than 35 hours; 66 percent of those with a bachelor's or higher degree wanted more influence, as compared with 61 percent of those with no college education. The relationship between skill and position in the firm with the desire for more influence does not, however, hold for all groups, as some highly committed workers already have considerable influence.

5. This is shown in two questions, the first regarding the problems of individuals and the second regarding the problems of groups. The first question was, "If employees as a group had *more say* in how the workplace problems of individual employees are solved at your company/organization, do you think this system would be *more* effective or *less* effective?" Seventy-six percent said more; 10 percent said less; 4 percent said the same; and 4 percent did not answer. The second question was asked of respondents in companies with no employee committee or union: "Imagine that *management* selected a committee of employees to discuss the problems employees have as a group with them. Do you think this would be *more* effective or *less* effective to resolve employees' concerns?" Seventy-three percent said more effective; 21 percent said less effective; 2 percent said the same; and 4 percent hadn't a clue.

6. The issue here is fundamental in economics, relating to the possible effect of the distribution of output on the level of output. If one side in a working arrangement (such as management) gives more decision-making power to the other side, such as workers, will the first side benefit or lose? If devolving authority raises the total value of the working arrangement, it is at least possible that both sides gain, although the workers' side might use its power to increase its share of total output.

7. The specific proportions who do not look forward to work: 39 percent for those earning between $200 and $599 a week; 43 percent among high school dropouts; 42 percent among black workers; and 42 percent among manufacturing workers.

8. Individual responses produces a bigger estimate of the proportion of workers whose trust of their employers falls short of their loyalty than the averages give, because the averages mix these workers with those whose trust exceeds their loyalty. We used the same four-point scale and wording to make it easier to compare the differences in responses.

9. Richard B. Freeman, "Evolving Institutions for Employee Voice," in *Exit and Voice in the Actual Working of the Economies*, ed. Luca Meldolosi (unpublished manuscript, 1998).

10. To see how the compression loses information, consider two workers who want a lot of influence. One reports that he has some influence on workplace decisions; the other says she has no influence. The latter is a more serious problem, but our measure does not distinguish between them. There are ways to check the seriousness of this problem, ranging from eyeballing cross-tabulations to computing separate item response variables for the importance of influence and for having influence, and examining the difference between those scales. Such analyses show that the summary statistic does not distort anything in the text.

11. To take an extreme case, if 60 percent of people wanted a lot of influence but had no influence and 40 percent had a lot of influence but did not want a lot of influence, 60 percent of workers would lack their desired influence, whereas our aggregate gap would be just 20 percent. Similarly, if someone wants a lot of influence on, say, workplace safety issues and has no influence, but has a lot of influence on training, which she does not want, the aggregate measure would show no representation/participation gap, when in fact such a gap exists in the safety area.

12. The average in this column does not give the percentage of workers who report that they have less influence than they want on *any* issue. The majority (83 percent) report some area in which they feel their influence falls short of what they want.

13. We performed a similar analysis using Rasch scaling and obtained comparable results.

14. Freeman, "Evolving Institutions for Employee Voice."

15. This was the view of some 80 percent of workers.

16. This group constituted 24 percent of our sample.

17. Forty-three percent said management opposed the union with information only; 23 percent said the firm threatened or harassed union supporters.

18. Thirty-six percent said they would certainly be willing to do so; 47 percent said that they were probably willing to do so.

19. In fact, this is not the whole story. Many U.S. managers set up EI committees, workplace teams, and other worker groups and delegate important decisions to those groups. But American labor institutions and laws make it difficult for nonunion firms to build on their interest in increasing employee voice. And the country's labor system provides no vehicle for workers to develop an organization to represent them at workplaces, short of a majority union. But these are not issues that we raised with workers.

20. The classic analysis of the interrelation between exit and voice is Albert Hirschman, *Exit, Voice, and Loyalty* (Cambridge, Mass: Harvard University Press, 1972).

CHAPTER 4

1. See Richard B. Freeman and Joel Rogers, "Who Speaks for Us," and Henry Farber and Alan Krueger, "Union Membership in the U.S.: The Decline Continues," in

Employee Representation: Alternatives and Future Directions, ed. Bruce Kaufman and Morris Kleiner (Madison, Wis.: Industrial Relations Research Association, 1993).

2. A 1993 Employment Policy Foundation survey did ask this question. They reported that 62 percent of private-sector union members would support the union; 15 percent (to whom the question must have been confusing) said they had a union; and 18 percent said they would vote against the union. If we sum the 62 percent and 15 percent we get 78 percent presumably supporting the union, as compared with 18 percent against it. The level of union support by union members is massive, although less than the 90 percent support found by the WRPS. Larger samples of union members are needed to pin down the proportion of supporters with certainty, but whether it is 62 percent or 78 percent or 90 percent for unions and 8 percent or 18 percent against, the qualitative story is the same: Union members support their union.

3. This question used a five-point scale, giving workers an option to provide a neutral (neither good nor bad) answer.

4. This is not true of the public sector, in which unions have organized many highly educated and skilled workers, such as teachers, nurses, police officers and firefighters, as well as the blue-collar workers they largely organize in the private sector.

5. Note also that because we do not have evidence on workers' desires for say or preference for dealing with workplace problems as a group prior to their current work experience, this calculation overstates the extent to which differences in views explain the differing intentions to vote for or against unions if, as seems likely, the union experience itself increases worker demands for say or their belief in the value of collective activity.

6. A linear probability regression of intention to vote union on dummy variables for gender, race, age groups, and education groups gave a significant positive coefficient of 0.095, with a standard error of 0.029 on former union members, implying that 9.5 percent more of them were likely to vote union. Adding the log of weekly pay reduced the coefficient to 0.065, with a standard error of 0.033. But the coefficient on former union members falls to an insignificant 0.024 with the addition of measures for employee-management relations. Thus, former members are always more likely to vote union than nonmembers, but the effect varies depending on the situation at their nonunion workplace.

7. Daniel Kahneman, Jack L. Knetsch, and Richard H. Thaler, "The Endowment Effect, Loss Aversion, and Status Quo Bias: Anomolies," *Journal of Economic Perspectives* 5, no. 1 (Winter 1991): 193–206; Daniel Kahneman, Jack L. Knetsch, and Richard Thaler, "Fairness as a Constraint on Profit-Seeking: Entitlements in the Market," *American Economic Review* 76, no. 4 (September 1986): 728–41. For a different analysis, see Tom Langford, "Involvement with Unions, Union Belief Perspectives, and Desires for Union Membership," *Journal of Labor Research* 15, no. 3 (summer 1994): 257–70.

8. Tom Kochan, "How American Workers View Labor Unions," *Monthly Labor Review* 102 (April 1979): 15–22. For a study of how local unions function, see Tove Hammer and David L. Wazeter, "Dimensions of Local Union Effectiveness," *Industrial and Labor Relations Review* 46, no. 2 (1993): 302–19.

9. See Wilson Center for Public Research, *Workers' Views of the Value of Unions* (May 1992).

10. We could do better by simply assigning to each worker the outcome vote against a union. Because two-thirds of nonunion workers vote against the union, this would give us, on average, a two-thirds correct classification. But this is obviously a cop out. It is equivalent to predicting that there will never be a stock market collapse or a hurricane or any other rare event, and then claiming success because these are rare events. The flaw in the cop-out prediction approach is that there is a big payoff to predicting the rare event correctly, only a small cost to predicting it incorrectly, and little payoff to predicting the normal event.

11. For earlier comparisons of how workers view unions, and the characteristics of workers that lead them to favor or oppose unionization for their workplace, see Karen E. Boroff and David Lewin, "Loyalty, Voice, and Intent to Exit a Union Firm: A Conceptual and Empirical Analysis," *Industrial and Labor Relations Review* 51, no. 1 (1997): 50–63; Gary Chaison and Dileep G. Dhavale, "The Choice between Union Membership and Free-Rider Status," *Journal of Labor Research* 13, no. 4 (1992); Gregory Defreitas, "Unionization among Racial and Ethnic Minorities," *Industrial and Labor Relations Review* 46, no. 2 (1993): 284–301; Richard B. Freeman and James Medoff, *What Do Unions Do?* (New York: Basic Books, 1984); Daniel S. Hamermesh and Albert Rees, *The Economics of Work and Pay* (New York: Harper & Row, 1988); Henry Farber and Daniel Saks, "Why Workers Want Unions: The Role of Relative Wages and Job Characteristics," *Journal of Political Economy* 88 (1980): 349–69; Henry Farber, "The Determination of the Union Status of Workers," *Econometrica* 51 (1983): 1417–37; Duane Leigh, "The Determinants of the Workers' Union Status: Evidence from the National Longitudinal Surveys," *Journal of Human Resources* 20 (1985): 555–66; Barry Hirsch, "The Determinants of Unionization: An Analysis of Interarea Differences," *Industrial and Labor Relations Review* 33 (1980): 158; William Dickens and Jonathan Leonard, "Accounting for the Decline in Union Membership, 1950–1980," *Industrial and Labor Relations Review* 38 (1985): 323–34; George Neumann and Ellen Rissman, "Where Have All the Union Members Gone?" *Journal of Labor Economics* 2 (1984): 175–92; Robert Flanagan, "NLRA Litigation and Union Representation," *Stanford Law Review* 38, no. 4 (1986): 957–89; Rebecca Demsetz, "Voting Behavior in Union Representation Elections: The Influence of Skill Homogeneity and Skill Group Size," *Industrial and Labor Relations Review* 47, no. 1 (1993): 99–113; John S. Heywood, "Who Queues for a Union Job?" *Industrial Relations* 29, no. 1 (1990): 119–27; Steve Hills, "The Attitudes of Union and Non-Union Male Workers toward Representation," *Industrial and Labor Relations Review* 38 (July 1985); Lisa Schur and Douglas L. Kruse, "Gender Differences in Attitudes toward Unions," *Industrial and Labor Relations Review* 46, no. 1 (1992): 89–102.

12. In addition to the models reported in the exhibit, we examined the effect of other measures of workplace conditions on workers' voting for a union. These measures–the state of employee-management relations at the workplace, the number of employees, the influence gap — gave similar results to those in the exhibit. This is because workers who report good or bad relations with their firm on one question give similar responses on others.

13. Henry Farber, "Trends in Worker Demand for Unionization," *American Economic Review* 79, no. 2 (1989): 166–71; Henry Farber, "The Decline of Unionization in the United States: What Can Be Learned from Recent Experience," *Journal of Labor Economics* 8, no. 1, part 2 (1990): S75–105; Henry Farber and Alan Krueger, "Union Membership in the United States: The Decline Continues," *NBER Working Paper No.* 4216 (1992). The predominant view that management resistance is critical to union success or failure is given by Paul Weiler, "Striking a New Balance: Freedom of Contract and the Prospects for Union Representation," *Harvard Law Review* 98 (1984): 351–420; Paul Weiler, "Promises to Keep: Securing Workers' Rights to Self-Organization Under the NLRA," *Harvard Law Review* 96 (1984): 1769–1827; Richard B. Freeman, "Why Are Unions Faring Poorly in NLRB Representation Elections?" in *Challenges and Choices Facing American Labor*, ed. Tom Kochan (Cambridge, Mass.: MIT Press, 1985); Freeman and Medoff, *What Do Unions Do?* The literature on union-organizing efforts is also voluminous: Stephen Bronars and Donald R. Deere, "Union Organizing Activity, Form Growth, and the Business Cycle," *American Economic Review* 83, no. 1 (1993): 203–20; Marion Crane, "Gender and Union Organizing," *Industrial and Labor Relations Review* 47, no. 2 (1994): 227–48; Gary Chaison and Dileep Dhavale, "The Changing Scope of Union Organizing," *Journal of Labor Research* 11, no. 3 (1990): 307–22; Gary Chaison and Dileep Dhavale, "A Note on the Severity of the Decline in Union Organizing Activity," *Industrial and Labor Relations Review* 43, no. 4 (1990): 366–73; William Dickens, "The Effect of Company Campaigns on Certification Elections: Law and Reality Once Again," *Industrial and Labor Relations Review* 36, no. 4 (July 1983): 560–75; Richard B. Freeman and Morris M. Kleiner, "Employer Behavior in the Face of Union Organizing Drives," *Industrial and Labor Relations Review* 43, no. 4 (April 1990): 351–65; Thomas Lee and Barbara Finnegan, "Strategies and Tactics in Union Organizing Campaigns," *Industrial Relations* 31, no. 2 (1992): 370–81; Terry Leap et al., "Discrimination against Pro-Union Job Applicants," *Industrial Relations* 29, no. 3 (1990): 469–78; Monty Lynn and Jozell Brister, "Trends in Union Organizing Issues and Tactics," *Industrial Relations* 28, no. 1 (1989): 104–13; Joseph B. Rose and Gary N. Chaison, "New Measures of Union Organizing Effectiveness," *Industrial Relations* 29, no. 3 (1990): 457–68; Donna Stockwell and John Thomas Delaney, "Union Organizing and the Reagan NLRB," *Contemporary Policy Issues* 5, no. 4 (1987): 28–45.

14. Employment Policy Foundation, *Fact and Fallacy: Updating the reasons for Union Decline*, May 1998.

15. This is a correct perception. In a study of NLRB elections in the Kansas City and Boston NLRB districts, Freeman and Kleiner found that on the order of one in five managers in firms that voted union were fired.

16. Nineteen percent said "a lot" better, and 45 percent said "a little" better.

17. Thirty-one percent said relations were more cooperative, as compared with 16 percent who said they were more confrontational and 42 percent who reported no change. For studies that examine how management views union efforts to be more cooperative, see Martin M. Perline and Edwin A. Sexton, "Managerial Perceptions of Labor-Management Cooperation," *Industrial Relations* 33, no. 3 (1994): 377–85.

18. The specifics are 66 percent, "no difference"; 23 percent, "makes job harder"; and 7 percent, "makes job easier."

CHAPTER 5

1. In the 1980s, when Japanese management practices were in vogue, two different publishers brought out copies of Miyamoto Mushashi's Samurai classic, *A Book of Five Rings*: Overlook Press (Woodstock, N.Y., 1982) and Viking Press (New York, 1982). A more recent edition was published by Random House (New York, 1993). *The Leadership Secrets of Attila the Hun*, by Wess Roberts (NY: Warner Books, 1991) was a big seller in the 1990s.

2. Among the many books in this vein are Jeffrey Pfeffer, *Competitive Advantage through People: Unleashing the Power of the Workforce* (Boston: Harvard Business School Press, 1994), and Thomas A. Kochan and Paul Osterman, *The Mutual Gains Enterprise* (Boston: Harvard Business School Press, 1994).

3. These percentages exceed the proportion of workers in firms with employee stock-ownership plans (ESOPs) that fall under the ESOP regulations or are counted by the National Council on Employee Ownership as employee-owned, largely because the WRPS did not probe workers about the specifics of their stock plan. Many companies have 401K and other retirement plans that hold company shares. This does not make them employee-owned, but workers may not have made the distinction.

4. Two other major studies have sought to identify the prevalence of advanced human-resource practices: Paul Osterman, "How Common Is Workplace Transformation and Who Adopts It?" *Industrial and Labor Relations Review* 47, no. 2 (January 1994): 173–88, and Edward Lawler, Susan Mohrman, and Gerald Ledford, *Employee Involvement and Total Quality Management: Practices and Results in Fortune 1000 Companies* (San Francisco: Jossey-Bass, 1992). Both pose questions about various practices to managers, as opposed to workers. Osterman's study is based on a sample of establishments from Dun and Bradstreet. The work by Lawler, Mohrman, and Ledford is based on a sample of Fortune 1000 firms. The general picture that they find on the breadth of practices is similar to what workers reported to us.

5. For instance, 84 percent of workers in large firms say their firm has a personnel/human-resource department; 77 percent of workers in manufacturing also report this. This exceeds the 68 percent in the table.

6. When data fit the Guttman model perfectly, they can be arrayed in a triangular matrix, so that the individual who has the lowest total score answers correctly only the easiest items; the individual with the next lowest score answers those items plus the next easiest, and so on:

Items (X = "correct" response)

	1	2	3	4
Individual 1	X	o	o	o
Individual 2	X	X	o	o
Individual 3	X	X	X	o
Individual 4	X	X	X	X

7. The key statistical assumption is that individual responses to an item follow a logistic probability distribution. David Bartholemew, *The Statistical Approach to Social*

Measurement (San Diego: Academic Press, 1996), shows that the sufficiency principle for conditional distributions of latent variables yields the Rasch logistic model on the assumption that individuals and items can be located on a single continuum. Gerhard H. Fischer and Ivo W. Molenaar, *Rasch Models: Foundations, Recent Developments, and Applications* (New York: Springer-Verlag TELOS, 1995), give alternative algorithms for estimating Rasch models.

8. We had ready access to a survey of establishments conducted by Paul Osterman of MIT (Osterman, 1996), and a survey of firms conducted by Cheri Ostroff. See Richard B. Freeman, Morris M. Kleiner, and Cheri Ostroff, "The Anatomy and Effects of Employee Involvement," mimeo, 16 July 1997. University of Minnesota, 1998. In both cases, we found that the number or scope of practices fit well a single latent scale, and that as we looked at more practices, the bell curve gave a more valid summary of the data than the alternative hypothesis that the distribution was sharply bifurcated between good and bad firms.

9. This is the case for the practices covered in the WRPS but not true of all practices. Osterman reports that some advanced practices are less likely to be found in the union setting.

10. The absence of small firms from the WRPS does not mean that we have no information on small establishments or workplaces. Many workers in large firms work in small establishments or workplaces. Citibank is a big fish in the banking industry, but the typical Citibank branch has a manager and five to ten employees.

11. Specifically, 21 percent used the system three or more times in the previous 12 months versus 24 percent who used it once or twice.

12. Specifically, 61 percent of managers and 58 percent of college graduates used the policy in the past year.

13. Specifically, 46 percent of 18- to 24-year-olds; 47 percent of those 55 and older; 47 percent of the semi-skilled; and 42 percent of laborers.

14. These figures are from Wave 2 of the survey, which had a special module on open-door policies. We also compared the reported effectiveness of EI on Wave 1 with reported use on Wave 2 and obtained similar results. In this case, 50 percent of the workers who said that their system was "very effective" used it three or more times in the past year, as compared with 35 percent of other workers.

15. Thirty-eight percent reported using it to deal with production/procedures/operations, and 22 percent reported using it to deal with general working conditions, giving a 60 percent use for these areas.

16. Specifically, 8 percent raised problems with a supervisor, 11 percent raised problems with wages or benefits; 18 percent of managers and 17 percent of union members raised problems about wages or benefits.

17. Nearly one-third (32 percent) of workers who used the open door for wage or benefit problems reported that it was ineffective, whereas just 12 percent of workers who used it to deal with production problems reported that it was ineffective. Twenty-two percent of workers said the open door was ineffective for dealing with a problem of working conditions.

18. See Charles J. Morris, "A Dialogue with the Chairman of the Labor Board: Challenging Conventional Wisdom on the Impact of Current Law on Alternative Forms

of Employee Representation,"*Hofstra Labor & Employment Law Journal* 15 (1998): 319–44, and "Alternative Labor Organizations under the National Labor Relations Act: a How-To Manual for Employees Councils, American Style (unpublished manuscript, 1998).

19. The WRPS asked both workers and managers about the frequency of suggestions and management's response to suggestions. The exhibit combines the information about which workers should have the most accurate knowledge — the frequency of their suggestions — and the information about which managers should have the most accurate knowledge — how useful they find suggestions. Alternatively, one can examine the perceptions of workers and managers separately. Here also EI appears to increase the frequency and value of suggestions, although workers report a greater difference between EI and non-EI settings than do managers.

20. Here are the percentages who supervise others: EI participants, 48 percent; nonparticipants in firms with EI, 28 percent; employees in other firms, 32 percent.

21. Specifically, 32 percent found it "very effective"; 55 percent, "somewhat effective"; 11 percent, "not too effective" or "not effective at all."

22. Exhibit 5.5 also shows that workers in a firm with EI who do not participate in the program have a less positive view of its effectiveness. Proportionately more of them rate the program as "not too effective" or "not at all effective" than rate it as "very effective." Whether this difference is due to nonparticipants' unfamiliarity with the program's effects or to participants' excessively favorable view of the virtues of something in which they were involved (a kind of endowment effect) is anyone's guess.

23. See, for example, Harry Katz, Thomas Kochan, and Jeffrey Keefe, "Industrial Relations and Productivity in the U.S. Automobile Industry," *Brookings Papers on Economic Activity* 3 (1987): 685–728.

24. For a general review of studies through the mid-1980s, see the various chapters in Alan Blinder, ed., *Paying for Productivity* (Washington, D.C.: Brookings Institution, 1990). Other studies include Joel Cutcher Gershenfeld, "The Impact on Economic Performance of a Transformation in Workplace Practices," *Industrial and Labor Relations Review* 44 (January 1991): 241–60; John Paul MacDuffie and John F. Krafcik, "Integrating Technology and Human Resources for High-Performance Manufacturing: Evidence from the International Motor Vehicle Research Program," in *Transforming Organizations*, Thomas A. Kochan and Michael Useem (New York: Oxford University Press, 1992), 209–26; Casey Ichniowski, Kathryn Shaw, and Giovanna Prennushi, "The Effects of Human Resource Management Practices on Productivity: A Study of Steel Finishing Lines," *American Economic Review* 87, no. 3 (June 1997): 291–313. For articles on the effects of EI programs, see Paul S. Aidler, Barbara Goldoftas, and David I. Levine, "Ergonomics, Employee Involvement, and the Toyota Production System: A Case Study of NUUMI's 1993 Model Introduction," *Industrial and Labor Relations Review* 50, no. 3 (1997): 416–37; Rosemary Batt and Eileen Appelbaum, "Worker Participation in Diverse Settings: Does the Form Affect the Outcome, and If So, Who Benefits?" *British Journal of Industrial Relations* 33, no. 3 (1995); 353–78; Avner Ben-Ner and Derek C. Jones, "Employee Participation, Ownership, and Productivity: A Theoretical Framework," *Industrial Relations* 34, no. 4 (1995): 532–54; Peter Berg, Eileen Appelbaum, Thomas Baily, and Arne Kolleberg, "The Performance Effects of Modular Production in the Apparel Industry," *Industrial Relations* 35, no. 3 (1996): 356–73; Denis Collins,

"Self-Interests and Group-Interests in Employee-Involvement Programs: A Case Study," *Journal of Labor Research* 16, no. 1 (1995): Edward M. Shephard III, "Profit Sharing and Productivity: Further Evidence from the Chemicals Industry," *Industrial Relations* 33, no. 4 (1994): 452–66; Mark Huselid, "The Impact of Human Resource Management Practices on Turnover, Productivity, and Corporate Financial Performance," *Academy of Management Journal* (June 1995): n.p.; Casey Ichniowski and Katherine Shaw, "Old Dogs and New Tricks: Determinants of the Adoption of Productivity-Enhancing Work Practices," *Brookings Paper on Economic Activity: Microeconomics* (1995): 1–65; Casey Ichniowski et al., "What Works at Work: Overview and Assessment," Industrial Relations 35, no. 3 (1996): 299–333; Ichniowski, Prennushi, and Shaw, "The Effects of Human Resource Management Practices on Productivity."

25. The change in output by 3 percent raises profits by four times that amount (12 percent) because profits are only one-fourth of output.

26. Lisa M. Lynch and Sandra E. Black, "How to Compete: The Impact of Workplace Practices and Information," *NBER Working Paper Series No.* 6120, 1 August 1997; Mary Ellen Kelley and Bennett Harrison, "Unions, Technology, and Labor-Management Cooperation," in *Unions and Economic Competitiveness*, ed. Lawrence Mishel and Paula B. Voos (NY: M.E. Sharpe, 1992). For articles on the union role in EI programs, see William Cooke, "Employee Participation Programs, Group-Led Incentives, and Company Performance: A Union-Nonunion Comparison," *Industrial and Labor Relations Review* 47, no. 4 (1994): 594–609; Adrienne E. Eaton, "The Survival of Employee Participation in Unionized Settings," *Industrial and Labor Relations Review* 47, no. 2 (1994): 173–88; Charles Hecksher and Sue Schurman, "Can Labor-Management Cooperation Deliver Jobs and Justice?" *Industrial Relations Journal* 28, no. 4 (1997): 323–30; Tom Juravich, Howard Harris, and Andrea Brooks, "Mutual gains? Labor and Management Evaluate Their Employee Involvement Programs," *Journal of Labor Research* 14, no. 2 (spring 1993): 165–85; Maryellen R. Kelley, "Participatory Bureaucracy and Productivity in the Machined Products Sector," *Industrial Relations* 35, no. 3 (1996): 374–99; Maryellen R. Kelley and Bennett Harrison, "Unions, Technology, and Labor-Management Cooperation," in Lawrence Mishel and Paula Voos, eds., *Unions and Economic Competitiveness* (New York: M. E. Sharpe, 1992), 247–86; John Paul Macduffie, "Human Resource Bundles and Manufacturing Performance: Organizational Logic and Flexible Production Systems in the World Auto Industry," *Industrial and Labor Relations Review* 48, no. 2 (1995): 197–221; Paul Osterman, "How Common Is Workplace Transformation and Who Adopts It?" *Industrial and Labor Relations Review* 47, no. 2 (1994): 173–88.

27. See Ralph T. King Jr., "Infighting Rises, Productivity Falls, Employees Miss Piecework System," *Wall Street Journal*, 20 May 1998, 1.

28. "Vast majority" in this case means 79 percent.

29. Forty-four percent said the management was "completely dedicated" to the program; 47 percent said it was "mostly dedicated"; and just 9 percent said it was "not too dedicated" or "not at all dedicated."

30. Recall that the gap is the difference between the share of workers who said it was very important to them to have a lot of influence in decisions and the proportion who reported a lot of direct involvement in those decisions.

31. Consistent with this, some 17 percent of employees in firms with EI who said they

had worked in a company at a time when employees were forming a union reported that the company had harassed or threatened union supporters, while 32 percent of employees in firms without EI said the company had harassed or threatened union supporters. As the question on the union drive did not ask whether the drive occurred at the employee's current firm or some other firm, this result might not relate to the current firm. It could be that the drive occurred at the current firm. It could also be that current EI participants have work histories that have disproportionately put them in more worker-friendly firms. Or it could be that their favorable attitudes toward their current management retrospectively colors their judgment of previous ones.

32. See United States Department of Labor. Commission on the Future of Worker-Management Relations, *Fact-Finding Report, Commission on the Future of Worker-Management Relations* (Washington, D.C.: U.S. Department of Labor: U.S. Department of Commerce, 1994).

33. Kelley and Harrison, "Unions, Technology, and Labor-Management Cooperation"; Lynch and Black, "How to Compete: The Impact of Workplace Practices and Information."

CHAPTER 6

1. The major legislation of the 1960s included the Equal Pay Act (1963), the Civil Rights Act (1964), and the Age Discrimination in Employment Act (1967). Legislation of the 1970s included the Equal Opportunity Act (1972), the Rehabilitation Act (1973), the Occupational Health and Safety Act (1970), the Federal Mine Safety and Health Act (1977), and the Employee Retirement Income Security Act (1974), as well as Executive Order 11246, which established affirmative action for federal contractors. Legislation of the 1980s included the Immigration Reform and Control Act (1986), the Employee Polygraph Protection Act (1988), and the Worker Adjustment and Retraining Notification Act (1988). The 1990s saw the Americans with Disabilities Act (1990), the Civil Rights Act (1991), and the Family and Medical Leave Act (1993).

2. Because we used a split-question design, half of the sample was asked about three of the items in the exhibit, and the other half about three other items. If people had simply guessed on the three items they were presented, 12.5 percent would have gotten all items correct. In fact, only 9 percent of employees got all three items correct; 51 percent got one question wrong, 35 percent answered two wrong, and 5 percent answered all three wrong.

3. This doctrine has been challenged in some courts. In 1987 Montana enacted a Wrongful Discharge from Employment Act that gives all nonunion employees broad legal protections from arbitrary dismissals. The National Conference of Commissioners on Uniform State Laws agreed on a model Employment Termination Act in 1991, but no state has adopted this act.

4. The 400,000 is the yearly average of 6 million visits to courts/agencies over 15 years. It is an underestimate of the actual number of individual complaints, as some persons might complain several times. Still, it is a ballpark figure.

5. Between 1971 and 1991, the number of federal district court cases on labor and

employment law increased from 6,800 to 25,000 (Commission on the Future of Worker-Management Relations, *Fact-Finding Report, May* 1994 [Washington, D.C.: U.S. Department of Labor, 1994], Exhibit IV-3). By 1996, American workers brought 23,000 lawsuits against their employers on discrimination grounds alone. From 1983 to 1993, complaints to OSHA increased from 15,601 to 32,359. Figures for other agencies show a similar pattern of rise. See U.S. Department of Labor, *Tables on Staffing, Workload, and Backlog: Five Agencies*, 3 March 1995.

6. State administrative agencies and courts in Wisconsin estimate at *least* 5,000 disputes (court cases, administrative complains, special hearings, whatever) in the enforcement annually. Simply extrapolating from Wisconsin's 5 million population to the rest of the United States would suggest a universe of state-based formal claims on the order of at least 250,000 annually. As Wisconsin is noted for its "progressive" traditions and strong state bureaucracy, it might have more legal disputes than other states, so in the text we used a 200,000 estimate.

7. Stephen Overall, "Court Out on Discrimination Law," *Financial Times*, 16 July 1997, 11.

8. Consider, for example, what happens when a worker goes to the National Labor Relations Board (NLRB) with the claim that an employer illegally fired him or her for union activity. Say the NLRB and perhaps later a court rules in the worker's favor, which entitles him or her to reinstatement and back pay one or two years later. Many workers will take a new job in the interim and choose to remain there rather than return to the firm that illegally discriminated against them in the first place. Back-pay settlements under the NLRA are modest. They are the difference between what the worker would have made at the firm that committed the unfair practice and what the worker earned elsewhere while waiting for the resolution of the problem.

9. A low-paid worker without the money to hire a lawyer probably cannot so threaten the firm, but a high-paid worker (often an older white male) might be able to so threaten the firm. U.S. labor law forbids firing for reasons of discrimination but generally permits firing for no reason.

10. As we did not ask workers whether their complaint was against their current employer or a previous employer, these data probably understate the true relationship between workplace problems and complaints to government regulators. Some workers who brought a case because management was treating them poorly surely moved to a different and better employment situation, weakening the still-noticeable pattern.

11. Consistent with the notion that access to resources increases the use of going to court/an agency, proportionately fewer unionized and high-paid workers (who have such access) than nonunion or low-paid workers report that they had thought about going to court or an agency but did not do so.

12. Specifically, 19 percent said they were afraid of employer reprisal, and 13 percent said they were intimidated. But many workers decided not to go to court for other reasons as well. More than one-third (36 percent) of workers who had thought about but decided against taking a problem to court said that the problem wasn't that important or worth the trouble; 13 percent said the problem got resolved in some other way; and 4 percent resolved the problem by quitting their job.

13. The average of the 61 percent in the upper panel and 55 percent in the lower panel of Exhibit 7.4. Note also that the question offered respondents only two choices, as if they were in a voting situation. Some respondents, however, volunteered that they thought current laws in particular areas offered the right amount of protection or restrictions, and we recorded those responses as well.

14. Specifically, 13 percent said "not too effective"; 8 percent said "not effective at all."

15. Twenty-five percent of persons who had never brought a complaint to court or an agency said arbitration would be "very effective" if management appointed the arbitrator, and 26 percent said it would be "very effective" if workers and management together appointed the arbitrator. By contrast, 17 percent of persons who had brought a complaint to a court/an agency said arbitration would be "very effective" if management appointed the arbitrator, whereas 35 percent said it would be "very effective" if workers and management together appointed the arbitrator.

16. Specifically, 22 percent had an excellent understanding; 55 percent has a good understanding.

17. Literature on the effectiveness (or the lack thereof) of current programs to increase health and safety in the workplace is extensive. Some analysts consider what might happen if workers had more authority in this area. See John F. Burton and James R. Chelius, "Workplace Safety and Health Regulations: Rationale and Results," in *Government Regulation of the Employment Relationship*, ed. Bruce E. Kaufman (Madison, Wis.: Industrial Relations Research Association, 1997), 253–93; Greg LaBar, "What If Your Workers Had the Right to Act?" *Occupational Hazards* 52, no. 2 (1990): 49–54; David Levine, "They Should Solve Their Own Problems: Reinventing Workplace Regulation," in *Government Regulation of the Employment Relationship*, 475–97; and Robert S. Smith, "Have OSHA and Workers' Compensation Made the Workplace Safer?" in *Research Frontiers in Industrial Relations and Human Resources*, ed. David Lewin, Olivia S. Mitchell, and Peter D. Sherer (Madison, Wis.: Industrial Relations Research Association, 1992), 557–86.

18. Commission on the Future of Worker-Management Relations (1994), 121–22.

19. Why are workers so divided on the decision-making power to give to a committee? We speculate that some workers feared that some regulatory issues would involve substantial capital investments with repercussions for the financial well-being of the entire firm, whereas others were thinking of standards that would be less expensive to attain.

CHAPTER 7

1. By choosing some attributes and not others, we have obviously limited what we can find out about worker preferences. In this sense, we have guided the discussion of workplace organizations. Our statement of the options are, however, as neutral as we could make them — factual with no adjectives or accompanying description tha might prejudice workers one way or the other.

2. The percentages given in the text are percentages for the entire sample. We did

not ask workers who said they did not want an organization if they would give time to the organization. They are included in the estimated 23 percent who reject a workplace organization.

3. Fifty-four percent of managers in firms with unions favor elected representatives versus 45 percent of managers in nonunion firms. Forty-three percent of managers in the union firms favor arbitration to resolve disputes, as compared with 37 percent of managers in nonunion firms. In both of these tabulations we included managers who said they want no organization or who refused to answer as valid responses.

4. Specifically, of the managers who favored employees electing representatives, 24 percent were "very satisfied" with their influence on workplace decisions, while 16 percent were "not very satisfied" or "not at all satisfied," giving an 8-point edge to being "very satisfied." By contrast, 35 percent of other managers were "very satisfied" with their influence, and just 11 percent "not very satisfied" or "not at all satisfied," giving a 24-point edge to being "very satisfied." Thirty-nine percent of managers who wanted employees to elect representatives trusted their firm a lot, as compared with 54 percent of other managers.

5. Twenty percent of the managers favoring elected employee representatives rated labor-management relations at their firm as fair or poor, as compared with 16 percent of other managers; 8 percent thought their firm's labor relations were worse than average, as compared with 4 percent of other managers.

6. To give an extreme example, assume the following distribution of preferences for two items with attributes A or B: AA, 20 percent; AB, 40 percent; BA, 40 percent; BB, 0 percent. Sixty percent choose attribute A for the first item. Sixty percent choose A in the second item. But only 20 percent want AA.

7. Specifically, of workers who favor electing representatives, 56 percent are for company funding; for workers who do not want elected representatives, 66 percent are for company funding. Conversely, of those who want company funding for a workplace organization, just 60 percent favor elected representatives, as compared with 69 percent of workers who want the organization to have its own funding and staff. We have excluded all "don't knows" and "want no organization" responses from this calculation.

8. There are 2^5 or 32 configurations for five features for which there are two choices. Multiplying this by 3 for the one feature where we have three choices gives 96.

9. These tabulations are based on the sample of respondents who answered all six items.

10. The specific proportion was 36 percent.

11. See Chapter 5, note 18.

12. These figures are for the entire sample. There are slight differences for those who were asked about the union option and those who were asked about the employee organization that negotiates option.

13. The estimated 9 percent are made up of workers who responded that they wanted a joint committee and a weak organization or who refused to answer the question about the type of organization they wanted. A small number of workers said they wanted

more laws or a union or an employee organization that negotiates but also did not answer the question about organizational attributes. We count them according to their answer as favoring laws, unions, or a negotiating organization.

CHAPTER 8

1. The other major English-speaking economies include Canada, the United Kingdom, New Zealand, Ireland, and (at least through 2005) Australia. See Richard B. Freeman, Peter Boxall, and Peter Haynes, eds., *What Workers Say: Employee Voice in the Anglo-American World* (Ithaca, N.Y.: Cornell University Press, 2006).

2. The Labor Management Relations Act (LMRA) that still governs workplace representation in the private sector consists of the National Labor Relations Act (the "Wagner Act") of 1935, as amended by the 1947 "Taft-Hartley Act," which has the same name as the consolidated statute.

3. Civil rights legislation, regulation of environmental and workplace safety, pensions and other tax-advantaged benefits, and laws on work-family issues, have produced a huge amount of "employment law" on workplace issues. But none of these goes directly to representation issues.

4. The penalties include injunctions against employers that violate the law during a drive for organizing or first contract, treble back pay for employees who are illegally discriminated against or discharged for exercising their LMRA rights, and civil penalties up to $20,000 per violation for employers found guilty of repeatedly and willfully violating employee rights during organizing or first contract negotiation.

5. Also, EFCA has thus far not gained anywhere near the support in the Senate (the graveyard for labor law reform in the late 1970s) that it had in the House, and we can easily imagine a successful Republican filibuster of the law even if Democrats gain a majority there again.

6. The LMRA orders employers to reinstate employees who have been illegally fired for union activity and to pay their back wages less anything they've been able to earn since. This is a "make whole" compensation of victims of illegal activity.

7. A 2003 Hart poll asked what was the better way to determine union representation at a workplace: "A: Hold a secret ballot election in which it takes a majority vote to establish union representation, or B: Pro-union employees can circulate a petition in favor or representation, and if a majority of employees sign it then union representation is established." Option A beat Option B among the general public by 60 percent to 32 percent and among union members by 69 percent to 28 percent. See Peter D. Hart Research Associates, Study no. 6924, 2003. A Zogby International poll said: "Congress is considering legislation that would repeal the right of workers to secret ballot elections on union representation and replace them with what are called "card check" elections. Under a card check system a union is certified as the representative of all the employees when a majority sign union authorization cards." It asked which views the person agreed with more. "Supporters say that such a system prevents employers from using threats and intimidation to influence secret ballot voting" and "Opponents say that

card check systems would allow unions to use deception and intimidation to get employees to sign cards." Card check won by 47 to 38 percent plurality (with 18 percent rejecting both statements or unsure). See Zogby International, *The Attitudes and Opinions of Unionized and Non-Unionized Workers Employed in Various Sectors of the Economy toward Organized Labor*, a report to the Public Service Research Foundation (August 2005). By referring to card check as an election, Zogby blurred the distinction between the card check and a secret ballot election.

8. David Moberg, "Labor Debates Its Future," *The Nation* (March 14, 2005).

9. This assumes that union density falls by 5 percent annually through normal turnover of unionized firms and jobs and growth of employment in nonunion workplaces, so that with 105 million private-sector employees, and a 7.5 percent union density, unions would lose 394,000 workers or about 400,000 per year.

10. The limited data available on organizing outside the NRLB show that "non-vote" organizing has become increasingly important in the 2000s. NLRB organizing is certainly down. Over 2002–05, NLRB elections declined from 2,724 to 2,117, and members gained through them from 81,315 to 63,744. (See *Daily Labor Report*, "Number of NLRB Elections, Win Rate by Labor Unions: Both Decreased in 2005," April 26, 2006, C1.) Meanwhile, unions claim roughly 200K new members organized in the private sector annually, making the current non-NLRB share of new member organizing about 70 percent. Note that the claimed new organizing (200K) is still half that needed to maintain density, and a fifth that needed to increase it one percentage point. Still, it represents an important shift in union organizing strategy, and one reflected in the EFCA proposal. (For a careful review of this shift, see James Brudney, "Neutrality Agreements and Card Check Recognition: Prospects for Changing Paradigms." *Iowa Law Review* 90 (2005): 819–96.) If such non-vote organizing can be brought to scale, or generalized through EFCA, it might significantly affect our estimates of the cost of organizing. In the meantime, readers should feel free to halve our estimates of organizing cost, which for convenience use an inflated assumed base of 100K in annual "traditional" (i.e., NLRB-election) organizing, rather than the 200K unions informally claim.

11. AFL-CIO, *Work in Progress* (2005) www.aflcio.org/aboutaflcio/wip/.

12. Our tabulations for 2001 are from www.aflcio.org/aboutaflcio/wip/.

13. The best study of the cost of organizing is Paula Voos, "Union Organizing: Costs and Benefits," *Industrial and Labor Relations Review* 36, no. 4 (July 1983): 576–91. Voos estimates that the average cost of organizing was $729, while the marginal cost ranged from $176 to $579 in 1967 dollars, depending on model specification. This translates into an average cost of $4,338 and a marginal cost of $1,047 to $3,445 in 2005 dollars. The midpoint of the marginal costs is $2,250.

14. Past attempts to mass union resources on particular locales (e.g., the AFL-CIO's Houston Organizing Project campaign in the 1980s, or the Las Vegas building trades project in the 1990s, or the Washington State apple industry campaign in the 2000s) are not encouraging.

15. This is not to say there have not been promising experiments, including the multi-employer regional labor market approach to organizing that SEIU has taken in New Jersey and Texas. But we do not know yet if they provide a model that is sustainable across many unions and at sufficient scale. It is just too early to judge.

16. *Hamlet* (Act V, Scene 1), modified by Freeman and Rogers.

17. Richard B. Freeman, "Spurts in Union Growth: Defining Moments and Social Processes," in *The Defining Moment: The Great Depression and the American Economy in the Twentieth Century*, ed. Michael Bordo, Claudia Goldin, and Eugene White (Chicago, Ill.: University of Chicago Press for NBER, 1998): 265–95.

18. We use the words de facto here because de jure the law provides equal protection to other forms of concerted employment action, as noted below.

19. See Richard B. Freeman and Joel Rogers, "Open-Source Unionism: Beyond Exclusive Collective Bargaining," *Working USA* 7, no. 2 (spring 2002): 3–4, and Freeman and Rogers, "A Proposal to American Labor," *The Nation* 274, no. 24 (June 2002): 18–24.

20. Daphne Taras and A. Gesser, "How New Lawyers Use E-Voice to Drive Firm Compensation: The 'Greedy Associates' Phenomenon," *Journal of Labor Research* 23, no. 4 (2002): 9–29.

21. Dorothy Sue Cobble, "Lost Ways of Organizing: Reviving the AFL's Direct Affiliate Strategy," *Industrial Relations* 36 (July 1997): 278–301.

22. Clyde Summers, "Unions without Majority — A Black Hole?" *Chicago-Kent Law Review* 66, no. 3 (summer 1990): 531–48, initiated recent reconsideration of the potential power of nonmajority unions. Subsequent scholarly debate and the historical record and original legislative intent are covered in Charles J. Morris, *The Blue Eagle at Work: Reclaiming Democratic Rights in the American Workplace* (Ithaca, N.Y.: Cornell University Press, 2005). The issue has been neglected so long that clarification of the NLRB's position is needed. That may be forthcoming from a case the Steelworkers, representing a nonmajority union, have brought against the giant retailer Dick's Sporting Goods. See Charles J. Morris, "Members-Only Collective Bargaining: Rejecting Conventional Wisdom," *Perspectives on Work: The Magazine of the LERA* (Fall 2005) www.lera.uiuc.edu/Pubs/Perspectives/onlinecompanion/Fall05-morris.htm.

23. For the experience in the United Kingdom and elsewhere, see Richard B. Freeman, "Searching outside the Box: The Road to Union Renascence and Worker Well-being in the U.S." in *The Future of Labor Unions: Restoring the Balance in a Market Economy*, ed. Julius Getman and Ray Marshall (Austin, Tex.: Ray Marshall Center for the Study of Human Resources, Lyndon B. Johnson School of Public Affairs, University of Texas at Austin, 2004): 75–110; Freeman, "From the Webbs to the Web: The Contribution of the Internet to Reviving Union Fortunes," in *Trade Unions: Resurgence or Demise?* ed. Sue Fernie and David Metcalf (London, UK: Routledge 2005); and Wayne J. Diamond and Richard B. Freeman, "Will Unionism Prosper in Cyberspace? The Promise of the Internet for Employee Organization," *British Journal of Industrial Relations* 40, no. 3 (September 2002): 569–96.

24. Linda Guyer, "Real World Experiences of Online Organizing," Conference on Unions and the Internet, London (May 11–12, 2001) (www.allianceibm.org).

25. Jay Greene, "Troubling Exits at Microsoft," *BusinessWeek* Cover Story (September 26, 2005).

26. Mitch Stacy, "Florida Wal-Mart Workers Start to Organize — without Union," Associated Press, *Akron Beacon Journal* website (October 1, 2005), www.ohio.com/mld/ohio/business/12792913.htm.

27. See www.aflcio.org/enron/connections.htm.

28. Steven Greenhouse, "Labor Federation Looks beyond Unions for Supporters," *New York Times* (July 11, 2004, Sunday, Late Edition — Final, Section 1): 26.

29. Kenneth McLennan, "What Do Unions Do? — A Management Perspective," *Journal of Labor Research* 26, no. 4 (fall 2005): 597–621.

30. Justin Hake, National Right to Work Legal Defense Foundation, as quoted in Randy Hall, "AFL-CIO's Non-Union Affiliate Tops 1 Million Members," *CSNNews.com* (September 4, 2005) www.cnsnews.com/Nation/archive/200509/archive.asp.

31. Harry Kelber, "Is 'Working America,' a New Affiliate, A Rising Star in AFL-CIO's Future?" *LaborTalk* (May 18, 2005) www.laboreducator.org/workgamer.htm.

32. Andrew Stern, www.seiu2004.org/press/keynote.cfm., June 21, 2004.

33. Leigh Strope, "Major Union Takes Organizing Drive to Web," *USA Today* website (June 23, 2004), www.usatoday.com/tech/webguide/internetlife/2004-06-22-unions-online_x.htm.

34. At present, Purple Ocean provides voice about broad work-related issues. It has over 100,000 members.

35. Seymour Martin Lipset and Noah M. Meltz, with Rafael Gomez and Ivan Katchanovski, *The Paradox of American Unionism: Why Americans Like Unions More than Canadians Do, but Join Much Less* (Ithaca, N.Y.: ILR Press, 2004).

36. For an earlier suggestion along these lines, see Joel Rogers, "United States: Lessons from Abroad and Home," in *Works Councils: Consultation, Representation, and Cooperation in Industrial Relations*, ed. Joel Rogers and Wolfgang Streeck (Chicago: NBER and University of Chicago Press, 1995): 375–410.

37. This could be done by administratively enforcing fines or injunctive action; by conditioning firm eligibility for government contracts or favored tax treatment on respecting associative rights; and/or by developing a private cause of action for their enforcement, with potential for punitive damages for their violation.

38. California Assembly Bill, AB 1889, Cedillo, 00-872, State Funds: Unionization (2000).

39. On September 2005, the U.S. Court of Appeals for the 9th Circuit affirmed the District Court decision in *Chamber of Commerce of the United States v. Lockyer*, No. 03-55166 (9th Cir. 2005). In January 2006, however, the Ninth Circuit announced it was going to rehear the case *en banc* (that is, with the full court present), and that its earlier decision should not be relied on as precedent. As we write, the fate of the California bill is unresolved.

40. Michael H. Gottesman, "Rethinking Labor Law Preemption," *Yale Journal on Regulation* 7 (summer 1990): 355–410.

41. *Building & Construction Trades Council v. Associated Builders & Contractors of Massachusetts*, 507 U.S. 218 (1993), known as "Boston Harbor."

42. Freeman and Rogers, "The Promise of Progressive Federalism," in *Making the Politics of Poverty and Inequality*, ed. Jacob Hacker, Suzanne Mettler, and Joseph Soss (New York, N.Y.: Russell Sage Foundation, manuscript in process) argue for greater state experimentation in a host of areas.

than desired, 1, 3, 21, 91; management co-operation and, 86–87; management resistance to, 2, 88–91; nonunion voice, 207, 210; productivity and, 131–33; representation/participation gap, 32, 75–79, 210; unions and, 21–22, 100, 106–10. *See also* Employee involvement (EI) programs

Internet: use of for organizing, 194–205; unions. *See* Open-source unionism

International Association of Machinists (IAM), 200–201

"It's the economy, stupid" objection, 37, 40–42

Job satisfaction, 4–6, 71–72, 211 n3–5; employee involvement (EI) programs and, 136–41; human-resource practices and, 125, 127; influence and, 73–76; survey variation, 5–6, 13; union support and, 105–10

Job security, 6, 10, 12, 50–51, 63

Job tenure, 37–39, 214 n9, 216 n4

Joint organizations, 33, 35, 67, 86–87, 180, 181. *See also* Organizational preferences; Workplace committees

Knights of Labor, 193, 198

Knowledge workers, 50, 52

Labor, national program to improve conditions for all workers, 195

Labor laws: assessing reforms, 149–50; decline of unions and, 95–96; disconnect from current business conditions, 185–87; elections and, 115; employment-at-will doctrine, 148, 225 n3; knowledge of; by management, 148–49; knowledge of; by workers, 47–48, 146–50; reform, 185–86; "spurts" in unions and, 193; support for stronger laws vs. opposition to penalties, 16, 186, 229 n6. *See also* Card checks; Employer Free Choice Act (EFCA); Government agencies; Labor Management Relations Act (LMRA); National Labor Relations Act; Secret ballot elections; Teamwork for Employees and Management Act (TEAM); Workplace committees

Laborers, Laborers' International Union of North America (LIUNA), 188

Labor Management Relations Act (LMRA), 28, 185–87, 198, 205–10, 229 nn2–4, 229 n6, 231 n22; de jure law vs de facto effects, 193, 230 n18. *See also* Federalism or States Rights

Labor market, 43–44, 91–92

Labor movement, split, 2, 188

Least-skilled workers, 50–51, 52, 71–72

Legal protection, 16, 24, 33, 34, 145–60, 179–80, 185; areas of, 9, 158; demographics, 159–60; worker preference for, 157–60. *See also*: Labor Management Relations Act (LMRA)

Legislation, 67, 145, 225 n1

Levi Strauss, 135

Living standards, 40–42

Lockyer (*Chamber of Commerce of the United States v. Lockyer*, No. 03-55166 (9th Cir. 2005), 232 n39

Loyalty, of worker to firm, 6–7, 39, 73, 74, 136, 137, 211 n6–n8, 216 n8

Majority certification, majority unionism. *See* Collective bargaining

"Make whole" compensation, 229 n5

Management: anti-union tactics, 16, 211 nn16–17; cooperative relations with, 33, 36, 62–63, 84–88, 143; distrust of, 6–8, 27, 49, 211 nn10–11; and employees, cooperative and conflictual relationships, 91; influence of workers and, 70–71; influence on Congress; politicking, 8, 211 n10; misperceptions of labor law, 148–49; organizational preferences, 84, 85, 172–73, 228 nn3–5; resistance of, 114–16; resistance of, to worker independence, 33; resistance of, to sharing power and authority, 2, 15, 88–91; trust of firm, 172–73; in union firms, 116; view of unions, 90, 109, 113–17, 220 n17; worker ratings of, 11, 49, 72–73, 88–90, 109–10, 176; WRPS involvement of, 31–32, 35–36, 53–58, 67, 107. *See also* Firms; Joint organizations; Management cooperation

Management cooperation, 33, 35, 62–63, 84–88, 169–70; arbitration and, 163; employee associations and, 86; employee involvement (EI) programs in, 142–44; workplace committees and, 166

Management-worker relations. *See* Worker-management relations

Managerial workers, 57–58; loyalty to firm, 39; management resistance and, 90–91; organizational preferences, 84, 85

Meet-and-confer legislation, 195

"Members only", "minority" or nonmajority unions, 195, 197–98, 231 n22

Methodology, 43–45, 53, 56, 58–59; Guttman scaling technique, 122, 123, 221 n6; latent variables, 216 n2; linear probability model, 100, 109–11, 218 n6; normal distribution, 123–125, 222 n8; Rasch scale, 123, 221–22 n7; split-sample design, 8, 56, 65, 68–70, 79, 157, 178, 225 n2; summary statistics, 78, 217 nn10–11; summated rating, 79–81, 122–23; workplace choices and, 168–69. *See also* Worker Representation and Participation Survey

Mineworkers. *See* United Mineworkers of America (UMWA)

Motorola, 135

NAFTA, 3

National Education Association, 193

United Steelworkers of America (USWA), 189, 198, 200–201

U.S. labor law, and limits on wage discussion, 130, 135, 149

U.S. Society of Human Resource Management, 151

Voice. *See* Influence, worker

Wages: decentralized wagesetting, 206; employee involvement (EI) programs and, 130, 135, 149; "equal pay," 11; human-resource practices and, 119–20, 126, 221n3; income inequality, 41–42, 91, 210; influence and, 21, 76, 79, 80; "living" wage, 10; organizational preferences and, 177; union support and, 24, 99. *See also* Collective bargaining

Wagner Act, 210, 229n2

Wal-Mart, 191, 201

Wave 1 telephone survey, 59–60, 65, 160

Wave 2 follow-up survey, 30, 61–62, 65, 86, 128; arbitration materials, 161

Worker-management relations, 1, 8–12, 49; framework, 29–30; open-door policies and, 128, 222n17; organizational preferences and, 175–76; power balance, 8, 15, 210; union support and, 109–12, 219n12; worker ratings of, 49, 72–73, 88–90, 109–10, 176. *See also* Employee involvement (EI) programs; Influence, worker

Worker Representation and Participation Survey (WRPS): background, 1, 30–32; basic findings, 2, 3, 31–36; British version, 64, 65; Canadian survey, 63, 64, 65; criticism of, 44–45; final design of, 4, 64–66; and management and labor advisors, 31–32, 35–36, 53–58, 67, 105, 180–81; German survey, 1; Japanese survey, 1; Korean survey, 1; omnibus survey, 61, 65; post-WRPS surveys and survey findings, 3–28; public-sector survey, 63–64, 65; redesign of, 55–57; representativeness of, 62–64; scaling of variables in, 60–61; student coding, 53; union involvement, 31, 60–61, 67; Web site, 213n5. *See also* Focus groups; Methodology; Surveys; Wave 1 telephone survey; Wave 2 follow-up survey

Workers: diversity of, 1, 50–51; importance of concerns of, 36–37; institutions preferred by, 24–27, 34–35; and labor law, knowledge of, 47–48, 146–50; knowledge, 50, 52; least-skilled, 50–51, 52, 71–72; loyalty (*See* Loyalty, of worker to firm); ratings of worker-management relations, 8–12, 49, 72–73, 88–90, 109–10, 176; rights (*See* Workplace characteristics). *See also* Focus groups; Influence, worker; Managerial workers; Nonmanagerial workers; Nonunion workers; Union worker

Working (Terkel), 43

Working America. *See* Open-source unionism

Workplace characteristics: fair treatment, 9, 13–14; governance. *See* Organizational preferences; legal protection and, 159–60; opportunities for advancement, 11; organizational preferences and, 177; relations, 11; rights, 9–10, 145–51, 198, 205-10, 229n3, 231n22, 232n37

Workplace committees, 2, 164–67; features of, 166–67; management initiated, forbidden by LMRA, 185; preference for, 25–27. *See also* Employee committees and Employee associations

Work in Progress (AFL-CIO), 190

Work schedule, worker influence and, 76, 79, 140

Works councils, 81–82, 164, 184, 206–7

Worldcom, 8, 202–3, 210

Wright, Erik, 57

WRPS. *See* Worker Representation and Participation Survey

Xerox, 135

Zogby poll, 18, 212n23, 229n7